Tax Havens

A VOLUME IN THE SERIES

Cornell Studies in Money

edited by Eric Helleiner and Jonathan Kirshner

A list of titles in this series is available at www.cornellpress.cornell.edu.

Tax Havens

How Globalization Really Works

Ronen Palan, Richard Murphy,
and Christian Chavagneux

CORNELL UNIVERSITY PRESS

Ithaca and London

First published 2010 by Cornell University Press
Printed in the United States of America
First printing, Cornell Paperbacks, 2010

Library of Congress Cataloging-in-Publication Data
Palan, Ronen, 1957–
    Tax havens : how globalization really works / Ronen Palan, Richard Murphy, and Christian Chavagneux.
        p. cm.—(Cornell studies in money)
    Includes bibliographical references and index.
    ISBN 978-0-8014-4735-8 (cloth : alk. paper)   ISBN 978-0-8014-7612-9 (pbk. : alk. paper)
    1. Tax havens.   2. Tax evasion.   3. International finance.
4. Globalization.   I. Murphy, Richard, 1958–   II. Chavagneux, Christian.
III. Title.   IV. Series: Cornell studies in money.
    HJ2336.P35   2010
    336.2'06—dc22   2009026884

Contents

Tables and Figures

Tables

Figures

Acknowledgments

They say in financial circles that "those who know do not talk and those who talk don't know." In tax matters, those who know talk, sometimes, but those who do not know talk a lot. The world of tax havens is opaque, confusing, and secretive. It is a world that is saturated with stories, rumors, and anecdotes. Yet the veritable flood of information can sometimes hide a dearth of solid data. The subject of tax havens has attracted the attention of a talented and dedicated group of academics, journalists, and activists from all around the world. These people have become our friends and colleagues, sometimes actual friends, sometimes virtual friends, but friends nonetheless. This book gives the reader an up-to-date assessment of the current state of knowledge about tax havens that this group has managed to accumulate. Our thanks go to all these friends.

They include first our colleagues on the Tax Justice Network. The contribution of John Christensen, its director, must be especially noted, but it is also important to note the contributions of Prem Sikka, Nicholas Shaxson, Sol Picciotto, Mark Hampton, and many others who have worked to create that organization over the last few years. The parallel work of Raymond Baker and his colleagues at the Global Financial Integrity Project in Washington, D.C., must also be noted.

We have relied on the work and conversation of a growing circle of academics from all over the world and from different disciplines. Jason Sharman, Greg Rawling, and Anthony Van Fossen from Australia; Jean-Christophe Graz and Sébastien Guex from Switzerland; Thomas Rixen and Philip Genschel from Germany; Jim Hines, Joel Slemrod, Simon Pak, Robert Kudrle, Lorraine Eden, and Bill Maurer from the United States and

Canada. In the UK, there has been some dispute along the way with the likes of Mike Devereux and Judith Freedman at Oxford, but the debate has been welcome. John Tiley at Cambridge has also added valuable comments on occasion.

Journalists have contributed significantly to this work, including Glenn Simpson and Jesse Drucker of the *Wall Street Journal*, Nick Mathiason of the *Observer*, Vanessa Houlder of the *Financial Times*, and David Leigh, Larry Elliot, Felicity Lawrence, and Ian Griffiths of the *Guardian*. Their dedication to publishing tax haven stories has helped bring much to light.

We also want to mention our friends in tax havens, from whom we have received many insights. Some have disagreed with us, but their insights also have been welcome. These include Colin Powell of Jersey, Tim Ridley of Cayman, and Malcolm Couch of the Isle of Man.

We have been very lucky with our publisher's choice of two anonymous referees. They both worked tirelessly to improve the quality of this book, gently coaxing us to clarify our ideas. We thank them for their help and support. We thank the team at Cornell University Press that worked with us on this project. We thank in particular Roger Haydon, who looked after the project from inception to publication. Roger not only commissioned the project but also edited the entire book, commenting on every aspect throughout the process. This book owes a lot to him.

This project owes also a great deal to the late professor Susan Strange, who many years ago encouraged two of the co-authors—Christian and Ronen—to learn about the obscure world of tax havens. Finally, we thank our wives, Anastasia, Jacqueline, and Béatrice, who inevitably ended up sharing our concerns and frustrations while writing this book. Their belief in the project was perhaps the most important support we had.

Introduction

In September 2007, only a month after the beginning of one of the most devastating financial crises ever experienced, the British bank Northern Rock was on the brink of collapse. Northern Rock had expanded rapidly prior to its failure, funding its growth as an aggressive player in the international market for Collaterized Debt Obligations (CDOs) and emerging as the fifth largest mortgage provider in the UK. However, those CDOs were issued not by Northern Rock itself but by what became known as its shadow company, Granite Master Issuer plc and Associates. What was intriguing about the arrangement was that Granite was owned not by Northern Rock but by a UK charitable trust established by Northern Rock. Much of the management of the resulting, supposedly independent structure was located in Jersey, a well-known European tax haven.

In March 2008 came the collapse of Bear Stearns, a leading U.S. investment bank. Bear Stearns had hemorrhaged money through its hedge funds, many of them registered in the Cayman Islands and Dublin's International Financial Centre—both well-known offshore finance centers.

That well-known tax havens became embroiled in the financial crisis was not a coincidence. If you think of tax havens as sun-kissed exotic islands reminiscent of the Garden of Eden where a few billionaires, mafiosi, and corrupt autocrats hide their ill-gotten gains, then think again. Tax havens are the underlying constant theme of the financial crisis of 2008–9. Lehman Brothers, whose collapse triggered a month of financial panic around the world, was registered in Delaware—a state that has served as an internal tax haven in the United States since the late nineteenth century. Lehman's collapse was followed by the Madoff scandal, a $50 billion ponzi scheme orchestrated by the well-known Wall Street financier Bernard Madoff. It took very little time to discover a link between Madoff's scam and tax havens. "Madoff Spotlight Turns to Role of Offshore Funds," announced the *New York Times* headline on December 30, 2008.

We do not suggest in this book that tax havens caused the financial crisis of 2008–9, but we do believe that they were one of the most important actors precipitating it. We argue that their regulation is key to any future plan to stabilize financial markets.

We are not alone. The French, German, British, the U.S. governments joined now by the G-20 are all keen to pressure these havens, for the sake of stability and, not unnaturally, for other, more traditional reasons as well. For tax havens are places where one can avoid or evade at least one of life's absolute certainties, taxes, and so they leave a gaping hole in most state finances. Tax havens also help those who use them escape other regulations, launder money, hide money from partners or spouses, and secure secrecy for their commercial activities.

The French call tax havens *paradis fiscaux*, financial paradises or financial havens, and it is perhaps a more appropriate term for them, for tax havens involve a wide variety of financial purposes in addition to taxation. In fact, there are slight variations in the translation of the concept in different languages, reflecting subtle differences in their roles and functions. The Spanish think of tax havens as *asilos de impuesto*, asylums from taxation but, like the French, they also use the term *paradisos fiscales*; the Italians talk about a *rifugio fiscale*, a financial refuge. In German tax havens are translated as *Steuerhafens*, which is the closest to the English meaning of the term, but in Russian they are "special tax zones," implying eased tax regimes or tax incentives for capital. International organizations eschew such popular terms in favor of "offshore financial centers" or even "international financial centers," implying that tax havens are no different from other financial centers—which as we demonstrate in this book, they are. Those campaigning for reform now call them secrecy jurisdictions. Such differences in terminology suggest that tax havens are complex, multipurpose phenomena.

The evidence is not difficult to find. If you took a stroll down Monaco's famous piers and tried to find a yacht that did not fly the flag of one of the principal tax havens discussed in this book—the Cayman Islands, Bermuda, the Isle of Man, Jersey, or even Luxembourg—you would be hard pushed. Because of the limited regulation typical of tax havens, even landlocked Luxembourg has emerged as one of the largest shipping nations of the world.

Alternatively, check the addresses of the scores of Internet casinos and see if any one of them is not registered in a tax haven. In general, it is clear that tax havens are not only about tax avoidance and evasion: undermining a broad range of regulations is now a significant part of the business model. Nonetheless, low taxation policies remain a core feature of their business.

Individually tax havens may appear small and insignificant, but in combination they play an important role in the world economy. First, they undermine the regulatory and taxation processes of the mainstream states by the provision of what may be described as "get out of regulation free" cards to banks and other financial institutions, to international business, and to wealthy individuals. Second, in doing so they skew the distribution of costs and benefits of globalization in favor of a global elite and to the detriment of the vast majority of the population. In that sense tax havens are at the very heart of globalization, or at least the heart of the specific type of globalization that we have witnessed since the 1980s.

Yet tax havens are legal entities, for the simple reason that they are sovereign states or suzerain jurisdictions, both of which have the legal right to write their own domestic laws. They may choose to write their tax codes and financial laws in ways that others consider harmful. Legal in this context means "allowed under the law," "recognized or established by a court of law," or "officially permitted." Legality has very little to do with either opinion or ethics. These places are exercising their rights, and their defense is that international law allows them to do so.

We think that blaming tax havens for their sovereign choice of law is a gross oversimplification of the argument. It is a fact that the majority of the tax havens of the world are very small jurisdictions; very few of them possess universities or research centers that teach the skills required to support a thriving global business community; and very few have local resources that would allow them to sustain a high standard of living. Tax havens are financial conduits that, in exchange for a fee, use their one principal asset—their sovereignty—to serve a nonresident constituency of accountants and lawyers, bankers and financiers, who bring a demand for the privileges that tax havens can supply.

As the modern "regulatory" state took shape toward the end of the nineteenth century, a number of advanced industrialized countries began the long and arduous process of reorganizing their revenue institutions. The state remained an important if still minor player in national economies until the great depression of the 1930s. Over time government outlay as a proportion of Gross National Product (GNP) rose from an average of 10% in the early twentieth century, to an average of 30 to 40% by the beginning of the twenty-first century. Paralleling these developments, tax avoidance and evasion became a topic of considerable interest. Nevertheless, tax havens have remained a specialized topic of interest to lawyers, accountants, and tax specialists. The period of sustained stagflation and the attendant fiscal crisis of the state in the 1970s stimulated renewed interest in tax havens, this time not only as facilitators of tax avoidance and evasion but as emerging financial centers as well (Park 1982; Johns 1983; Johns & Le Marchant 1993). The study of tax havens remained, nonetheless, a secondary area of expertise, and it has made little or no impact on mainstream scholarship. Things have changed dramatically since the late 1990s. Starting with an important Organization for Economic Cooperation and Development (OECD) study of harmful tax competition published in 1998, a number of international financial organizations have made tax havens one of their key priorities. At the same time, a growing number of academics (see box 2.1), as well as journalists, have turned their attention to tax havens, as indeed have civil society organizations. The result has been a veritable explosion of new information and theoretical debates.

This book provides an up-to-date evaluation of the role and function of tax havens in the world economy. It also provides an account of the origins and development of the tax havens of the world from the late nineteenth century through the latest tax havens in post-communist countries, the Middle East, and Africa. In addition, the book offers an up-to-date estimate of the size of the phenomenon, explains the various uses of tax havens, and analyzes the impact of tax havens on the state and business. We conclude the book with the impact of the OECD and European Union attacks on the offshore world and consider what might happen next. Although the literature on tax havens is growing by leaps and bound, this book, to our knowledge, offers the first comprehensive synthesis of the disparate strands of research and knowledge on tax havens.

Our principal contention is that most accepted ideas about tax havens are false. Tax havens are not working on the margins of the world economy, but are an integral part of modern business practice. Furthermore, they exist not in opposition to the state, but in accord with it. Indeed, we take the view that tax havens not only are conduits for tax avoidance and evasion but belong more broadly to the world of finance, to the business of managing the monetary resources of an organization, country, or individuals. They have become one of the most important instruments in the contemporary, globalized financial system, and one of the principal causes of financial instability. Their sovereignty sets them apart, yet it is their sovereignty that gives them the means to integrate themselves into the world on terms they have, at least in part, been able to set for themselves.

Money, Wealth, and Tax Havens

The names of offshore jurisdictions have appeared with monotonous regularity in every financial crisis or scandal that has erupted over the past twenty years—whether financial crises in East Asia, Russia, and Argentina, or the corporate fiascos associated with companies such as Long Term Capital Management, Parmalat, Refco, Enron, and, in the 2008/2009 crisis, Northern Rock, Bear Stearns, and Madoff's ponzi scheme.

The sense of fiasco perhaps reached its pinnacle when it was revealed in February 2008 that a dog named Günter joined 1,400 of his fellow German citizens (most of the conventional homo sapiens variety) and set up anonymous trusts managed by Liechtenstein's LGT bank to avoid German taxation (Dinmore and Williamson 2008). In June 2008, an employee of UBS, the premier Swiss bank, pleaded guilty to helping a Russian oligarch evade millions of dollars' worth of taxes in the United States. In November 2008, a senior Swiss-based employee of the same bank was indicted on charges of tax evasion in the United States. The UBS employee estimated that $20 billion of assets were involved and the total fee income to UBS each year might have amounted to $200 million. UBS reportedly is cooperating with the inquiry (Balzli and Hornig 2008). He stated that UBS chose to ignore regulations with regard to the operation of offshore accounts for its U.S. clients and in the process facilitated tax evasion.

The evidence is clear that tax havens and the tax evasion that at least some of them facilitate are serious business. At some point quantitative growth accumulates to a qualitative change, and the impressive figures associated with tax havens suggest that they play an important if often overlooked role in the contemporary world. We hope that anyone who still believes that tax havens are a mere sideshow, the playground of the rich and famous, will think differently after reading this book.

The statistics are certainly impressive. In our estimate there are between forty-six and sixty active tax havens in the world right now (table 1.4). They are home to an estimated two million international business companies (IBCs)—a term used to describe a bewildering array of corporate entities, most of which are extremely opaque, and thousands (if not millions) of trusts, mutual funds, hedge funds, and captive insurance companies. About 50% of all international banking lending and 30% of the world's stock of Foreign Direct Investment (FDI) are registered in these jurisdictions. Some very small islands are among the world's largest financial centers: the Caymans, a small set of islands in the Caribbean and a British Overseas Territory, is the fifth-largest international financial center in the world. That list also contains the small British Crown jurisdictions of Jersey, Guernsey, and the Isle of Man, as well as what we call intermediate havens, such as Switzerland, Luxembourg, Ireland, and Singapore.

The global rich—the "Richistanis" as Frank (2007) calls them—held in 2007 approximately $12 trillion of their wealth in tax havens. It is as if the entire U.S. annual GNP were parked in tax havens.

The hedge fund industry has discovered the delights of tax havens. According to some estimates the big four Caribbean havens—the Caymans Islands, the British Virgin Islands, Bermuda, and the Bahamas—are home to 52% of the world's hedge fund industry. But these figures are disputed. The Cayman Financial Services Authority claims that 35% of the world's hedge fund industry is located in its territory alone (Cayman Islands Monetary Authority figures as reported in GAO 2008), and some cite an improbably high figure of 80% (Zuill 2005). This unresolved debate is disconcerting: it shows how little we really know about the hedge fund industry.

The statistics are staggering, but these are only numbers, and numbers need interpretation, a critical task we undertake in this book. We interpret them from the perspective of a political economist; we aim to decipher the political and social trends embedded in the numbers. We argue that the numbers represent a profound paradox of the modern world And what these figures represent can be captured in one word—avoidance. They are the abstract expression of the collective efforts of the state, corporate, and business elites of the world to avoid the very laws and regulations that they have collectively designed.

Such elites primarily seek to avoid taxation. They seek to avoid or reduce their share in the collective effort that pays for the "collective goods" provided (or supposedly provided) by states, such as security, economic, political, and social stability, health, education, and infrastructure. However, elites also seek to avoid regulations. The regulations they seek to avoid are often the financial and business rules and norms that states introduced to maintain order and stability—without which the rich would not have gotten so rich in the first place. Tax havens allow people to manage many other, more esoteric social regulations, among them the avoidance of gambling and pornography laws.

Granted, not all taxes and regulations are necessary or socially beneficial. Until the 1970s, most advanced capitalist countries heavily regulated their broadcasting industries, allowing only state-sponsored broadcasting companies to operate. The growth of offshore radio stations such as Radio Luxembourg and Radio Caroline, both of which operated on the tax haven principle (Palan 2003), appears in retrospect to have been a beneficial development. Once governments realized how popular these offshore stations are, and how futile were their aims of controlling the airwaves, they responded by liberalizing their domestic broadcasting regulations. Here, "offshore" proved to be a modernizing force compelling governments to abandon intrusive regulations. Broadcasting, however, is uniquely accessible to all. In most cases—indeed, in all the cases discussed in this book—entry barriers to the range of benefits offered by tax havens are high, limiting their clientele to a small and extremely wealthy minority. As a result, unfortunately, tax havens benefit the rich and the powerful, while the costs are largely borne by the rest of society.

When we say that tax havens are at the very heart of globalization, we mean that tax havens are among the most significant, if persistently overlooked, structural factors that are determining the distribution of the benefits and costs of globalization among the world's peoples. That they skew the benefits of globalization to favor a small minority of the world's rich and powerful is a matter of high political import.

We can find examples of people taking advantage of collective goods for private pleasure at every level of society, of course, from the poorest to the richest. The tax haven phenomenon is a massive organized attempt by the richest and most powerful to take advantage of collective goods on a scale rarely seen; and it is, perhaps for the first time, taking place globally. Tax havens are, therefore, at the heart of a particular type of globalization—globalization that is characterized by a growing gap between the very rich and everyone else. Such globalization is neither necessary nor inevitable. Rather it is a product of a complex set of factors, key among which has been lenient and forgiving attitudes toward tax havens that have characterized international politics, especially those in which the United States has been involved.

Regulatory Responses

The astonishing statistics associated with tax havens tell us that they have played a central role in skewing developments in the world economy. First, they have helped to undermine the international financial regulatory environment and taxation policies of all those countries and regions that participate in globalization, as well as those that do not. Second, they have served collectively as a vehicle for skewing the allocation of costs and benefits of globalization. The degree to which modern business, large and small, have become embedded in tax havens, while astounding, is rarely acknowledged. An international company or business with no links to tax havens is a rare species nowadays. But the impact of tax havens is felt largely indirectly, revealed through the statistics that show a persistent growth in the gap between rich and poor since the 1980s all over the world (see, e.g., Duménil and Lévy 2004). The role that tax havens are playing in undermining financial regulations has come to light only recently.

Yet all this was known for a while. How could the leading industrial countries allow these small jurisdictions to rise and flourish? Well, they did and did not. Countries such as the United States, UK, France, and Germany sought from time to time to close certain loopholes, pressuring this or that tax haven to change some of its rules and policies. There were also some feeble attempts, dating back to the interwar period to try to develop a coordinate international response to tax havens. But frankly, not much was accomplished. Worse, the very same countries, with the possible exception of France and Germany, were major players in the development of the tax haven phenomenon after World War II.

For reasons discussed later in this book the sentiment began to change toward the end of the 1990s. Since then a number of initiatives, led initially by the OECD "harmful tax competition" campaign, began to gather steam. However, in an excellent detailed analysis, Jason Sharman (2006) exposed these efforts largely as futile. Yet only three years later, it appears that tax havens are under greater threat than ever.

Concern about tax havens has been bubbling for a long time, but the full impact of tax havens on the world economy took a long time to mature and may have dawned first on the leaders of the European Union. While the OECD campaign was largely in the doldrums, the EU has emerged as the effective leader in the global struggle against tax havens—a mantle unlikely to pass to the United States despite the results of the November 2008 election. The issue was certainly known to both the Clinton and the George W. Bush administrations, and the former was one of the drivers of the multilateral efforts against tax havens. But one of the first acts of the Bush administration was to withdraw support from multilateral efforts to combat harmful tax competition. The new Obama administration is an entirely different kettle of fish. As a senator, Barack Obama played an important role in various initiatives to combat tax havens. Once in power, he signaled important changes in policy allying the United States with France and Germany in the fight against tax havens.

The crisis of 2007–9 may prove an important watershed in the evolution of regulatory response to tax havens. We discuss recent developments in the regulatory response to tax havens in the conclusion to this book.

What Are Tax Havens?

It is not easy to define tax havens, and in fact we devote an entire chapter to the subject. At this point we suggest that tax havens are places or countries (not all of them are sovereign states) that have sufficient autonomy to write their own tax, finance, and other laws and regulations. They all take advantage of this autonomy to create legislation designed to assist nonresident persons or corporations to avoid the regulatory obligations imposed on them in the places where those nonresident people undertake the substance of their economic transactions.

An additional characteristic that most tax havens share is an environment of secrecy that allows the user of structures created under local law to do so either completely anonymously, or largely so. The third common characteristic is ease and affordability in gaining access to the entities incorporated in the territory.

Evasion and Avoidance

Tax havens are used, as their name suggests, to avoid and evade taxes. However, these two terms are often confused, and so some clarification is essential at this stage.

Individuals and companies just about anywhere in the world have the opportunity to undertake what might be described as "tax planning" within the law of the territory in which they live or operate. For the vast majority of the world's population, including most people in advanced industrialized countries with reasonable wages, the concept of "tax planning" is largely meaningless: tax is normally deducted at source from earnings, and that is more or less that with regard to the settlement of tax liabilities.

For the wealthy minority of the world's population and for most companies, tax planning is, in contrast, an important part of their business and personal lives. There is even a special term to describe the life experience of some: they are called PTs, the "permanent tourists" or those who are for tax purposes the "permanently not there" (Maurer 1998). This is an extreme, however, and in practice tax experts distinguish among three basic approaches to tax strategy.

The first is "Tax compliance." This happens when a company or an individual seeks to comply with tax law in all the countries in which they operate, makes full disclosure of all relevant information on all their tax claims, and seeks to pay the right amount of tax required by law at the right time and in the right place, where "right" means that the economic substance of their transactions is consistent with the form in which they are declared.

At the other end of the scale is tax evasion. Tax evasion is an illegal activity undertaken to reduce an individual or company's tax bill. It occurs when a taxpayer fails to declare all or part of his or her income or makes a claim to offset an expense against taxable income that he or she did not incur or was not allowed to claim for tax purposes. Tax evasion is a criminal offence in most countries but a civil offence in a minority of countries, such as Switzerland and Liechtenstein. The difference is significant. Such countries cannot legally cooperate in civil matters; hence the Swiss authorities' most common response to other countries' requests for assistance in cases connected to tax evasion has been that eager and keen as they are to stamp such unsavory practices, sadly they are unable to cooperate because tax evasion is a civil matter in the Swiss Federation.

This characteristic response has been highlighted in recent events. In 2008, when massive tax evasion through highly secretive Liechtenstein foundations was made public, a Liechtenstein spokesperson explained how surprised and disappointed they were to discover that these secret foundations, set up under a law passed in 1926, could be abused by foreigners for tax evasion purposes. Liechtenstein, she said, was perhaps a tad naive, believing that most people in the world would behave just like its own citizens and would cheerfully pay all taxes due—but naivety, she added, was not a crime. The implication was clear: Liechtenstein wished us to believe that it was taken for a ride by those nasty foreigners. Few were deceived by the response.

Finally, there is tax avoidance. Tax avoidance is the gray area between tax compliance and tax evasion. This is the favorite area occupied by an army of accountants, lawyers, bankers, and tax experts. Strictly speaking, a tax avoiding individual or a company seeks to ensure that one of three things happens. First, they might seek to pay less tax than might be required by a reasonable interpretation of a country's law. Second, they might hope that tax is paid on profits declared in a country other than where they were really earned. Third, they might arrange to pay tax somewhat later than the profits were earned.

Legally, there is a clear difference between evasion and avoidance. Tax professionals like to cite a series of court rulings, mainly from the major countries in the world, which appear to support the legality of tax avoidance. The reality, however, is more complicated. First, the tax rules of almost every country are complex, and much avoidance relies on the existence of doubt. Second, when transactions take place across international boundaries in a world that has no global tax rules, the opportunities to play off the taxation law of one state against that of another (a process that tax professionals call "arbitrage") is often difficult to resist. The consequence is that the line differentiating tax evasion from avoidance is often too difficult to determine in general terms, and is way beyond the ability of most of those who participate in tax haven practice to either know or understand—a fact that the tax professional can easily exploit. For that reason, we talk of avoidance and evasion throughout this book without significant differentiation, relying in doing so on the maxim of former UK chancellor of the exchequer Dennis Healey who famously described the difference between the two as being "the thickness of a prison wall."

The British Empire Strikes Back

Finance is thought of as a hyper-mobile, decentralized, and globalized web of impersonal units of risk trading. In this web London is normally ranked as either the largest or the second largest wholesale financial center in the world (Yeandle et al. 2005). We believe that London is in practice the leading *international* financial center, whether one thinks of international banking credit activities, foreign exchange and over-the-counter derivatives transactions, marine insurance premiums, or international bonds issues.

Conventional rankings of international financial centers are founded on a debatable assumption, that British Crown Dependencies such as Jersey, Guernsey, and the Isle of Man, as well as British Overseas Territories such as the Cayman Islands, Bermuda, British Virgin Islands, or Gibraltar are independent and separate from the UK. Remove this assumption, and a far larger string of international centers emerges, accounting for nearly one-third of cross-border bank assets and liabilities in June 2008. If we add former colonies of the British state such as Singapore and Hong Kong, the impact of a political entity long considered defunct—the British Empire—on the contemporary financial system appears decisive, accounting for a 37% share of all international banking liabilities and a 35% share of assets.

A closer examination of the list of international financial centers reveals two additional anomalies. One is the importance of mid-size European states such as Switzerland, the Benelux countries, and Ireland in international finance. Each is a significant financial center in its own right; combined, they account for nearly 20% of international banking liabilities.

A second anomaly involves political entities long thought insignificant in the modern world: city-states. Among those, best known are Singapore, Hong Kong, and Luxembourg, but we could certainly add the Caymans, Jersey, Guernsey, Bahrain, Monaco, and, of course, the City of London, as modern variants. City-states, excluding London, accounted for nearly 17% of cross-border banking liabilities in March 2008, and with the City of London, they account for roughly 28% of international banking liabilities.

Granted, there are overlaps and some degree of double counting in these figures, but this little exercise in reconfiguration of well-known statistics raises some intriguing questions. The exercise suggests that we should pay special attention to the role of the British Empire in the creation of a British-dominated offshore economy. And we also should pay attention to the unique role played by the European intermediate havens. Both are used for tax avoidance and evasion purposes, which is the British-dominated pole of the offshore economy. However, these same British-influenced locations have also been closely linked to the rise of investment banking since the 1980s, whereas the European havens have specialized instead in what may be described as the harvesting of profits from intangibles (such as logos, brand names, etc.), in which they encourage companies to relocate into specialized low-tax vehicles registered in their domains.

Tax Havens and the Professionals

So far, we have approached tax havens as a state strategy. Such an approach is common, but it can be highly misleading. We will miss a crucial aspect of tax havens unless we pay close attention to the commercial firms that service them.

The biggest accounting firms, together with lawyers and bankers, tax experts and financial traders, plus their associated trust and corporate services companies, are to be found in most tax havens, but most prominently in the thirty or so largest jurisdictions. These professionals are crucial: as far as we can tell, they were present at each and every legislative innovation designed to avoid tax and regulation. They advised and coaxed the politicians to provide the legislation they needed to pursue their trade, and on occasions they drafted that legislation for the states in which they had located themselves. The professionals have also been present in each and every redrafting of the laws of offshore and they are the ones who actually set up the offshore facilities that such legislation enables. They also innovate new techniques of evasion and avoidance, which they sell to clients; lobby against changes in the laws against tax havens; and argue that tax havens are an entirely legitimate form of business.

The professionals are therefore absolutely irreplaceable, for they ensure that the business of tax havens flourishes. Most tax havens are very small jurisdictions and do not have the manpower and skills to operate on a global scale. The State of Jersey provides a perfect example. Probably few if any members of the State of Jersey have any real understanding of how "the offshore finance community" within Jersey works or what it is its denizens really do. They are simply a legislature for hire, doing what is asked of them. For example, Jersey's obnoxious Trust Law of 2006 was passed without a vote since no one objected, or as far as we can tell even commented on it, in the island's State Assembly. But legislators did do exactly what was asked of them: they provided what the local financial services industry demanded. In so doing they implied their understanding of something very simple and straightforward: in exchange for legislation the tax havens collect revenue from some activities that the offshore community brings into their jurisdiction without encountering any obvious costs. It seems to be a win-win situation serving the interests of all, and so why spend time on the boring details of trust laws?

These professionals make up the so-called Offshore Financial Center (OFC) community. They are international, transient, and interested only in following the money. If for any reason the money leaves a tax haven, you can be fairly sure that the OFC community will follow it. The perfect example of this type of behavior is found among the Big Four accountant firms, which are all, almost without exception, present in all the world's significant tax havens, including the most abusive. The people who service these firms are rarely local, and, as it is becoming increasingly clear they rarely integrate into the local community. They service a client base that is almost never local, unless it be the local lawyers who are servicing offshore clients, and their reason for being there has little to do with geography but all to do with the money flows they are managing.

Precisely because these people are transient, they have little real regard for local regulation. They may pay lip service to it as part of their costs of operation, but they can also afford to ignore it, as they evidently did in the case of UBS in the United States. Their belief is simple: if a problem of compliance were to arise, they could simply move on. As a result, compliance is not a real issue for them, and that is why, we suggest, it is obvious that despite the theoretical soundness of the local regulatory systems, actual compliance rates are so low.

Any effective regulation of the offshore world (a hot topic of debate since the publication of the OECD report in 1998, and likely to be equally hot in the next decade), would require not just that tax havens be regulated, but that the professional operators be regulated as well—and not just with regard to what they do in such places, but with regard to what they facilitate. They will resist such moves, but this is a battle that must be won. Not only because tax havens are not really home to the vast amount of money that the figures suggest. They are, as we explain in this book, very largely "recording havens" or, to use the jargon, "booking centers" that serve as legal domains for the registration of contractual relationships that take place elsewhere (although they collect license fees and other revenues in return). The staggering statistics belie the fact that at heart, tax havens are largely a fiction, one almighty fictional world that is aimed at one thing: at the avoidance of taxation and regulation in the world in which the transactions they record actually take place or have real impact. Their activity is entirely parasitic, feeding on both the world economy and the system of states. That is why tax havens are one of the most important political issues of our times.

Part I

Tax Havens and Their Uses

Chapter 1

What Is a Tax Haven?

The term "tax haven" has been widely used since the 1950s.[1] Yet there is no consensus as to what it means. The influential U.S. Treasury's Gordon Report concluded: "there is no single, clear, objective test which permits the identification of a country as a tax haven" (1981, 21). Twenty-five years later, Jason Sharman reached similar conclusions. The term "tax haven," Sharman writes, still "lacks a clear definition and its application is often controversial and contested" (2006, 21). Nevertheless, and despite controversies and debates, the list of countries considered to be tax havens has changed remarkably little since the 1980s, and the same is true of their roles and functions.

Competitive Policies in an Integrated World

Most studies of tax havens focus on the territories themselves. We believe, however, that to understand tax havens, one needs to appreciate the geopolitical and environmental conditions that gave rise to them in the first place. They did not produce that environment, nor can they influence it in

---

1. The term tax "avoidance" can be found as early as the 1850s. "However, there was no consistent, ongoing administrative or public discussion of the issue during the nineteenth century" (Likhovski 2007, 203). In 1927 there was discussion in the House of Commons of the use of the Channel Islands for the purpose of tax avoidance (Likhovski 2007, 206). The term "tax haven" is rarely found in journalistic or academic literature before the 1950s.

a significant way; they simply learned to take advantage of the conditions they faced.

The modern state system is founded on the principles of sovereignty and sovereign equality. Each sovereign state has the right to write its own laws and pursue its own policies, including tax laws and regulations, within its own territory. During the twentieth century, each state developed its own system of taxation and regulation, and each reached for a different balance between competing domestic interests. Consequently, the world contains as many variants of tax and regulatory regimes as there are states.

Furthermore, particularly since the late nineteenth century, business has become increasingly mobile and international. Cross-border trade has grown at a tremendous pace, as have foreign direct investment and international portfolio investments. A related trend has been the rise of the large-scale economic units—internally differential, hierarchical, and bureaucratic—which are now known as Multinational Corporations (MNCs) or Multinational Enterprises (MNEs).

The traditional craftsman-turned-capitalist combined many skills in one person, acting as owner, buyer of raw material, producer, designer, salesperson, finance officer, and legal adviser. The modern corporation has evolved into a highly specialized bureaucratic machine in which different departments perform different functions. A typical modern MNE may set up manufacturing facilities in different countries, locate its headquarters, design, engineering, and finance departments elsewhere, and place its sales department in yet another location. As a result, an estimated 60% of all international trade takes place across frontiers but between different arms of the same company (OECD 2002). In an alternative model, many MNEs have chosen the "hollow" route, in which they subcontract out most if not all of their manufacturing, finance and legal services, advertising, sales, and so on.

These developments gave rise to what is often labeled interdependence and globalization. Even the largest economies in the world, such as the United States and China, have become specialists in manufacturing goods or services. Historically, country specialties have developed either because of active state or regional policy, or in many cases spontaneously, and they have developed for a great variety of reasons, including access to raw material, geographical location, topography, availability of human capital.

Many governments use their sovereign right to enact law in order to help successful sectors within their economies to compete in the world economy or, alternatively, to spur the development of new competitive sectors. They often employ some combination of fiscal subsidies and sweeteners, including reductions in taxation (sometimes by informal or highly opaque set of arrangements) and removal of "red tape" (i.e., regulation) to attract or retain mobile capital.

The fiscal portions of such policy packages are called Preferential Tax Regimes (PTRs) and include a wide array of initiatives and regulations designed to attract foreign capital. When in the late 1990s the European Commission decided to investigate tax abuse among European Union (EU) member countries, it discovered 206 PTRs—and that figure does not include PTRs in dependent territories of EU member states such as the Channel Islands and Gibraltar. The attractions ranged from generous depreciation allowances to subsidies to peripheral regions and various other types of tax holiday schemes (ECOFIN 1999). EU member states are not alone in this practice, and many states all over the world offer a bewildering variety of PTRs. Such behavior has led to considerable political tension between states and accusations of harmful competition, dumping, free riding, and cheating. Often such accusations are accompanied by calls for protectionism and economic retaliation.

At heart, tax havens are merely another type of economic specialty practiced by states—albeit a specialty that is created and sustained with the help of particularly aggressive, and some would say virulent, PTRs. It is a specialty favored by the smallest independent jurisdictions in the world, and as a result, it is numerically the most popular type of competitive strategy (Palan and Abbott 1996). Dharmapala and Hines calculate that for a country with a population under one million, the likelihood of becoming a tax haven rises from 24% to 63% (2006). The figure is probably higher if dependent jurisdictions such as the Caymans and Jersey are added to the list. Like other competitive state strategies, tax havens enact a range of legislation and tax rules that are aimed at attracting and developing what they call their offshore sector. Equally, and perhaps unsurprisingly, they are subject to the same accusations of harmful competition, free riding, parasitical behavior, and cheating.

Finance, Intangibles, and Tax Havens

The vast majority of the world's PTRs were established to attract manufacturing and assembly lines. Tax havens, in contrast, are aimed primarily at other sectors. To understand what tax havens offer, we need to dwell briefly on some of the more spectacular and esoteric developments in the area of finance.

The financial system is normally divided into two branches, retail and wholesale. Retail banking (and other financial services such as insurance) tends to be a highly profitable business, which handles the financial requirements of individual savers and borrowers. Wholesale finance manages specialized, bulk financial transactions, often of unimaginable sums of money, traded between the financial institutions themselves, and it tends to be even more profitable. The Bank for International Settlements (BIS) estimates that about $3 trillion exchanges hands in the foreign currency market every day; and that there are outstanding derivative contracts in excess of $600 trillion, or twelve times the world's GDP (BIS 2007). It is this wholesale financial market that "froze" during the 2008–9 crisis.

The wholesale financial markets burst the national boundaries in which they had operated since the end of World War II. Since the 1960s, they have been operating more or less as one globally integrated financial system. The wholesale financial system primarily trades in "incorporeal" properties: currencies, equities (shares), debt instruments (bonds), claims on existing and future earnings, hedging contracts and indices. However obscure and complex some of these instruments may appear, they are all contracts for the exchange of property titles. The existence of a global market simply means that a legal framework that supports such exchanges is global as well. Incorporeal properties have no tangible physical existence; they are represented as contractual agreements that are either printed out or, more commonly now, stored electronically.

Financial centers, retail and wholesale, which trade in these incorporeal properties evolved to service the financial needs of the economy that hosts them. Theoretically, the size of a financial center is linked to the size of the economy it services. However, the complexity of financial products and the vast sums of money involved have led to the development of highly skilled groups of workers in the various branches of banking, capital and credit markets, insurance, brokerage, accounting, and of course the law. As a result, financial systems have tended to congregate geographically in the major cities of the world. Profits generated in such centers are taxed by the countries in whose territories these centers are located, and the countries concerned serve as regulatory authorities over these financial centers.

The wholesale financial market trades in incorporeal assets which, by definition, are highly mobile, so the market possesses a flexibility that other sectors do not enjoy. The usual rules of economics still apply—like every other type of economic activity, financial transactions involve costs and income. Costs include the intellectual labor that goes into the making and arranging of a deal, including sunk overhead costs. Income is generated only at the point of the contract and can therefore be risky. However, financial actors can avoid taxation on profits, as well as regulations, by "booking" a contract somewhere other than the place where it was negotiated. For example, a financial transaction can be arranged in London, New York, or Frankfurt—places where specialists tend to be found. But to avoid UK, U.S., or German taxation and regulations, the transaction can be registered or "booked" in low-tax or lightly regulated jurisdictions such as the Cayman Islands. In such centers, almost all the bank branches are "shell" operations. In other words, the branches exist but do not actually do any business or have any assets.

It is not only banks and financial institutions that use tax havens for booking purposes. MNEs operate through complex set of subsidiaries, affiliates, and sub-contractors in many countries, and they are supposed to pay tax on profits made in the territory of each of these countries. MNEs, therefore, also have an incentive to book financial transactions in low-tax, lightly regulated countries. In addition, large MNEs have their own pension funds and may take advantage of lightly regulated/low-tax countries to reduce the handling costs of these funds. Because MNEs operate in many countries, they employ specialized holding companies to register management and financial activities in low-tax countries whenever possible. Banks and companies use a great variety of instruments to achieve these aims (discussed in detail in chapter 3). There are many more techniques that help companies, financial institutions, and rich individuals to avoid taxation or certain sorts of regulation. We discuss those in chapter three.

Tax havens offer particularly aggressive PTRs that are aimed at capturing mobile capital. They are largely repositories of contractual relationships and serve almost entirely as booking devices. It is rarely the case that the substance of the transactions booked in a tax haven actually takes place there. Hence, there is very little actual activity in tax havens, and they are often described as "virtual" centers (Palan 2003). We may define tax havens, therefore, as "legislative spaces." They are jurisdictions that deliberately create legislation to ease transactions undertaken by people who are not resident in their domain. Those international transactions are subject to little or no regulation, and the havens usually offer considerable, legally protected secrecy to ensure that they are not linked to those who are undertaking them. Such transactions are "offshore"—that is, they take place in legal spaces that decouple the real location from the legal location. We should note that, defined in this context, "offshore" has little to do with geography, let alone small islands, but rather with legislative spaces (Palan 2003).

Definition Problems: PTRs and Tax Havens

This basic definition of tax havens raises several practical problems. Although some tax havens are easily recognizable, a highly mobile environment combines with the proliferation of PTRs to create a situation whereby any country may serve as a potential haven from the taxation of some other countries. As a result, the lines separating PTRs, aggressive PTRs, and tax havens are highly contested.

As early as the 1980s, Vincent Belotsky, a high-ranking U.S. Internal Revenue Service (IRS) official, noted that many countries, including the United States, fit the conventional definition of tax haven. The United States, he wrote, "applies a zero rate of tax on certain categories of income, including interest received by nonresident alien individual or a foreign corporation from banks and savings institutions" (1987, 59). Foreigners could use the U.S. banking system to avoid paying tax to their home countries on their savings. In addition, "United States banks offer a high level of banking secrecy to their foreign clients. Unlike domestic clients, foreign clients are excused from obtaining taxpayer identification numbers, their accounts are not reported to the IRS and there is no withholding tax" (1987, 60). Belotsky even suggested that the United States actively promoted itself as a tax haven (1987, 60). Indeed, when the German authorities began to worry about the erosion of the tax base in the late 1980s, topping their list of offending countries were not Switzerland and the Cayman Islands, but rather the United States, Belgium, the Netherlands, and Ireland (Weichenrieder 1996).

The line separating tax havens from other PTRs is arbitrary; it is a "matter of degree more than anything else" (Irish 1982, 452). Some tax havens even deny that they exercise a PTR, let alone an aggressive PTR. Colin Powell, while Jersey's acting chief officer, said: "It is not the island that has made itself more and more attractive; it is the relatively high tax structures of the main industrial countries that have made them relatively unattractive" (Jeune 1999). In reality, we suggest, most tax havens are not as innocent as they pretend. Although we agree that on occasion particular legislation or tax rules may be used opportunistically for tax avoidance and evasion purposes, we believe that the states we discuss in this book have adopted tax haven legislation as a conscious, intentional, and long-term developmental strategy.

Tax haven regimes are set up not to suit the academic's fondness for classification but for the commercial purposes of capturing "rent" from mobile capital. Any activities that become movable because of technological developments instantly become targets of the more agile tax havens. Tax was an obvious first target, and still is the major rationale for setting up these legislative spaces. However, many tax havens have realized the commercial value of extending the principle of tax haven legislation to capture other mobile businesses, such as shipping, casinos, and pornography. The Internet, for instance, created new opportunities for distant casinos, which were grabbed by Bermuda, Costa Rica, and the small island of Alderney.

As this happens, the "consumers" of tax havens—wealthy families, companies, and the professionals that set up tax haven entities—are discovering innovative ways of using them, often killing two birds with one stone. Diamond and Diamond (1998), for instance, believe that the main reason for the spectacular growth in the use of Caribbean tax havens by wealthy individuals during the 1980s and 1990s was not taxation per se but rather matrimonial, family, and insolvency issues. Such assets are hidden not from the tax authorities but from spouses, other family members, and creditors—although the tax haven's location probably also helps to reduce taxation. Similarly, a U.S. regulation subjects hedge funds to U.S. banking and financial regulation if the fund involves more than one hundred partners. A tax haven avoids this rule—and supplies better tax treatment to boot.

Driven by competition, technological advance, and market needs, many tax havens have been branching out into new activities. The literature on tax havens has dealt with this proliferation of activities in two ways. One approach is to describe all these new businesses under the umbrella term of "tax havens." Some experts, for instance, call the flag of convenience (FOC) arrangements practiced by countries such as Liberia or Panama as a form of tax haven (Irish 1982). The argument holds that tax remains the core but no longer the only defining characteristic of the tax haven. The other approach argues that a tax haven is a restricted category, but that some tax havens may also offer other services. This approach is particularly useful when it comes to controversy about the role of tax havens as offshore financial centers.

Definition Problems: The Confusion between Tax Havens and OFCs

The tax havens naturally exploit the proliferation of tasks that they perform for public relations purposes. Because of the association of tax havens with tax evasion, money laundering, criminality, and embezzlement, few tax havens wear the tag with pride. In fact, most if not all deny any association with tax evasion, and seek to present their policies as benign forms of PTR. At best (or worst), some tax havens are prepared to accept the less pejorative designation "offshore financial center" (OFC). Some advertise their offshore business sector on their official websites, and over the last few years OFC has become the description of choice, particularly by international economic organizations such as the International Monetary Fund (IMF), the Financial Action Task Force on Money Laundering (FATF), and the Financial Stability Forum (FSF). Yet the concept of OFC raises its own nightmarish definitional problems, to the point that the IMF abandoned its OFC program in 2008.

Tax havens and OFCs evolved, as we will see in part II of this book, for different purposes and at different times. Yet today it is difficult to distinguish in practice between the activities of tax havens and those of OFCs. Tax havens have existed since the early twentieth century, and were used primarily but not exclusively to evade and avoid taxes. They served other purposes as well, including money laundering and capital flight, and offered stringent secrecy provisions, which proved attractive to couples seeking to avoid punitive divorce settlements.

The concept of OFC, in contrast, is more recent. As far as we can tell, the term came into use only in the early 1980s. However, it has not been used in a clear and consistent manner. The term OFCs is used most commonly to describe financial centers specializing in nonresident financial transactions, especially those known as Euromarket transactions. The original OFC, as we show in chapter 5, developed in September 1957 in London. The market became known as "offshore" because it escaped nearly all forms of financial supervision and regulation. As an unregulated market, it soon became global in reach. According to this criteria, the biggest OFCs now are the City of London in the United Kingdom, the International Banking Facilities (IBFs) in the United States, and the Japanese Offshore Market (JOM).

With their array of secrecy provisions, lax regulation, zero or near-zero taxation, and no capital controls, tax havens proved a magnet for Euromarket transactions. In fact, developing an offshore financial center was a logical extension to the traditional tax haven as both are the product of, and benefit from, avoidance. Furthermore, the lack of regulation or light supervision that characterize OFCs, can easily be used (or abused) for tax avoidance and money laundering purposes. British banks and corporations, for instance, quickly realized the advantages of tax havens. They established subsidiaries in the Crown Colonies to serve essentially as booking offices for Euromarket transactions in the early 1960s. They were soon followed by North American banks that preferred Caribbean havens. Hence, several tax havens developed their own OFCs but were known primarily as either "booking" centers or funding centers.

International financial organizations, including the BIS and the IMF, then began to use OFC in a more restrictive manner to describe specifically the financial services that were evolving in tax havens. The term OFC was used as a polite reference to tax havens, and this has become the prevalent meaning.

At the same time, international financial organizations have periodically acknowledged the strange anomaly that the largest OFCs are located in London, New York, and Tokyo. This became conceptually confusing, because not all tax havens were OFCs, and some OFCs were not tax

---

Box 1.1 The four types of OFCs

In a seminal article written in 1982, Y. S. Park (1982) identified four types of OFCs. Primary OFCs such as London or New York serve worldwide clientele and act as international financial intermediaries for their market regions. Primary centers are not only banking centers but also financial capital market centers. "The key ingredient of a successful centre," writes William Clarke, "is the provision of new money and this in turn depends not only on flexible bank finance, but also on the existence of financial instruments and of financial institutions capable of absorbing a growing volume of securities" (2004, 42). In the case of London, for instance, the capital market is comprised of a stock market, inter-bank market, currency and securities markets, derivatives, and includes an array of financial institutions such as investment banks, hedge funds, insurance companies, pension funds, investment trusts, private equity firms, and so on.

The second type are booking centers such as the Bahamas or the Cayman Islands. Booking, collecting, and funding centers do not have capital market capacity, at least not in any significant measure; they are banking centers at best and have not matured into capital market centers.

The third type are funding centers, such as Singapore or Panama, which play the role of inward financial intermediaries, channeling offshore (or Euromarket) funds from outside their markets toward local or regional uses. In 1968, for instance, Singapore set up a specialized market called the Asian Currency Unit (ACU), in response to a request from the Bank of America to act as a local branch to handle Euromarket transactions.

Finally, collection centers like Bahrain engage primarily in outward financial intermediation. Irish (1982) believes that the latter two categories combined booking and operational activities. All three remain, however, banking rather than capital market centers.

---

havens, who launched a campaign to distance themselves from the concept of OFC.

To complicated things further, OFC is used in a third way, to describe the community of experts and financial services located in tax havens. OFC, in this case, is applied to the community of professional services, consisting largely of expatriates that are visibly an offshore enclave located in these islands-turned-financial-centers, having little to do with the local population. As the various campaigns against tax havens began to evolve, the semantic confusion was no longer tenable.

BIS statistics regarding the international assets and liabilities of banks show that some tax havens have taken a place among the world's premier financial centers. The Cayman Islands are ranked as the sixth largest financial center in the world in terms of assets (table 1.1), Jersey is sixteenth,

Table 1.1 Financial centers ranked by bank's external assets, all sectors (in billions US$; December 2007)

Assets		Liabilities	
United Kingdom	$6,844,744	United Kingdom	$7,310,789
Germany	3,561,009	United States	3,717,692
United States	2,959,285	France	2,806,73
France	2,816,618	Germany	1,992,697
Japan	2,401,783	Cayman Islands	1,864,468
		Switzerland	1,393,45
Cayman Islands	1,927,233	Netherlands	1,192,895
		Ireland	1,151,69
Switzerland	1,539,29	Belgium	968,998
Netherlands	1,341,471	Italy	941,947
Belgium	1,162,452	Singapore	802,822
Luxembourg	1,063,835	Luxembourg	732,594
Ireland	1,029,579	Japan	711,981
Hong Kong SAR	798,302	Spain	701,686
Singapore	785,447		
Italy	646,663	Australia	495,631
Spain	612,778	Hong Kong SAR	476,491
		Bahamas	413,923
Jersey	518,968	Sweden	405,35
Austria	483,104	Jersey	348,968
Bahamas	407,3	Denmark	343,63
Sweden	340,698	Austria	324,341
Canada	302,618	Canada	263,118
Guernsey	246,337	Portugal	241,884
Denmark	222,926	Guernsey	204,686
Bahrain	208,26	South Korea	203,683
Australia	184,963	Bahrain	201,587
Taiwan	177,271		192,5
Portugal	138,932	Norway	173,06
Greece	124,202	Greece	143,92
Finland	101,712	Finland	120,417
Isle of Man	93,469	India	97,917
South Korea	85,675	Brazil	92,167
Norway	82,178	Taiwan	83,701
Brazil	65,192	Isle of Man	68,571
Turkey	44,05	Turkey	54,228
Panama	28,416	Mexico	25,704
India	27,737	Panama	23,363
Mexico	26,734	Netherlands Antilles	20,643
Macao SAR	25,169	Macao SAR	12,987
Netherlands Antilles	23,02	Chile	9,182
Bermuda	11,027	Bermuda	3,241
Chile	6,293		

Source: BIS, 2008.

and the Bahamas is seventeenth. In fact, if we add the intermediate (or as they are sometimes called onshore/offshore) centers such as Switzerland (7th), the Netherlands (8th), and Luxembourg (9th), then tax havens dominate the list of OFCs.

Semantics aside, the more interesting question is whether these jurisdictions have developed into genuine OFCs or whether they remain mere "paper centers," providing a home for shell companies and trusts, proxy banking institutions and captive insurance companies.

Writing in the early 1980s, Irish observed that "typically, these branches [in the Caymans] are nothing more than a set of ledgers managed and kept by an agent rather than a physical location where business is transacted. While deposits and loans are lodged in these shells, the transactions are physically negotiated elsewhere and the funds may never actually be present in the shell" (1982, 464). Fifteen years later, Marvin Goodfriend of the Federal Reserve Bank of Richmond maintained that "Eurodollar deposits and loans negotiated in London or elsewhere often are booked in locations such as Nassau and the Cayman Islands to obtain more favorable tax treatment" (1998, 50). A report written for the Bank of England in 2001 takes the view that "financial intermediation undertaken by entities based in many OFCs [i.e., tax havens] is almost entirely "entrepôt" (Dixon 2001, 104).

Sylla (2002) believes that the early spillover of financial activities to tax havens such as the Bahamas and the Caymans were motivated less by tax concerns and more because it was cheaper to set up branches of banks in these locations, which had the added advantage of sharing New York's time zone. In addition, for technical reasons described in chapter 5, British banks and corporations could access the London offshore market only by using offshore subsidiaries (because the latter rendered them technically nonresident).

There are good reasons to believe that the bulk of financial transactions booked in the purer type of tax havens is still arranged elsewhere. The assets and liabilities of the Cayman Islands are roughly one-third of the UK financial center's (table 1.1). Yet while the Corporation of the City of London reports 338,000 people working directly in the Square Mile (a misleading figure in that it refers to every worker, including cleaners and security guards), the UK's National Audit Office reports that only 5,400 people work in the Cayman OFC (NAO 2007, table 15). The disparity between the two figures suggests that either Cayman is exceedingly efficient, or it is still largely a booking center with relatively little "real" banking activity.

Another instructive figure can be divined from the Caymans' own financial reports, which boasts that by December 2005, there were over 70,000 companies incorporated on the Cayman Islands, including 430 banks and trust companies, 720 captive insurance firms, and more than 7,000 funds (www.gocayman.com). The figures suggest that if we exclude all IBCs, and just add up banks, captive insurance entities, and funds (the majority in hedge funds); we end up with roughly 8,000 such entities, and so each one has on average about one-half of one employee! In other words, on average one person runs, as well as serves as the employee of, two banks, insurance companies, or hedge funds in the Cayman Islands.

On Jersey, a forty-five square mile island with a population of 87,000, approximately 12,000 people are employed in the offshore sector. This figure is equivalent more or less to the employment figures of a decent-sized international investment bank. The Northern Rock's SPV (special purpose vehicle) arm, Granite, handled £49 billion and was based in Jersey (see chapter 6). However, when journalists went searching for Granite's employees to interview, they found no one. Granite was in fact managed by Northern Rock's staff from the UK. From Greg Rawling's survey, we also know that 97% of his respondents cited tax as the primary motivation for using these types of OFCs (2005, 305). Similarly, investigative journalist Brittain-Caitlin writes:

> Most of the largest companies in the world are well installed in Cayman. But what you will not find there is any physical presence of an office completed with logos, staff, and a smile and a hello from a receptionist. No, in Cayman you will find blandly named companies whose names are as purely functional as the companies themselves. (2005, 47)

Table 1.2 suggests that despite being nominally among the largest financial centers in the world, none of the small island tax haven has so far managed to develop any international bank of a significant size. Indeed,

Table 1.2 International positions by nationality of ownership of reporting banks (amounts outstanding in billion US$)

	Assets		Liabilities		World GDP ranking	GDP, 2006, billions US$
Germany	(1)	$4,763.6	(1)	$3,811.4	3	$2,906
Switzerland	(2)	3,569.4	(2)	3,593.5	20	380
France	(3)	3,227.8	(5)	3,062.0	6	2,230
United States	(4)	3,075.4	(3)	3,442.0	1	13,201
UK	(5)	3,020.0	(4)	3,178.8	5	2,345
Japan	(6)	2,316.7	(7)	1,236.7	2	4,340
Netherlands	(7)	2,056.1	(6)	1,885.7	16	657
Belgium	(8)	1,255.3	(8)	1,185.7	18	392
Italy	(9)	863.0	(9)	858.2	7	1,844
Spain	(10)	654.8	(10)	703.2	9	1,223
Offshore centers		11.9		21.7		

Source: BIS, 2007.

the combined assets of the booking centers' own banks are a mere one-twentieth of Portugal's banking system, a country that otherwise does not even make it into any of the tables in this book.

The situation concerning the medium-size centers such as Switzerland, Luxembourg, Ireland, and Singapore is more complex. The most remarkable success is Switzerland, which has produced very large and powerful international banks (table 1.2). Much less of a success is the UK, ranked only fifth in the world by this measure (consistent with its GDP position in the world). Medium-size centers were able to benefit from their tax haven status and developed well-functioning OFCs. However, the question whether OFCs such as Luxembourg, Switzerland, and Singapore could survive the elimination of their tax haven provisions is a matter of dispute—many believe they would be unlikely to remain major OFCs without these provisions.

Box 1.2 The IMF definition of OFC

The IMF was first among international organizations to raise the alarm about tax havens (Cassard 1994). By the early years of the twenty-first century, and facing its own crisis, the IMF attempted to wrest the lead in analytical and research work on tax havens from other organizations. Ever since it has been leading innovative analytical work on tax havens. In a widely cited background paper, the Fund defined OFCs as:

> centers where the bulk of financial sector transactions on both sides of the balance sheet are with individuals or companies that are not residents of OFCs, where the transactions are initiated elsewhere, and where the majority of the institutions involved are controlled by nonresidents. Thus, many OFCs have the following characteristics:

1. Jurisdictions that have financial institutions engaged primarily in business with nonresidents;
2. Financial systems with external assets and liabilities out of proportion to domestic financial intermediation designed to finance domestic economies; and
3. More popularly, centers which provide some or all of the following opportunities: low or zero taxation; moderate or light financial regulation; banking secrecy and anonymity. (IMF 2000)

In 2007, the IMF released another working paper written by Ahmed Zoromé, who argues that all existing definitions fail to capture the essence of the OFC phenomenon, which, he argues, is "the provision of financial services to nonresidents, namely, exports of financial services" (2007, 8). The peculiarity

(continued)

Box 1.2 *(continued)*

of OFCs, he argues, "is that they have specialized in the supply of financial services on a scale far exceeding the needs and the size of their economies" (2007, 6) Zoromé offers the following definition:

An OFC is a country or jurisdiction that provides financial services to nonresidents on a scale that is incommensurate with the size and the financing of its domestic economy (2007, 12–13).

Zoromé's methodology is deficient in several respects. First, a statistical methodology shows only the relatively successful tax havens. There are, however, a good number of "failed" tax havens—mostly small Pacific Islands but some also in the Caribbean (Antigua, for instance), some in the former Soviet bloc countries (Moldova), and a few in Africa—that strive to become tax havens but fail. Second, he fails to acknowledge "inner" tax havens. These are states or regions within federal states such as the United States (Nevada, Delaware), Russia (Ingushetia), or Malaysia (Labuan), which use domestic autonomy to enact the type of laws that we associate with tax havens. Third, we question the wisdom of thinking of offshore financial centers as a "service" economy in the traditional sense of the word, or of ignoring completely the issue of taxation.

In 2008, the majority of the directors of the IMF decided to abandon its separate OFC program, acknowledging the semantic and conceptual difficulties associated with the term (IMF 2008).

Ideal Type Description of Tax Havens

The above discussion shows the great difficulties we encounter as we try to move from theory to the real world of taxation. One analytical tactic favored by academics is to use a Weberian ideal type of definition. An ideal type is formed from the characteristics and elements of a given phenomenon, but it does not correspond to all its characteristics or particulars. We can supply an ideal-type description of the tax haven on the understanding that very few places in reality correspond closely to this ideal type. It so happens that most tax havens tend to be very small jurisdictions, and the smaller and more successful among them happen to align with the ideal-type description. However just because larger states or territories, with population of say half a million to ten million, will have more varied economies does not mean they are not tax havens. The principal "ideal-type" attributes of tax havens are as follows.

Low or Nil Taxation

The quintessential tax haven is a country that offers either zero or near zero rates of taxation to nonresident companies and savers. This is perhaps the best-known characteristic of tax havens, yet in many ways it can be highly misleading. The reality is that, however small or efficient a tax haven may be (or claims to be), none has been able to perform the miracle of running a properly functioning state without raising revenues through taxation. There are, as a result, some genuinely low-tax jurisdictions on our list of tax havens, but these tend to be highly dysfunctional states that are both unsatisfactory places to live in and unsuccessful in their bid to become flourishing havens. Alternatively, there are "clever" tax havens that are able to raise sufficient revenues to operate, at the same time presenting themselves as nil- or low-tax jurisdictions. They do so by employing one or more of the following three methods.

First, tax havens typically differentiate between resident and nonresident taxpayers. The apparent taxation rates for nonresident taxpayers can be very low or even nominally zero. Tax havens separate domestic and nonresident population through what is called "ring fencing," which arises when a haven decides to charge its resident population a tax that it does not wish to apply to those using its haven services. Many of the well-known tax havens—such as Jersey, Guernsey, the Isle of Man, Switzerland, and Liechtenstein—impose income tax on the worldwide income of their resident populations, but ensure that tax exiles using their domains do not suffer some or all of these charges. The UK, too, conducts a ring fencing operation by applying the domicile rule—one reason the UK is considered a tax haven (see box 1.3). The UK Crown Dependencies and some other tax havens charge locally owned companies income tax on their corporate profits but do not do so on companies owned by nonresidents. Jersey has even enacted some of the most stringent anti-tax-avoidance legislation in the world to penalize its own residents who want to use the services of other tax havens.

However, it would be wrong to think that nonresidents are not taxed at all. In reality, nonresident taxpayers are taxed by other means, such as licensing and registration fees and/or requirement to maintain "dummy" local directors. All tax havens charge fees for the operation of nonresident entities. For example, in Vanuatu it costs US$150 to register a company and $300 a year to maintain it on the registry of companies. In the Isle of Man, the annual fee for a nonresident company is approximately £320 a year. In addition, even "pure" havens tend to impose employment, customs, duty, and property taxes, with nonresident businesses—which are required by most tax havens to employ local residents and maintain small local offices—paying some tax indirectly. These sums can constitute a significant contribution to the economy of a small tax haven, and may compensate handsomely for the loss of direct tax revenues, particularly if the tax haven is able to attract many paper or shell companies. Revenues generated by the offshore sector serve as supplementary income and can reduce domestic taxation.

Unsurprisingly, tax havens rarely advertise this gain in net revenue, and so it is very hard to assess. For example, a breakdown of government income was not included in the hundreds of pages of data in the Cayman Islands' published budget for 2004/5 (Caymans 2004)—and the Caymans is one of the more transparent tax havens. We know, however, that the Cayman Islands raises most of its taxes from tourist levies and import duties.

A second popular method used by tax havens to reduce taxation involves subsidies from larger states. Some of the most successful "pure" tax havens are dependent jurisdictions; they rely on larger states for their security, diplomatic relations, and maintenance of the currency and broader macro-economic environment, as well as the collection of VAT (value-added tax) receipts. They pass some of these savings to residents and to nonresident taxpayers. These include the highly successful Crown Dependencies of Jersey, Guernsey, and the Isle of Man, plus Gibraltar in Europe and the Caymans, Bermuda, and the British Virgin Islands (BVI) in the Caribbean. Others include the Netherlands Antilles; Monaco and Andorra, both of which rely on the French state for most of its essential services, France; and Liechtenstein, which relies on Switzerland.

The Isle of Man has been particularly successful in this game. It has enjoyed subsidies from the UK government amounting to more than £200 million a year—a fact little known even to its direct competitors, Jersey and Guernsey. This is the result of the so-called common purse agreement by which some revenues between the UK and the Isle of Man are supposedly shared. Since 1911, when the island's population was suffering near-famine conditions, the agreement of 1911 has been designed to provide subsidy to the Isle of Man. The UK's National Audit Office notes other smaller subsidies such as the considerable cost the UK bears for regulating civil aviation in places like the BVI, even though the latter has a GDP per head higher than that of the UK (NAO 2007).

Ironically, some forms of regulation intended to prevent tax haven abuse have actually boosted the coffers of the havens. For example, the EU Savings Tax Directive (discussed in chapter 10) requires that banks and other financial institutions in havens for which the UK and the Netherlands hold responsibility, as well as Switzerland and Liechtenstein, deduct tax at a current rate of 20% from payments of interest to residents of an EU state. This was a compromise arrangement applied to cases where the account holder refuses to disclose information on income he or she has earned to the home state. These havens receive 25% of the sum deducted as an "administration" cost! According to one EU report, Liechtenstein collected €2.5 million in 2005, Jersey €48 million, Guernsey €4.5 million, and Switzerland a hefty €159.4 million (European Commission 2006, 16).

We have already alluded to the third method. In some rare cases, low-tax regimes may be historical. Since 1869, for example, the Principality of Monaco has not imposed taxation on revenue of any sort; its state income being derived primarily from the casinos that have long been its major attraction and from municipal taxation. But it is also true that jurisdictions like Monaco can appear to be a low-tax jurisdiction only because of very high municipal taxes, which are normally not registered in the official statistics as taxation. Municipal taxes are typically regressive; hence Monaco is very attractive to the superrich, for whom its regime of municipal taxation appears relatively inconsequential compared to taxes in other countries. And of course Monaco, as mentioned above, also relies on France for most of its essential services.

In sum, the reality of this interdependent world is that when one comes across low- or zero-tax jurisdiction, someone else is paying additional tax elsewhere, thereby permitting that jurisdiction to offer low-tax services.

Secrecy Provisions

The other defining characteristic of tax haven is strict confidentiality. Indeed, some prefer to call tax havens "secrecy havens," arguing that opacity, rather than nominal or declaratory levels of taxation, is the key trait that distinguishes these jurisdictions from other PTRs (Hampton 1996).

Opacity is realized in three ways. Perhaps the most commonplace is a banking secrecy law. It is normal for all banks to provide secrecy for their customers, but in many locations this is considered best commercial practice and is not mandated by law. As a result banking secrecy is far from sacrosanct. All UK banks, for instance, are required to report interest earned on all accounts they maintain in the UK to HM Revenue & Customs on an annual basis. This is in direct contrast with what prevails in many tax havens and in some locations that are not considered havens but where banking secrecy is protected by law. Switzerland is considered the originator of the legal concept of banking secrecy, enshrined in its 1934 banking laws (see chapter 4). The law makes it a criminal offence for any bank employee to disclose bank information for any reason whatsoever. The right of the government to obtain bank information is also severely limited.

Switzerland, however, is no longer alone in this practice. Liechtenstein, the Bahamas, the Cayman Islands, and others have adopted even more stringent laws. In some countries, banking secrecy is so deeply enshrined in law that it would require constitutional change for it to be removed. Chile, which is not considered a tax haven, is one such case. The combination of legalized banking secrecy and limited government right of inquiry (usually restricted nowadays to criminal matters, which may exclude tax evasion) is the norm in most tax havens.

Bank secrecy laws have attracted a great degree of criticism and political pressure in the past few years. Austria repealed its bank secrecy laws in 2000, and Switzerland is now prepared to cooperate with foreign authorities on criminal cases. UBS has announced at a recent shareholders meeting in Lucerne that it was poised to bow to U.S. pressure and release the names of an unspecified number of U.S. customers who may have committed tax fraud in squirreling away their assets. Lichtenstein's prime minister said on October 6, 2008 that a new agreement to share tax information about its banks' clients with the United States was "imminent." Yet there are places that are holding out. Panama, for one, has no information exchange provisions at all. Singapore is the new Switzerland, without doubt, and Dubai is not far behind. Andorra, as well, is also holding out

Although in some locations where secrecy was considered absolute it can now be permeated, this will only happen in extremis. For the vast majority of people secrecy will still work. There is no automatic information exchange and Tax Information Exchange Agreements (TIEAs) are used sparingly. Jersey's agreement with the United States has only been used four times in the past five years. We believe that some cracks might be appearing, but they are hardly going to undermine the whole structure of offshore as yet.

The second popular method of creating opacity is to allow the establishment of entities whose ownership and purpose is difficult to identify. Trusts are perhaps the best known and most popular mechanism for achieving this aim (see chapter 3). Most jurisdictions do not require any registration of trusts, and even where registration is required it is not a matter of public record.

Trusts and companies are the most prevalent forms of offshore entities. Most companies registered in tax havens are limited by shares, and in contrast to onshore companies, information on governance structure, ownership, and purpose is usually kept secret. Very often, a bearer instrument is used (FATF rules on money laundering have tended to limit access to this mechanism in recent years). A bearer instrument is a document that indicates that the bearer of the document has title to property, such as shares or bonds. Bearer instruments differ from normal registered instruments in that no records are kept of either the ownership of the underlying property or transactions involving transfer of ownership. Whoever physically holds the bearer papers owns the property.

Bearer instruments are useful for investors and corporate officers who wish to retain anonymity—although ownership is extremely difficult to recover in the event of loss or theft. The use of such instruments means that ownership of a company can be not only hidden but also transferred at will without stamp duty or capital gains being paid and without any organization that deals with the company being none the wiser. Money laundering regulations are virtually impossible to apply in such circumstances. Consequently, tax haven companies offer opportunities for abuse to almost anyone who might trade with them.

Finally, foundations are also secretive structures. Most commonly associated with Liechtenstein and Panama, foundations might best be described as a form of trust that is recognized as having separate legal existence akin to a limited company. Recent adverse publicity for Liechtenstein may diminish the market for foundations in the short term, but it is noteworthy that places like Jersey are now investigating the possibility of making foundations available to the clients of their local professional firms.

The third method of creating opacity may be described as passive, in that it relies on inactivity or intentional negligence. Many tax havens do not perform serious due diligence and have perfected the practice of purposeful looseness in regulations. They have erected bureaucratic hurdles against information exchange with other countries, and their regulatory bodies have scant resources and ask no questions. For example, the BVI, which boast the largest number of IBCs registered in any territory, does not maintain records of those that have discontinued operations. Because BVI has no idea how many of the IBCs logged in its official statistics are currently functioning, there are serious questions about the quality of its administration.

Light and Flexible Incorporation

Another characteristic of a tax haven is the ease with which entities may be incorporated, and the ease with which anonymity can be secured when doing so, and subsequently the ease to operate the resulting limited company. Tax havens make it easy and cheap to set up companies, trusts, even banks. Companies can be literally bought "off the shelf," and the cost of incorporation is very low. Many tax havens do not require financial institutions and corporations to have any real presence in their territory.

Competition among Tax Havens and Evolution of Niche Strategies

Because of the proliferation in the number of tax havens, competition is intense. Consequently, many tax havens are developing niche strategies, creating legislative differentiation for themselves. A different typology of tax havens can be based on these niche strategies. This typology suggests the following:

Box 1.3 Mid-size states as tax havens

Larger states or territories with populations of half a million to ten million possess more varied economies and may not, at first sight, conform to the ideal of a tax haven. Yet some such countries offer tax haven attributes to such a degree that they should be considered, often despite their protestations, tax havens.

Among the most significant tax havens of the world, Switzerland, Luxembourg, and Singapore claim that they are not low-tax jurisdictions. Strictly speaking, they are correct: they are certainly not low-tax jurisdictions for their own citizens. Yet through a complex set of loopholes and formal and informal rules they can serve as low-tax jurisdictions to nonresidents. In addition, all three offer very strict secrecy provisions and relatively easy and cheap mechanisms to set up nonresident companies.

On the face of it, there is nothing unusual about Luxembourg's rate of taxation. The normal corporate tax rate, including municipal business tax, is approximately 37.5%. But Luxembourg has all sorts of special tax provisions, such as the one for so-called co-ordination centers. Such centers are approved on a case-by-case basis, and must be established by a company that operates in at least two other countries. Such centers are liable to all Luxembourg taxes, but the profits of the co-ordination center are determined on a cost-plus basis and at least 5% of the deductible expenses. This method of calculating profits ensures that despite the nominal 37.5% tax levied, companies that take advantage of the provision pay a very small amount in tax.

The Luxembourg holding companies are of greater significance, as they are subject to capital contribution tax at the rate of 1% and a subscription duty at the rate of 0.2% of the paid up value of the shares (ECOFIN 1999, 37). Luxembourg offers many other such arrangements. Most have come under intense scrutiny in the last decade but continue in operation nonetheless.

Belgium offers the same co-ordination center arrangements. These centers are liable to Belgian income tax at the normal rate of 40.17%. But instead of levying tax on actual profits as shown in financial statements, income tax is levied on a notional tax base determined as a percentage of certain operating costs (ECOFIN 1999, 30). In reality, a Belgian co-ordination center pays light taxes.

Hong Kong, Panama, and Costa Rica all have income taxes, but because they rely on the territoriality principle to determine the scope of their tax jurisdiction, foreign-sourced income is generally not taxed at all. Arrangements such as these, deliberately adopted by intermediate tax havens, gain them a place on the list of tax havens.

---

a) Incorporation locations. This category is used primarily for the registration of entities such as offshore companies that are then used in transactions recorded in other tax havens. They tend to be associated with very low effective regulation, examples being Montserrat and Anguilla, and have no OFC to speak of.

Table 1.3 Select foreign affiliates in the Irish financial service center, assets and number of employees

Name of ultimate parent company	Name of affiliate	Pre-tax profits, millions	Gross assets, millions	Number of employees
3Com. U.S.	3Com. (Cayman)	$4.6	$153	0
Albany Inter. U.S.	A1 fin. service (Switzerland)	€3.0	€117	0
Airbus, France	Airbus, fin. ser (Netherlands)	0	€2	0
Analog Development, U.S.	Annalog Development Int. finance (Netherlands)	$11.6	$592	6
BBA, UK	BBA finance (Luxembourg)	0	$433	0
Boston Scientific, U.S.	Bost. S. Int. Fin (Netherland)	$2.8	$312	0
Tyco Inter. Bermuda	Brangate (Lux)	$26.6	$907	6
Bristol-Meyers Squibb, U.S.	BR. Mey, Sq. Int (Switzerland)	€15.1	€947	4
Cisco Systems, U.S.	Cisco Fin Int. (Bermuda)	$–109.0	$235	27
Coca-Cola, Greece	Coca-Cola holding (Cyprus)	€–3.7	€2179	0
CNH, Netherlands	CNH, Capital (Netherlands)	€–6.3	€94	49
IBM, U.S.	IBM, Int, fin. holding (Netherlands)	$50.2	$2653	4
Eli Lilli, U.S.	Kinsale Fin. (Switzerland)	$32.9	$1409	1
Pfizer, U.S.	Prizer, Services (Isle of Man)	$33.6	$6501	10
	Pfizer int bank, Europe (Isle of Man)	$23.6	$485	0
Vivendi, France	Polygram int. (Luxembourg)	$22.0	$3919	0
Sea Container, Bermuda	See Container, fin. (Bermuda)	€0.5	€26	0
Black & Decker, U.S.	Black & Decker, int. (Netherlands)	$5.9	$888	7
Volkswagen, Germany	Volkswagen, inv. (Cayman)	€15.9	€566	7
Xerox, U.S.	Xerox leasing (Jersey)	€29.7	€645	0
General Motors, U.S.	RFC (Ireland)	$2.1	$108	0
Sigma-Aldrich, U.S.	Sigma-Ald. serv (UK)	£1.2	€645	0
INGKA, Holdings, Netherland	IKEA, Invest. (Netherlands)	SEK 53.7	2052 SEK	1

Source: based on Stewart 2005, 281.

b) Registration centers. These havens are associated with locally owned money being invested in its country of origin via an offshore location to benefit from a preferential tax regime, or what is known as "round tripping." The Chinese reputedly use BVI entities for such purposes. Other examples are Panama to serve the U.S. market, and Jersey to target the London market, while Vanuatu serves the Australian market. In contrast to incorporation locations, these places have developed local expertise to service customers who use entities registered in their location.

c) Secrecy locations. In these jurisdictions—including Liechtenstein, the Turks and Caicos Islands, Singapore, and Dubai—secrecy is considered absolutely paramount and is heavily protected.

d) Specialist service providers. These havens aim to secure a specific type of business activity. For example, Bermuda and Guernsey target the reinsurance market, the Caymans the hedge fund industry, and the Isle of Man has set out to secure a market in companies floating on the UK's Alternative Investment Market (AIM).

e) Market entry conduits. These havens seek to earn a margin from the routing of transactions through their domain. Most seek to exploit their network of double tax treaties in the process. They include Malta and Cyprus, which compete for funds routed from the developing world into the EU; Mauritius, which is a conduit for investment in India; the Netherlands, which acts as a location for holding companies for investment throughout Europe; and Belgium and Luxembourg, which have at various times sought similar roles for themselves using mechanisms noted above.

f) High net worth providers. These havens—Switzerland, New York, and London—developed the resources needed to manage funds deposited by the world's wealthiest people and can ensure that their clients can get to see their fund manager with relative ease.

g) Tax raiders. These countries seek the relocation of profits to their domains, where they are taxed at a lower rate than elsewhere, but where they offer a high degree of financial security and limited risk that the transactions may be identified as taking place in a tax haven. Foremost among these locations is Ireland.

Box 1.4 Is the UK a tax haven?

U.S. tax officials admit that the United States may be considered a tax haven. The case for arguing that UK is a tax haven is stronger. As we see in chapter 4, the UK invented the concept of the offshore company, where registration takes place in one location but residence is considered to be elsewhere. The UK also introduced the concept of the trust and codified regulations with regard to their use in the 1925 Trustee Act, which is still in use. Crucially, the UK enshrined the secrecy of trusts, requiring neither that they be registered unless taxable nor that they have accounts in the public record. By doing so the UK created the perfect instrument for offshore secrecy. The UK has also been characterized as an OFC by the IMF (Zoromé 2007).

In September 1957 the Bank of England created, perhaps unwittingly, the regulatory concept of offshore when it accepted that transactions that took place in London but were undertaken between two parties resident outside the UK were not subject to UK financial regulation. They were deemed to take place "elsewhere" and not London, even though it was obvious to all involved that this was a fiction.

Finally, the UK has literally created more of the world's tax havens than any other state. It has been the deliberate policy of the Foreign & Commonwealth Office over many years to encourage its small island dependencies to develop as tax havens.

UK-domiciled international banks are often caught in money laundering activities. A French parliamentary inquiry into the City of London released in 2001 uses a 400-page dossier to demonstrate that London is a secrecy space on a par with any tax haven, and is frequently unwilling to comply with foreign requests for the exchange of information.

The domicile rule is the quintessential piece of evidence that the UK is a tax haven. Albeit modified and reduced in scope in April 2008, the UK domicile rule states that any person who immigrates to the UK but declares their wish to return to their country of origin at some point in the future, is not liable to pay local tax on their worldwide earnings. Note that the person need not actually return to their country but only declare that this is their intention. In fact, that person's children, whether born in the UK or not, are usually exempt from paying tax on their worldwide earnings as well. This law is exploited by a horde of Russian oligarchs, Arab sheiks, U.S. corporate raiders, and European magnates, who flock to London, declaring their intention to return home one day, and use the UK as a tax haven.

The UK makes it exceedingly easy to set up companies. It is possible to form a company within hours. No proof of identity of any sort is requested by the UK state agency responsible, Companies House. Companies can be bought "off the shelf" from registration agents, again with no evidence of identity being required. As such, it is easy to establish a company using false names and information. It is possible, in addition, to issue bearer shares in UK companies, even though this practice is frowned on. This is not a mistake or an oversight: the right to issue bearer shares survived into section 779 of the Companies Act 2006. UK companies can also use nominees as directors, company secretary, and shareholders, all of whom can be recorded as being located at an accommodation address.

In effect, you can set up and run a company in the UK without the Companies House or the public having any idea who is behind the activities it is pursuing.

One other form of UK entity, the Limited Liability Partnership, is "tax transparent." This means that the entity itself, although incorporated with limited liability under UK law, is not taxable. Instead, its profit is apportioned to its members who are then taxed only if resident in the UK. Such entities can book income as arising in the UK on which they can seek to avoid UK tax liability.

It should come as no surprise that a study conducted by several economists has concluded that the UK must be classified as a tax haven (Becht, Meyer, and Wagner, 2006).

(continued)

Box 1.4 (*continued*)

In July 2007, the Chancellor of the Exchequer Alistair Darling said that "claims that the UK was a tax shelter were seriously flawed. . . . The government is committed to ensuring that everyone pays their fair share of tax" (Neveling 2007b). The UK government believes that some UK dependencies are tax havens. We beg to differ. We believe that the UK itself is a tax haven.

Tax Havens of The World

Several lists have been prepared over the years that seek to identify the places known as tax havens. Table 1.4 shows a "list of lists" of such havens over approximately the last thirty years.

There is a remarkable degree of agreement regarding some locations. The Bahamas, Bermuda, the Cayman Islands, Guernsey, Jersey, Malta, and Panama appear on every list. Twenty-two states and jurisdictions appear on at least eight lists. In practice, those that appear on fewer than three lists are unlikely to be of consequence, with the exceptions of Dubai, Latvia, Uruguay, the U.S. Virgin Islands, the United States, the Netherlands, and Belgium. In addition, Austria has not appeared on any list, even though it has had significant tax haven characteristics. Ghana, although not currently on any of these lists, is creating the basis for becoming a tax haven, joining Somalia as the only other country on mainland Africa with such a status. In sum, we believe, there are about fifty-six countries worthy of serious consideration as tax havens in 2009. It should be noted, however, that our list excludes some countries such as Tonga, which the OECD calls tax havens but where such activity appears to be inconsequential.

Conclusion

There is no universally accepted definition of a tax haven. The difficulty in offering such a definition is twofold. First, the majority of states in the world offer a plethora of fiscal incentives to selected industries and sectors, described in academic and policy jargon as Preferential Tax Regimes. Because there is no clear line dividing PTRs from tax havens, the use of tax as the criterion for assessing whether a location plays a questionable role in the financial markets is always going to be fraught with difficulties. Second, the unique secrecy rules provided by tax havens, or "secrecy havens" as some (e.g., Hampton 1996) have called them, provides a better

Table 1.4 Tax havens of the world

Rank	Location	Int'l Bureau Fiscal Docs 1977	Charles Irish 1982	Hines Rice 1994	OECD 2000	IMF 2000	FSF 2000	FATF 2000/02	TJN 2005	IMF 2007	STHAA 2007	Low-TaxNet 2008	Total
1	Bahamas	1	1	1	1	1	1	1	1	1	1	1	11
2	Bermuda	1	1	1	1	1	1	1	1	1	1	1	11
3	Cayman Islands	1	1	1	1	1	1	1	1	1	1	1	11
4	Guernsey	1	1	1	1	1	1	1	1	1	1	1	11
5	Jersey	1	1	1	1	1	1	1	1	1	1	1	11
6	Malta	1	1	1	1	1	1	1	1	1	1	1	11
7	Panama	1	1	1	1	1	1	1	1	1	1	1	11
8	Barbados	1	1	1	1	1	1	1	1		1	1	10
9	British Virgin Islands	1	1	1	1	1	1	1	1		1	1	10
10	Cyprus	1		1	1	1	1	1	1	1	1	1	10
11	Isle of Man	1	1	1	1	1	1	1	1		1	1	10
12	Liechtenstein	1	1	1	1	1	1	1	1		1	1	10
13	Netherlands Antilles	1	1	1	1	1	1	1	1		1	1	10
14	Vanuatu	1	1	1	1	1	1		1	1	1	1	10
15	Gibraltar	1		1	1	1	1	1	1		1	1	9
16	Hong Kong	1	1	1		1	1		1	1	1	1	9
17	Singapore	1	1	1		1	1		1	1	1	1	9
18	St Vincent & Grenadines	1		1	1	1	1	1	1		1	1	9
19	Switzerland	1	1	1		1	1		1	1	1	1	9
20	Turks & Caicos Islands	1	1	1	1	1	1		1		1	1	9

(continued)

(Table 1.4—cont.)

Rank	Location	Int'l Bureau Fiscal Docs 1977	Charles Irish 1982	Hines Rice 1994	OECD 2000	IMF 2000	FSF 2000	FATF 2000/02	TJN 2005	IMF 2007	STHAA 2007	Low-TaxNet 2008	Total
21	Antigua & Barbuda	1		1	1	1	1	1	1		1		8
22	Belize			1	1	1	1	1	1		1	1	8
23	Cook Islands			1	1	1	1	1	1		1	1	8
24	Grenada			1	1	1	1	1	1		1	1	8
25	Ireland	1	1	1		1	1		1	1		1	8
26	Luxembourg	1		1		1	1		1	1	1	1	8
27	Monaco	1		1	1	1	1	1	1		1		8
28	Nauru	1	1		1	1	1	1	1		1		8
29	St Kitts & Nevis			1	1	1	1	1	1		1	1	8
30	Andorra	1		1	1	1	1	1	1			1	7
31	Anguilla			1	1	1	1	1	1		1	1	7
32	Bahrain		1	1	1	1	1		1	1			7
33	Costa Rica	1	1			1	1		1		1	1	7
34	Marshall Islands			1		1	1	1	1		1	1	7
35	Mauritius				1	1	1	1	1	1	1	1	7
36	St Lucia				1	1	1	1	1		1		7
37	Aruba				1	1	1		1		1	1	6
38	Dominica			1	1	1		1	1		1		6
39	Liberia	1		1	1				1		1	1	6
40	Samoa				1	1	1	1	1		1		6
41	Seychelles	1			1	1	1		1			1	6
42	Lebanon		1	1		1	1	1	1				5
43	Niue				1	1	1	1	1				5

#	Jurisdiction									Total
44	Macau			1	1	1			1	4
45	Malaysia (Labuan)			1		1	1		1	4
46	Montserrat	1		1	1	1				4
47	Maldives			1	1	1				3
48	United Kingdom					1	1	1		3
49	Brunei					1			1	2
50	Dubai					1			1	2
51	Hungary				1	1				2
52	Israel				1			1		2
53	Latvia					1	1			2
54	Madeira					1			1	2
55	Netherlands				1	1				2
56	Philippines	1				1				2
57	South Africa					1	1			2
58	Tonga		1			1				2
59	Uruguay		1			1				2
60	US Virgin Islands					1	1			2
61	USA					1			1	2
62	Alderney					1				1
63	Anjouan								1	1
64	Belgium					1				1
65	Botswana								1	1
66	Campione d'Italia					1				1
67	Egypt					1				1
68	France					1				1
69	Germany					1				1
70	Guatemala					1				1
71	Honduras					1				1

(continued)

(Table 1.4—cont.)

Rank	Location	Int'l Bureau Fiscal Docs 1977	Charles Irish 1982	Hines Rice 1994	OECD 2000	IMF 2000	FSF 2000	FATF 2000/02	TJN 2005	IMF 2007	STHAA 2007	Low-TaxNet 2008	Total
72	Iceland								1				1
73	Indonesia							1					1
74	Ingushetia								1				1
75	Jordan			1									1
76	Marianas								1				1
77	Melilla								1				1
78	Myanmar							1					1
79	Nigeria							1					1
80	Palau					1							1
81	Puerto Rico		1										1
82	Russia							1					1
83	San Marino				1								1
84	Sao Tome e Principe								1				1
85	Sark								1				1
86	Somalia								1				1
87	Sri Lanka		1										1
88	Taipei								1				1
89	Trieste								1				1
90	Turkish Republic of Northern Cyprus								1				1
91	Ukraine							1					1
		32	29	40	41	46	42	37	72	22	34	41	436

Sources: Irish 1982; Hines and Rice 1994; OECD, IMF, FSF, FATF listings in the year noted; Hampton and Christensen 2005; Stop Tax Haven Abuse Act 2007; Tax Net, http://www.lowtax.net/lowtax/html/jurhom.html.

indication of the key product that these locations supply and facilitates all the abuses that they permit, including aggressive tax avoidance and tax evasion.

This focus on secrecy does not entirely solve the definition problem because the majority of states in the world offer a great variety of secrecy provisions not only with regard to national security issues—and many states take a very broad view on what they consider national or strategic interests—but also with regard to the commercial world.

The definition of a tax haven is, therefore, inevitably subjective. We define tax havens as jurisdictions that deliberately create legislation to ease transactions undertaken by people who are not resident in their domains, with a purpose of avoiding taxation and/or regulations, which they facilitate by providing a legally backed veil of secrecy to obscure the beneficiaries of those transactions. We accept that this definition leaves the judgment as to whether a country is a tax haven or not to be a matter of opinion. Thus, in table 1.4 we adopt a consensual approach to identifying tax havens: the more authorities believe that a state serves as tax haven, the more likely it is to be one.

Chapter 2

Tax Havens: Vital Statistics

The head of the OECD offshore unit, Jeffrey Owens, declared in 2007 that "between five and seven trillion US dollars are located in tax havens." Others tout that "half of the global stock of money goes through offshore" (Cassard 1994). BIS data suggest that Cayman-registered banks have accumulated in excess of $1.5 trillion in deposits, that Luxembourg-registered mutual funds have amassed more than $2.3 trillion of assets, and Swiss "private" bankers manage about US$4 trillion of assets (Sullivan 2007a). These are some of the staggering figures associated with tax havens. How reliable are these figures? And what do they tell us?

Statistics about tax havens are notoriously confusing. We have already seen that the definition of tax havens is contested, and inevitably, statistics about havens vary a good deal. In addition, tax havens are often confused for OFCs and vice versa, and that confusion is repeated in the statistics as well. Official data gathering methods are not standardized, which creates more confusion. As Sullivan notes, "in the Cayman Islands, the monetary authority does not report dollar amounts on non-bank activity. That leaves Cayman's huge investment and hedge fund industry off the official radar" (2007b). Indeed, most jurisdictions produce little or no information about wealth managed through shell corporations and private trusts. To confuse matters further, the boundary separating tax evasion from tax avoidance is not entirely clear (and differs from one state to another), and much avoidance and evasion takes the form of transfer pricing, which is notoriously difficult to identify and calculate.

Some tax havens are known for having exaggerated or "massaged" the figures. "In the highly competitive marketplace for offshore financial services," notes Sullivan "puffed-up numbers can heighten a jurisdiction's perceived prominence . . . data [are] often presented so that offshore financial services appear more significant than they really are" (2007b). Available data and headline figures can be misleading, and require a critical eye and sophisticated interpretation.

In this chapter, we sift through the available data to provide an estimate of the impact that tax havens are having on the world economy. We stress, however, the enormous difficulties involved in gathering reliable data.

Box 2.1 Sources of information on tax havens

Objective difficulties in obtaining detailed and accurate information have long hampered research into tax havens. The vast majority of "consumers" of tax havens facilities, corporations, financial institutions and rich individuals, let alone criminals, seeking avoidance of one thing or another, are extremely reluctant to provide information about their activities in tax havens. Even if, strictly speaking, the vast majority are not breaking any laws, they are still residing or running some of their operations through tax havens and OFCs in order to avoid one thing or another and prefer to remain anonymous and shun the limelight.

The providers of tax haven services, states and the professionals, are also reluctant to supply detailed accurate information on the offshore sector for fear of losing their clientele. In addition, the vast majority of tax havens do not have strong incentives, nor do they possess the logistical capacity to regulate, let alone research in depth, their offshore sector. As a result, it has been difficult to obtain detailed and accurate information on tax havens, and the sector remained for a long time shrouded in secrecy. Nevertheless, our knowledge of the phenomenon has grown tremendously in the past few years.

There are seven principal sources of information on tax havens. Much of the initial descriptive information on tax havens was collated and provided by various manuals and reference books aimed at practitioners, that is those who are using tax havens for avoidance purposes. Country specific studies are typically produced by independent publishing houses. Various books, guides, and encyclopedias "amount to a recital of a few sections of the laws and local procedures (how to incorporate, how much it costs, etc.) of several tax havens without necessarily relating these to a specific target audience" (Ramati, 1991, 19). Best known are the Tolley's series (2003), the Grundy series (1987), the Economist Intelligence unit reports (Doggart 2002), Ginsburg (1991), Beauchamp (1983), Chambost (1977), and the papers of the so-called granddaddy of tax haven research, Walter Diamond (Diamond and Diamond 1998).

Several international organizations—including the BIS, the IMF, the FSF, UNCTAD, and OECD—provide a wealth of statistical information, as well as

(continued)

Box 2.1 (*continued*)

analysis and discussions of the role and functions of tax havens and OFCs in the world economy. International organizations normally rely on national statistical officers for their aggregate data, leading independent academics to question the reliability of data emanating from tax havens and used by international organizations. The BIS provides national statistical bureaus with detailed guidelines on methods of information gathering and seek to standardize principles of data gathering throughout the world. There has been marked improvement in the past few years in the quality of statistical information and analysis of the offshore sector supplied by these organizations. The IMF and BIS, in particular, have devoted considerable resources toward researching the analytical and conceptual problem associated with existing locational (i.e., state-centered) statistics and data in a globalized financial system and are producing increasingly diverse and detailed data of financial flows worldwide. Economists and accountants have learned to apply innovative statistical techniques and work with these goldmines of aggregate international data. Among those, the work of Desai et al. 2002, 2004a, 2006; Dharmapala and Hines 2006; van Dijk et al. 2006; Hines 1999; Hines and Rice 1994; Murphy and colleagues 2006, 2007, 2008a, 2008b; Slemrod 1994; Slemrod and Wilson 2006); and Sullivan (2004a, 2004b, 2007a, 2007b) deserve specific mention. The ongoing debate among these organizations, academic researchers, and civil society groups is pushing the boundaries of research forward. As a result, we can begin to construct a fairly detailed profiles of the role and function of the offshore sector in the global economy.

The third source of information is the tax havens themselves: the great majority of the major havens provide annual reports on their offshore sector, including information on the type of incorporation available and relevant tax and financial laws in their territories. (Some even provide a useful historical account of the evolution of their tax and regulatory regimes.) Most tax havens also publish their responses to the various initiatives of the OECD, the FSF, and the IMF. Some also publish annual reports on the number of companies and banks incorporated in their territory. These annual reports are used partly in order to attract business; hence some tax havens have been accused of over-estimating the number of offshore entities located in their territories to improve their visibility vis-à-vis their competitors. The more successful tax havens, such as the Cayman Islands and the Channel Islands, have learned that they stand to gain more by cooperating (or appearing to cooperate). The more they are engaged in discussions with these organizations and adopt their methods of data gathering and information exchange, the more they are treated as sovereign states and are able to protect their core interests. Tax haven authorities have also learned that it is to their advantage to cooperate with academic researchers who can then present, at the very least, their side of the argument in their research. Some tax havens, such as Jersey and the Isle of Man, have gone as far as inviting members of the Tax Justice Network, including one of the authors of this book, Richard Murphy, to consult them on compliance with various initiatives. The result is a wealth of new information.

The fourth useful source of information are the banks, financial institutions, law and accountant firms specializing in offshore, who publish reports on their offshore activities in order to attract new clients. Some of the better known firms, such as KPMG and Ernst & Young, publish research papers on various aspects of offshore finance and tax havens. This kind of research is conducted probably as part of the same international initiative to legitimate tax havens as OFCs and/or present a particular bank as reliable. In addition, dedicated web journals such as lowtax.net and the Schmidt report seek to inform corporate clients. Although the various reports and studies published by these institutions and web journals tend to be biased, they give us an idea of the main issues and debates within the business and "consumer" sector of tax havens.

A fifth source of valuable information is provided by national tax authorities, particularly by inland revenue and custom services of developed countries, who provide their own estimates of the magnitude of the phenomenon. The French parliament has published on its website a study of the five principal European tax havens, including London (Peillon and Montebourg 2000, 2001). The U.S. Congress commissioned a series of research reports beginning with the famous Gordon Report (1981), which provided the first comprehensive study of tax havens. U.S. tax officials were among the first to publish learned studies of the tax haven phenomenon (Belotsky 1987; Irish 1982). The U.S. and Irish revenues (and others) are funding academic research on the effect of tax havens on revenues. The Norwegian government has commissioned a major research paper from the Tax Justice Network. However the national agencies do not speak with one voice: the U.S and British treasury departments adopt a relatively "pro" OFC attitude. The U.S and British inland revenues and custom services, as well as the British National Audit Office, in contrast, are far more critical of tax havens. Some inland revenues—including the U.S., British, and Irish—are soliciting the help of academics to comb through confidential corporate and individual tax returns in order to understand better the impact of tax havens on their revenues. Although the data remain confidential, some of the findings are presented in international conferences. The net result of these internal debates is a wealth of new information, as each agency seeks to advance its political stance by releasing research and data.

A sixth source is the academic work that has flourished in the past few years. Tax havens are no longer the exclusive realm of tax experts but have attracted research interest of economists, geographers, sociologists, international relations scholars, and even anthropologists. To the pioneering work on tax havens that was conducted in the 1980s and early 1990s (Johns 1983; Johns and Le Marchant 1993; Naylor 1987, 2002; Picciotto 1992, 1999; Roberts 1994), we should add the work of political scientists and international relations scholars in the late 1990s and early twenty-first century (Hampton 1996, 2007; Hampton and Christensen 1999; Chavagneux and Palan 2006; Palan 2002, 2003;

(*continued*)

Box 2.1 *(continued)*

Vleck 2008). Recent years have seen a veritable explosion of academic re-
search, most notably the invaluable research of three Australian academics:
Jason Sharman (2005, 2006; see also Sharman and Mistry 2008; Sharman and
Rawlings 2006), Greg Rawlings (2004, 2005; see also Rawlings and Unger,
2005), and Anthony Van Fossen (2002, 2003). Also noteworthy is the work of
Lorraine Eden and Bob Kudrle in the United States (2005), Philip Genschel
(2002, 2005) and Thomas Rixen (2008) in Bremen; Michael Webb (2004) and
Roland Paris (2003) in Canada; and Claudio Radaelli (2004) at Exeter University, UK. We know quite a lot about the origins of Switzerland as a tax haven
courtesy of research conducted by Sebastian Guex at Zurich (1998, 1999) and
Christian Chavagneux in the Paris archives (2001). We also have considerable
information on the Dublin financial center due to the excellent detailed work
of the economist Jim Stewart (2005).

A group of researchers at Sciences Po, Paris, is conducting a long-term research project on the relationship between money laundering and criminality (Godefroy and Lacoumes 2004), as are Raymond Baker and colleagues
supported by the Ford Foundation (Baker 2005; Kar and Cartwright-Smith
2008); Simon Pak and colleagues at Penn State University (Boyrie et al. 2001;
2005); and Richard Blum (1984) and Jack Blum and colleagues (Blum et al
1998). Among accountants, the work of Prem Sikka (2003) deserves special
mention. Geographers as well have contributed to tax haven research. One
strand of research is on the nature of the small states in the world economy
(Baldacchino 2006; Tschoegl 1989); other studies focus on specific states (for
instance, Cobb 1998). The anthropologist, Bill Maurer (1998) has conducted
some of the most innovative work on the subject.

Last but not least, civil society associations such as the Tax Justice Network
in the UK and ATTAC in Germany, France, and Switzerland are providing a
constant stream of research and serve as important sources of information on
the nature of tax havens. An opposing view and information is found at the
website of the Center for Freedom and Prosperity (http://www.freedomand
prosperity.org/).

"Half of the Global Stock of Money Goes through Tax Havens"

In a 1994 report, the IMF surprised many seasoned observers by declaring that more than half of cross-border lending is conducted through
offshore jurisdictions (Cassard 1994). The IMF's declaration drew public
attention to figures that had been floating among experts for a while
(Ginsburg 1991).

The BIS began collecting data on what it called OFCs in the last quarter
of 1983—interestingly, the date corresponds with an abrupt rise in the

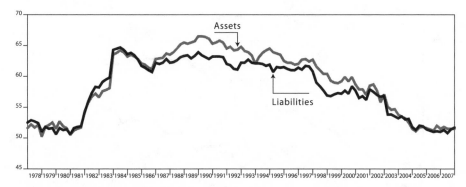

Fig. 2.1 Banking assets and liabilities location in offshore financial centers, 1977–2007. Source: BIS, 2007.

flow of money going through these same territories according to BIS statistics (see figure 2.1). The United Kingdom dropped exchange controls in 1979, the United States in 1980, and France and Germany soon after. These actions may have triggered the abrupt increase. Nevertheless, the rise may have been exaggerated simply because the BIS began gathering data at around that date. The original data set produced by the BIS consisted of information on international assets (bank loans and obligations) and liabilities (deposits, shares, and obligations). It showed that the proportion of banks' cross-border assets and liabilities in OFCs peaked in the late 1980s at 65% but declined thereafter and in 2007 was at 51%. A related set of figures compiled by the BIS since 1995 shows that on average, by the end of 2007, offshore banks were receiving little more than 47% of total cross-border deposits and little more than 43% of all cross-border loans from banks in other tax havens.

Estimates of global cross-border lending for 2007 were approximately $24.5 trillion, so the figure for offshore banks translates to roughly $12.2 trillion. However, the BIS does not distinguish between OFCs and tax havens. Therefore, the mind-boggling figure of "half of the world's stock of money" refers not only to the Caymans and Bermudas of this world but also to London, the IBFs in the United States, and Tokyo's JOM.

The statement that half of the global stock of money goes through tax havens is misleading, but it is safe to say that that money goes through tax havens and OFCs. But even these figures are only approximations. The BIS data are incomplete and its reporting confined to the major tax havens. Moreover, there is no reporting of business managed off the balance sheet (Over-the-Counter, OTC), which anecdotal information and the subprime crisis both suggest can be of enormous magnitude.

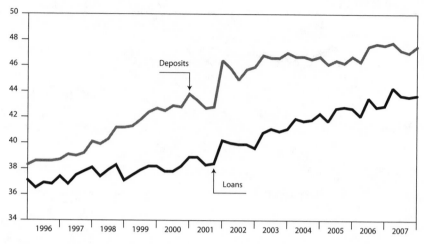

Fig. 2.2 Share of international loans directed to and originating from tax havens and OFCs as percentage of world total. Source: BIS, 2008.

Tax Havens and Foreign Direct Investment

Another astonishing set of statistics relates to global investment. Available data show with striking consistency that approximately 30% of all foreign direct investment (FDI) is invested, or at the very least passes, through tax havens. UNCTAD data show a slight increase in FDI flows through tax havens since the mid 1990s. Why do tax havens play such a central role in global FDI?

We should be clear from the outset that the technical meaning of foreign direct investment can be misleading. Economists distinguish broadly between two types of cross-border investments. Portfolio investment was traditionally the passive holding of foreign securities such as stocks, bonds, and financial assets; whereas foreign direct investment involved "real" facilities in foreign lands, including factories, offices, distribution networks, subsidiaries, and so on. Since the mid-1970s, however, the OECD has adopted a new definition of FDI: "an incorporated or unincorporated enterprise in which a foreign investor owns ten per cent or more of the ordinary shares or voting power of an incorporated enterprise or the equivalent of an unincorporated enterprise" (OECD 1999, 8). The OECD is perfectly aware that the 10% cutoff line is arbitrary. Nonetheless, the term FDI now represents the holding, active or passive, of 10% or above of shares in a foreign enterprise. As a result, FDI figures no longer register "real" investment in production, manufacturing, or services in foreign land, but rather represent ownership structures. This important distinction goes a long way in explaining some of the surprising statistics relating to FDI in tax havens. They suggest that MNEs use their tax haven subsidiaries on a massive scale to invest in foreign countries.

Such statistics beg the question whether MNEs are truly investing in OFCs or merely using haven subsidiaries to invest elsewhere (i.e., do they serve merely as entrepôt centers as Dixon [2001] believes), and why would MNEs choose to re-route their investments through tax havens?

They do so primarily, we believe, for tax reasons. The OECD notes an aberration in FDI statistics, which, it argues, can be explained only as tax related. When in 1968 the United States introduced mandatory controls on direct investment abroad, constraining U.S.-registered companies from raising funds for foreign operations at home, the U.S. bureau of statistics discovered a suspicious rise in the number of U.S. bank affiliates registered in the Netherlands Antilles (N.A.). These affiliates raised capital on the Euromarket, but due to a treaty between the United States and the Netherlands, interest payments on borrowings channeled through N.A. affiliates were not subject to withholding taxes. In addition, most taxes on affiliates in the N.A. generated offsetting tax credits for the U.S. parent companies. By 1984, the year in which the 30% U.S. withholding tax on interest paid to foreigners was repealed, the United States was running a cumulative negative FDI position vis-à-vis the N.A. of $25.1 billion. In addition, U.S. parent companies had "borrowed" $42 billion from their N.A. finance affiliates. Once withholding tax was repealed, the situation rapidly reversed itself. At the close of 1993, the net outstanding debt of U.S. companies vis-à-vis N.A. affiliates had been reduced to $8.7 billion and the negative direct investment position had become negligible (OECD 1999, 43). The repeal of U.S. withholding rules explains, in no small part,

Table 2.1 U.S. multinationals investment in tax havens, top twelve destinations (flows of foreign direct investment in 2006, in billions US$)

UK	$364
Canada	246
The Netherlands	215.7
Australia	122.6
Bermuda	108.5
Germany	99.2
Japan	91.8
Switzerland	90.1
Mexico	84.7
Ireland	83.6
Luxembourg	82.6
British Caribbean dependencies	80.6

Source: Bureau of Economic Analysis, 2006.
Note: Countries in italics are considered to be tax havens.

Table 2.2 Top ten FDI sources in China

Jurisdiction	2006 (in billion US$)	2007 (in billion US$)
Hong Kong	$21.31	$27.70
British Virgin Islands	11.68	16.55
South Korea	3.99	3.68
Japan	4.76	3.58
Singapore	2.46	3.18
United States	3.00	2.62
Cayman Islands	2.13	2.57
Samoa	1.62	2.17
Taiwan	2.23	1.77
Mauritius	1.11	1.33

Source: Mofcom, 2007.

the subsequent fall in the significance of the N.A. as an OFC. (For further discussion see chapter 6.)

The Netherlands Antilles is not an isolated story. There is considerable evidence that multinationals re-route much of their investments via tax havens (Vleck 2008). A detailed study of U.S. affiliates based on the data of the Bureau of Economic Analysis—which by law is not allowed to share with any U.S. agencies and is considered by experts to be relatively reliable—supports this view. Analysis shows that U.S. multinational firms have made "extensive use of tax havens: in 1999, 59% of U.S. firms with significant foreign operations had affiliates in tax haven countries" (Desai et. al. 2006, 514).

A U.S. Congressional Budget Office report (CBO 2005) notes a paradox: by the end of 2004, foreigners owned $12.5 trillion of assets in the United States, that is $2.5 trillion more than the value of U.S.-owned assets abroad. Nevertheless, U.S. residents consistently earned more income from their foreign investments than foreigners earned from their larger U.S. investments, thereby holding down the size of the U.S. current-account deficit. As late as the end of 2007, foreigners were still holding roughly $2.5 trillion more assets in the United States than Americans were holding abroad. Nonetheless, the U.S. residents still earned almost $90 billion more than they had to pay abroad.

The CBO (2005) provides several explanations for this difference in returns, including the risk factor of investment in politically unstable countries (which in theory should yield higher returns). The assumption is that the United States represents a low-risk investment. Interestingly, the study states that U.S. subsidiaries abroad may appear more profitable in part because those subsidiaries may overstate their overseas profits for tax reasons, whereas foreign-owned subsidiaries in the United States may understate their profits for the same reason. Irish-registered U.S. subsidiaries perform, on average, three times better than U.S. FDI overall, and Bermuda-registered U.S. subsidiaries are twice as profitable as the average. Why should Irish or Bermudan subsidiaries outperform other subsidiaries? The CBO identifies no definitive data but believes that transfer pricing is the main reason' for the profit differentials. Desai et al. (2006) suggest, in contrast, that deferral of home-country taxation is a more powerful inducement to establish tax haven operations than is transfer pricing. (This may be true for the United States but not for other countries where there is less potential for deferment.) Whatever the motivation or mix of motivations (and a mixture is more probable), tax is the most likely explanation for the staggering amount of FDI routed through tax havens.

The U.S. Congress commissioned a study from the U.S. Government Accountability Office (GAO) into foreign-owned U.S. corporations between 1996 and 2000. The GAO report (2004) worked on the assumption that foreign-controlled corporations—some of which may have been U.S.-owned companies operating via tax havens—might be shifting income to lower-tax countries. The study found that the majority of corporations—71% of foreign-controlled corporations and 61% of U.S.-controlled corporations—reported no tax liabilities during·this period. Indeed, more than 60% of U.S.-controlled corporations with at least $250 million in assets (representing 93% of all corporate assets) reported no tax liability to the IRS. As we might expect, a higher percentage of foreign-controlled companies do not pay any tax in the United States. A Citizens for Tax Justice Report reaches similar conclusion: 82 of the 275 top U.S. corporations paid no taxes between 2001 and 2003, although they declared $102 billion in pre-tax profits. Forty-six companies with a combined profit of $42.6 billion paid no federal income taxes in 2003 alone. Instead, they received rebates totaling $5.4 billion.

In addition, the one-year tax amnesty announced by President Bush at the end of 2004, allowing a low level of taxation (5.25% instead of 35%) on foreign-earned profits reinvested in the United States, proved to be a great success. By the beginning of 2006, more than 840 companies had repatriated a little more than $310 billion, that is, the equivalent of almost 40% of the U.S. external deficit (Browning, 2008). The amnesty reinforced the belief that U.S. companies relocate massively to tax havens, thereby contributing to apparent U.S.-generated FDI. These studies and other anecdotal evidence suggest that tax havens help U.S. corporations to avoid paying tax, but it is not clear by how much.

The European FDI map is broadly consistent with the U.S. version, with approximately 30% of all FDI by European multinationals bound for OFCs. Forty-seven percent of all inward FDI into France, for example, is held by companies installed in tax havens, a third of this in intermediate

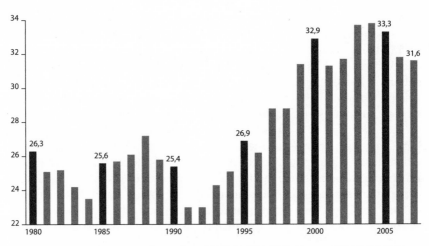

Fig. 2.3 FDI in tax havens as share of world's FDI, 1980–2008. Source: UNCTAD, 2008.

havens such as the Netherlands (first holder) and the United Kingdom (second). France is not unusual among European Union counties.

Tax, however, is not the only cause of statistical oddities. Some of the small British Caribbean dependencies are among the largest recipients of U.S. FDI, and BVI is still the second largest source of FDI to China. Although there is much talk of the rise of China in the world economy, in 2006 Bermuda alone received five times more U.S. FDI than China. Similarly, data concerning the United Kingdom (first destination), the Netherlands (third), Switzerland (fifth), Ireland (sixth), Switzerland (eighth), and Luxembourg (tenth) are misleading. The UK apart, it is very unlikely that this so-called FDI remains in these countries. We know that FDI from Hong Kong and BVI is largely a matter of Chinese capital being re-routed either for political reasons or in order to gain tax advantages (Vleck 2008). In other words, a considerable portion of FDI into China is not FDI at all but is local money being invested via an offshore location, a process called "round tripping." The same pattern has been witnessed in Mauritius (Srinivasan 2005), which has emerged as the largest foreign investor in India, about 50% more than the United States (Rixen 2008). This is solely, many experts believe, because of the benefits included in the taxation treaty between India and Mauritius.

Tax havens are used, therefore, primarily as intermediaries to the world's FDI flows or as entrepôt centers. They are not only the largest recipients but also the largest providers of FDI. Data for the first five months of 2007 issued by the Ministry of Commerce of China showed that during that period, ten countries contributed 86% of all the money invested in new Chinese ventures. They were (in order) Hong Kong, the BVI, Japan, South Korea, Singapore, the United States, the Cayman Islands, Samoa, Taiwan, and Mauritius.

The Number of Offshore Entities

Most tax havens provide information on the number of entities registered in their territories. Table 2.3 draws primarily on a detailed International Narcotics Control Strategy Report on money laundering prepared by the Bureau for International Narcotics and Law Enforcement Affairs of the U.S. Department of State (INCSR 2008). The report is concerned primarily with money laundering. Not all tax havens are considered a serious threat for money laundering, and so the report is not comprehensive in its coverage. We supplement it with the number of international business companies in offshore jurisdictions as compiled by *STEP* magazine in 2004.

The British Virgin Islands are the largest supplier of international business companies (IBCs), reaching 800,000 in 2007, followed by Hong Kong with 500,000, Panama 370,000, and the Bahamas 115,000. These figures must be taken with a grain of salt, as we have no way of telling how reliable they are. We do know, for example, that the BVI fails to keep track of companies that have stopped operating in its domain.[1] In contrast, the Bahamas does report data of this sort, and of the 115,000 IBCs listed in its territory, only 42,000 are currently active. We do not know whether this ratio is applicable to other countries.

Although our information must include accounting errors, the signs are that the number of IBCs continues to rise at an average rate of between 10% and 15% a year. For example, 81,783 IBCs in the Caymans by 2006 included a rise of 27% from 2005 (Ridley 2007). We estimate the current total worldwide number of IBCs to be in excess of two million.

Sullivan (2007a) has conducted a survey of the number of offshore hedge funds by working with two estimates. One estimate compiled by Hedge Fund Research Inc. reported the number of hedge funds at the end of 2006 as 7,241. Another useful data source was compiled by Lipper Tass Data (www.lipperweb.com/products/tass.asp). Sullivan concluded that the big four Caribbean islands of Cayman, Bermuda, BVI, and the Bahamas hosted between them 52.3% of the world's hedge funds in 2006, followed by the United States with 30.1%. Estimates of assets in these

1. One of the authors of this book raised this issue with BVI administrators. The response suggested that they had little idea which of the companies registered in their domain may or may not be in use.

Table 2.3 Number of offshore entities in tax havens

	IBCs	Banks	Trusts	Insurance companies	Mutual funds/ hedge funds	Internet gaming companies
Anguilla	7,400 STEP					
Antigua Barbuda	3,255	17	3	2		23
Aruba	372 NVs 2,763 Aruba exempt companies	2	4 captives			11
Bahamas	115,000 Of which 42,000 active	139[a]				4 casinos 10 gaming cites
Bahrain	n/a	54 OBUs				n/a
Barbados	4,635	55	7 mutual funds 1 exempt	164 exempt 55, qualified exempt		0
Belize[b]	32,800	8	30	1	1 M	
BVI	802,850	9	208	402 captive	2,550 m	
Brunei, Step	2,500					
Cayman[c]	62,572	450		740 cap	8,600	
Comoros[d]	1,200	300				
Cook Ils. STEP	15 000	6				
Costa Rica						250
Cyprus	54,000	26[e]				
Dominica	12,787	1		20		3
Gibraltar STEP	31 142					
Grenada	1,580[f]		1			

Guernsey	18,800	47		632	851
Hong Kong	500,000[g]	53		177 cap	164
Isle of Man[h]	35 821 (STEP)	48	953	175	1,086
Jersey	33 936 (STEP)	16			
Labuan (STEP)	4 915				
Liechtenstein	75,000[i]			95 insurance 260 reinsurance	2,238 2nd largest mutual fund in the world
Luxembourg[j]	15,000				
Monaco	21392 (STEP)	60[k]			
Mauricios	20,000[l]				
Netherland	14,191	18	84	15	
Neth. Antilles	9 678 (STEP)	34			
Niue	369 652 (STEP)				
Panama	25,383	6	182	3	
Samoa	34,000		160	3	
Seychelles		82[m]			
Singapore		1	3,684	90	12
St. Kitts and Nevis	33,165 IBC 9,840 LLCs 1,201 exempt companies				257 exempt foundations
St. Lucia	2,851[n]		66	24	
St. Vincent and the Grenadines	8,573	6	154	13	55

(continued)

(Table 2.3—cont.)

	IBCs	Banks	Trusts	Insurance companies	Mutual funds/hedge funds	Internet gaming companies
Switzerland		331				
Turks and Caicos	17,000	4	20	2,500		
Vanuatu	3,603	5		70		

Sources: INCSR 2008. Where INCSR figures are unavailable or incomplete, we use a table compiled by Step Survey 2004 and lawtax.net, 2004 indicated as (STEP)

[a] The figure is for banks and trusts combined. The number has declined from 301 in 2003 to 139 because of the new requirement placed by the central bank in 2001 that "managed banks" are to have physical presence in the Island.

[b] Belize introduced the Offshore Banking Act in 1996. Offshore banks cannot serve customers who are citizens or legal residents of Belize

[c] The Cayman Financial Reporting Authority (FRA) began operation and has a staff of six: a director, a legal adviser, a senior accountant, a senior analyst, a junior analyst, and an administration officer.

[d] Regulation of Banks and Comparable Establishment enacted in 1999 license offshore banks. IBCs were introduced in 2001.

[e] The figure is for Banks conduct operations mainly with nonresident. Cumulative assets of such banks $112 billion.

[f] Grenada saw significant decrease in reported number of IBCs in its territory from 6,000 in 2006.

[g] HK IBCs are established with nominee directors, and many are owned by other IBCs normally registered in the BVI. Hong Kong and BVI are used together for money rerouting purposes.

[h] Latest available data, September 30, 2004.

[i] The figures are for corporations and trusts. Two hundred thirty licensed fiduciary companies and sixty lawyers serve as nominees for/or manage all these entities.

[j] $3.1 trillion in domiciled assets.

[k] Banking system manages approximately $ 102.8 billion. Approximately 85% of the banking customers are nonresidents.

[l] The figure is for Special Financial Institutions (SFIs). van Dijk et. al. (2006) estimates that there were about 20,000 "mailbox companies," which do not have substantial commercial presence in the Netherlands.

[m] Total assets under management in Singapore grew 24% between 2005 and 2006 to $581 billion.

[n] St. Lucia saw a 49% increase in 2006.

Table 2.4   Estimates of hedge fund assets by domicile, end of 2006 (in millions US$)

Domicile	Method I	Method II	Average of two
Bahamas	$24,172	$24,531	$24,352
Bermuda	107,028	64,321	85,675
B.V.I.	129,384	171,733	150,559
Cayman Islands	470,450	497,977	525,503
Total	**731,035**	**761,558**	**746,296**

Source: Sullivan 2007b.

jurisdictions are presented in table 2.4. The size of the hedge fund industry is believed to be approximately $1.5 trillion in 2006.

How Much Tax Is Evaded through Tax Havens?

How much in the way of tax payments is evaded or avoided through tax havens? The most candid and accurate answer we can give at this point is that we simply do not know. The recent scandals involving Liechtenstein and UBS reaffirmed what many have suspected for a long time.

When one of the authors of this book wrote a study of offshore in 2003 (Palan 2003), not even rough estimates of tax avoidance and evasion were available. Since then several dedicated critical accountants have produced some useful gross estimates of avoidance and evasion that we can report here.

Tax Havens and Wealthy Individuals

Sophisticated accounting techniques can provide estimates of national tax avoidance (Murphy 2008a). But because not all or even the bulk of individual tax avoidance is routed through tax havens, the best estimates of individuals' evasion/avoidance are worked out through estimates of the value of wealth held in offshore locations.

Such data are hard to come by, because neither governments nor international financial institutions seem either able or willing to research the global picture. We believe that the best available estimates are: one calculated by one of the authors of this book, Richard Murphy (2006), and the other a series of studies conducted by the editor of *Tax Notes* magazine, Martin Sullivan, of Jersey, Guernsey, the Isle of Man, Switzerland, and the hedge fund industry (Sullivan 2007a, 2007b).

Murphy triangulated three sets of published data to reach an estimate of the assets maintained by individuals in tax havens. The first set of figures is from the BIS: in June 2004 offshore bank deposits totaled $2.7 trillion off-shore out of a $14.4 trillion total in all bank deposits. This means that approximately one-fifth of all deposits are held offshore (not "half of the global stock of money"). The BIS figures relate solely to cash and exclude other financial assets such as stocks, shares, and bonds and also the value of tangible assets such as real estate, gold, and even yachts held offshore, as well as shares in private companies. These assets are typically controlled through offshore companies, foundations, and trusts—the latter are not even registered let alone required to furnish annual statements of account. The value of these assets is therefore unknown and harder to determine.

The second source of data Murphy uses was included in the annual Merrill Lynch/Cap Gemini "World Wealth Reports" (2002). The 1998 report estimated that one-third of the wealth of the world's high net-worth individuals (HNWIs as banks refer to them) was held offshore. According to the 2002 wealth report, the value of assets held by HNWIs with liquid financial assets of $1 million or more was $27.2 trillion in 2002/3, of which $8.5 trillion (31%) was held offshore. A more recent estimate is not available, although Murphy notes that this figure is increasing by approximately $600 billion annually, which would bring the 2008 figure to about $9.7 trillion.

A slightly different estimate was published by the Boston Consulting Group (BCG) in their Global Wealth Report for 2003. BCG estimated the total holdings of cash deposits and listed securities of HNWIs at $38 trillion. The geographical region of origin is noted in table 2.5. These figures also exclude real estate, non-financial assets, and privately owned businesses.

Corroborative data were published in a report by the research arm of the global consulting group McKinsey & Company, which showed that total global financial capital amounted to $118 trillion in 2003. The McKinsey data include the balance of bank-to-bank debts, which are not included in BIS data. BIS data, therefore, reflect the sums held by individuals, non-banking corporations, and trusts, and are more accurate for calculating how much individual wealth is held in tax havens.

Table 2.5   High net worth individuals (HNWI) total wealth

Continent	Total wealth US$ trillions	Probable amount in offshore US$ trillions [4]
North America	$16.2	$1.6
Europe	10.3	2.6
Middle East & Asia	10.2	4.1
Latin America	1.3	0.7
Total	38	9.0

Source: Murphy 2006.

According to McKinsey the ratio of cash to total financial assets ranged, between 3.3 and 3.85 over the period reviewed. Applying an average of 3.5 to the BIS offshore holdings yields a figure for total financial assets held offshore of $9.45 trillion. This gives us a third estimate within the range of $9 to $10 trillion.

However, this estimate does not include real estate and other tangible assets, the ownership of private businesses held offshore, and intangible assets such as the right to receive royalties and licensing fees. No one can be sure of the precise value of these assets, but a modest estimate would add no more than $2 trillion to the value of offshore holdings (which given the value of real estate may well be very modest indeed). Based on that Murphy concludes that the total value of assets held offshore lies between $11 trillion and $12 trillion.

BIS figures do not distinguish between individual and corporate savings in tax havens, so this estimate may include some corporate savings as well. Nevertheless, if we assume that $11.5 trillion yields for the investor an average annual return of 7.5%—which is a very average return—than the gross return on assets is $860 billion a year. What are the tax losses arising from $860 billion, estimated at an average tax of 30%? Because wealthy individuals (and perhaps some corporations) hold their assets offshore, the annual tax loss amounts to approximately $255 billion.

Murphy's figures are remarkably close to the calculations of the Levin Congressional Committee, which reports that "According to a 2001 estimate, financial assets of five trillion US $ are invested in tax havens" (Levin 2003). The committee assumed an average rate of return of 5% and a moderate average tax rate of 25%, and calculated that the result would amount to $62.5 billion in revenue forgone each year in residence countries. Considering that the U.S. economy is 20% of the world's economy, a simple extrapolation gives us $310 billion for the entire world—well within an acceptable margin of error compared to Murphy's calculations.

Table 2.6 Estimates of individual's nonresident assets that could be avoiding tax on those assets in their home jurisdictions (in billions US$)

	End 2006	Est. first half 2007
Jersey	$491.6	$500
Guernsey	293.1	300
Isle of Man	150.5	200 (end 2007)
Switzerland	607.4	
Hedge funds (big four): Cayman Islands, BVI, the Bahamas, Bermuda	262.8	

Source: Sullivan 2007b.

Sullivan (2007b) has done remarkable work on individual tax haven accounts. Unfortunately, his work is not yet complete and provides only snapshot estimates of some of the most significant tax havens.

Unsurprisingly, Sullivan's estimates are criticized by those working in the locations he has reviewed, but they have the considerable merit of being based on data published by the jurisdictions themselves. We believe that Sullivan's work is an important contribution to understanding and hope that it can be extended to other locations.

There is additional evidence to corroborate these rough estimates and suggest, in fact, that they are, as both Murphy and Sullivan argue, conservative figures. Ireland collected almost €840 million from 15,000 Irish residents hiding undeclared income abroad (Benoit and Houlder 2008). In Italy, a recent amnesty resulted in the disclosure of €75 billion of assets held offshore. In 2007, the UK raised £500 million in an "offshore disclosure facility" after legal rulings forced banks to hand over details of hundreds of thousands of offshore accounts (Benoit and Houlder 2008).

Multinational Corporations and Tax Havens

There is a massive lacuna in research on tax havens: there are simply no figures, approximations, or even wild guesses concerning the amount of corporate tax evasion and avoidance. The statistics already mentioned in this chapter, as well as the excellent empirical research by economists such as Hines and his colleagues (Desai et al. 2004a, 2006; Hines and Rice 1994; Slemrod 1994; Stewart 2005), demonstrate conclusively that tax is a major consideration in most companies' portfolio of subsidiaries and affiliates, and tax havens host many subsidiaries and affiliates set up for tax avoidance/evasion purposes. Yet not the OECD, or the United States, or the UK inland revenue services, or even the Tax Justice Network, is prepared to provide any estimate of corporate tax avoidance/evasion. This is not for lack of interest. The simple fact is that as long as companies can publish consolidated accounts that leave their tax haven activities hidden from view, it is almost impossible to produce reliable estimates of the trade that they undertake in tax havens or of the profits that are recorded there. This is a major weakness that the Tax Justice Network and others are tackling by calling for country-by-country reporting, which would show activities in tax havens.

The Debate about Corporate Taxation

The debate on corporate taxation is rather, well, taxing. There are conflicting views on whether corporate taxation has been declining in the past three decades, and if so, to what degree the decline in corporate taxation is attributable to tax havens. To confuse matters further, another debate questions whether existing cross-national comparative statistics, collated since the early 1980s, are particularly helpful.

Economists are generally of the opinion that the unweighted mean statutory tax rate has been declining steadily in OECD countries over the past three decades (Baldwin and Krugman 2004; Devereux et al. 2002; Garretsen and Peeters 2006). Devereux et al. (2002) and colleagues have calculated that the mean statutory tax rate declined between 1982 and 2001 from 48% to 35% (2002, 456). Others point out that the decline in statutory tax rates has been accompanied by a broadening of the tax base and hence should not be interpreted as a decline in the overall rate of corporate taxation. Baldwin and Krugman (2004) found that corporate tax revenue/GDP in the EU remained more or less static at 8% to 9% between 1956 and 2000, while corporate taxes for the poorer EU members rose gradually from 4–5% to 8–9% by 2000 (2004, 7).

In light of these developments, tax economists are now leaning toward a different set of measures known as Effective Average Tax Rates (EATR). EATR is a complex set of computations that attempt to simulate the real tax environment as seen from the perspective of the corporation. Although different researchers adapt different EATR models, the consensus is that EATR fell from around 40% in 1981 to 28% in 2001 in OECD countries.

Some evidence suggests a long-term decline in income from corporate taxation. The Congressional Budget Office reports that between 2000 and 2003 overall corporate income taxes collected by the U.S. federal government dropped from $207 billion to $132 billion. The figure rose to $183.8 billion in 2004, but it still represents just 9.6% of total federal revenues, down by almost half from the 17% in 1970. The U.S. corporate tax rate is also declining in comparison to the size of the economy (i.e., as a percentage of GDP). According to the CBO's Historical Budget Data, corporate income taxes declined from 4.2% of GDP in 1967 to 1.2% in 2003, rising only slightly to 1.6% in 2004. Corporate tax cycles tend to be heavily linked to the economic cycle and to resulting levels of corporate profitability. In 2007, the UK's National Audit Office reported that 30% of the largest companies in that country had not paid tax in the previous year.

The Tax Gap
The relative decline in corporate tax receipts can be caused by myriad reasons, and in and of itself tells us next to nothing about avoidance and evasion. Furthermore, declared profits for tax purposes tend to be very different from declared profits to stock markets. Tax paid is frequently lower than what is declared in corporate accounts. Tax authorities have developed a method called the tax gap to measure the difference between declared profits and paid taxes and actual taxes paid. Others, such as the Tax Justice Network, have developed a slightly different method based on publicly available information, which they call the expectation gap.

The expectation gap is the difference between the rate of tax set by the government where a company operates and the actual rate of tax that the company pays. It provides an indication of the amount of tax likely to be collected considering current tax levels and declared profits. Part of that gap is the result of tax evasion and avoidance.

The IRS March 2005 press release defines the tax gap as "the difference between what taxpayers should pay and what they actually pay on a timely basis." The UK's Revenue & Customs has a slightly more complicated definition: "the tax gap measures the amount of tax we ultimately fail to collect, or, alternatively the amount of uncorrected non-compliance" (HMRC 2008). There are debates concerning the use of a tax gap (see Murphy 2006), but it is the best available measure we have. Murphy studied the taxes of the fifty largest UK companies for the British Trades Union Congress, and his work confirms that the UK follows trends similar to those in the United States (Murphy 2008a). Murphy shows that these companies paid on average 5% less of their profits in tax than they actually declared from 2000 to 2006. Moreover, the average tax rate paid by these companies fell by more than 0.5% a year over a seven-year period, even though the UK tax rate for these companies was constant during those years. As a result, the de facto corporation tax rate for UK companies in 2006 was 22.5% when the actual rate agreed by Parliament was 30%. This difference was due primarily to the ability to defer tax payments using tax-planning techniques, some of which undoubtedly involve offshore arrangements where the remittance of funds from low-tax jurisdictions can be deferred. In fact, at the end of 2006 the amount of deferred tax on the balance sheets of the fifty largest companies in the UK amounted to more than the total corporation tax paid in the UK in the previous year! Although companies are required to reconcile the differences that arise within their corporate accounting statements, reconciliation is not disclosed.

Murphy (2008a) calculates that annual avoidance in the UK stands at about £25 billion. In addition, he has, in unpublished work using data from HM Revenue and Customs, estimated that tax evasion may cost the UK Exchequer at least £72 billion a year. He concludes that gross annual avoidance in the UK is about £97 billion—16.6% of expected tax receipts or 6% of GDP. In a related study, Murphy calculates that the total tax losses to the UK due to tax evasion and related activities through tax havens stand at approximately £18.5 billion a year (2008b).

The IRS believes that the U.S. tax gap is about $330 billion a year or 16% of federal revenue and 2% of GDP. The proportion of total tax loss for the UK and the United States is strikingly similar. Official figures in France indicate that the French state loses €40–50 billion a year, roughly 3% of GDP. The European Union estimates the tax gap for the entire Union at 2–2.5% of GDP. These estimates exclude sub-state and local taxation, both of which are substantially more important outside the UK, thereby explaining the disparity in GDP ratios. The tax gap gives no clue as to the relationship between domestic and offshore avoidance/evasion.

Corporate Taxation and Tax Havens

How much of this loss can be attributed to tax havens? Desai et al. contend that all "available data for the US shows that the reallocation of profits to tax havens has increased substantially in recent years. In 1990, low-tax countries accounted for 20.7 per cent of foreign manufacturing profits of US multinationals and that share rose to 46.8 per cent by 2000" (2005, 188). While in 2002 "high-tax" countries such as Canada, France, Germany, Italy, and the UK accounted for 44% of U.S. foreign sales, plants, and equipment, and 56% of foreign-employee compensation, they accounted for only 21% of reported foreign profits of U.S. corporations (Sullivan 2004a). The rise of corporate use of tax havens has contributed significantly to the precipitous decline in corporate taxes raised by the U.S. government in recent years, particularly when it comes to U.S. multinationals that are able to shift their pretax income offshore. U.S. corporations shifted $75 billion of their taxable profits into tax havens in 2003, which, according to Sullivan, deprived the IRS of between $10 billion and $20 billion in expected tax revenues. At the same time, the profits of foreign subsidiaries of U.S. corporations in eighteen tax havens soared from $88 billion in 1999 to $149 billion in 2002 (Sullivan 2004a). Pre-tax rates of return in low-tax countries were significantly higher than in high-tax countries, strongly suggesting that companies are shifting their profits without relocating real economic activity (Sullivan 2004a). Note that Sullivan's figures do not include the offshore holdings of corporations.

Table 2.7 Effective taxation of U.S. subsidiaries, 2004

Rank	Country	Before-tax profits (millions US$)	Effective tax rates (%)
1	Ireland	$26,853	8%
2	Bermuda	25,212	2
3	Netherlands	20,802	9
4	UK	19,717	31
5	Canada	19,626	26
6	Luxembourg	18,405	1
7	Switzerland	14,105	4
8	Japan	11,526	39
9	Mexico	7,699	37
10	Singapore	7,533	11
11	Germany	5,371	27
12	Cayman Islands	2,809	5

Source: Sullivan 2004, 1190.

Another interesting study (Becht et al. 2006) assesses the impact of a recent ruling by the European Court of Justice, which allowed freedom of incorporation within Europe. Beginning with the 1999 Centros ruling, a ruling that prevented member states from refusing to register branch companies formed under the law of another European member state, even if the company has never conducted any business in the latter state (see Looisjestijn-Clearie 2000). The analysis uses data for 2.14 million private and public limited companies incorporated in the UK between 1997 and 2005. They show that "the Centros rulings are directly responsible for creating large international flows of companies. Between 2002 and 2005, over 55,000 new private limited companies have been set up from other EU member States in the U.K. In absolute terms, the largest flows of companies come from Germany, France, the Netherlands and Cyprus, with over 26,000 firms from Germany alone. Most of the new foreign Limited companies are small, having only one or two directors" (Becht et al. 2006, 7).

We suggest that a considerable portion of the decline in corporation tax revenues may be attributed to the use of tax havens. However, there are no reliable estimates of the loss of tax revenue.

Transfer Pricing

All the evidence suggests that the main vehicle of tax avoidance/evasion and capital flight through tax havens is the mundane practice of transfer pricing. Transfer pricing is the price companies charge for intra-group, cross-border sales of goods and services. Raymond Baker (2005) believes that about 70% of all capital flight is conducted by means of transfer pricing. A survey of 850 multinationals in twenty-four countries carried out by Ernst & Young in 2007 found that 77% of the respondents placed transfer pricing at the heart of their tax strategy for 2008-9. The results vary across industries. For example, in the pharmaceutical industry 76% of tax directors considered the issue to be of great importance compared to only 8% in insurance. In a survey conducted in late 2005, 68% of multinational companies (43% in 2000) said they now integrate transfer pricing into the product design phase. U.S. companies were particularly active in transfer pricing; their rate of involvement doubled from 40% in 2000 to 80% by 2005. The 2007 poll also indicated that governments are equally involved in the hunt for abusive tax practices in this area. Fifty-two percent of companies reported having being investigated for transfer pricing abuses since 2003, and 27% of the cases led to an adjustment of their tax liability.

As mentioned earlier, it is believed that 60% of all international trade is intra-company trade, and as a result the potential for abusive transfer pricing is considerable. That said, transfer pricing is a legitimate practice so long as it is undertaken using what is called an "arm's length principle"—that is, companies charge for their goods and services at prices equivalent to those that unrelated entities would charge in an open market (OECD 2001).

In practice prices based on the arm's length principle are often difficult to establish within highly complex international production networks, where companies use trademarks, patents, brands, logos, and a variety of company-specific intangible assets. The technique, therefore, is open to abuse. Abusive transfer pricing involves the manipulation of prices of transactions between MNEs's related affiliates. The practice is widespread and can be applied to any two affiliates of a company, whether in tax havens or not. The veil of secrecy makes abuse much easier through tax havens.

The techniques of transfer pricing consist essentially of misinvoicing for trade transactions. This can be done by:

a. Under-invoicing the value of exports to a tax haven from the country from which cash is to be expatriated. The goods are then sold from the tax haven at full value, the excess earned on onward sale being the value of the flight capital;
b. Over-invoicing the value of imports into the country from which cash is to be expatriated. The excess part constitutes capital flight, and is often deposited in the importer's offshore bank account;
c. Misreporting the quality or grade of imported products to assist the value of the over- or under-statement for the reasons noted above;
d. Misreporting quantities to assist the value of the over- or under-statement for the reasons noted above;
e. Creating fictitious transactions for which payment is made. One well-worn tactic is to pay for imported goods or services that never materialize.

Simon Pack and John Zdanowicz (2002) studied the transfer pricing tactics used between parent and subsidiary companies of U.S. multinationals. They were able to identify flagrant anomalies such as water plastic seals from the Czech Republic quoted to the parent company at an astronomical price of $972.98 per unit; gloves from China quoted at $4,121.81 a kilo; and locks from France at $3,067.17 per kilo. Meanwhile U.S. missiles were exported to Israel for the modest sum of $52.03 each, diamonds were exported to India at $13.45 per carat, 35mm cameras went to Colombia at $7.44 per unit, and car seats were sold to Belgium at $1.66 each. These are the tell-tale signs of transfer pricing abuses. Aggregating their findings, the two researchers suggest that such practices amounted to a loss of $53.1 billion in tax revenues to the United States in 2001, up from $35.7 billion in 1998.

Transfer pricing is used not only to shift profitable business to low-tax countries but also to upload costs in countries that offer subsidies. This practice is particularly popular in the extractive industries. Logically, the mining and drilling equipment used at a mine is owned in the country in which it is used. In tax planning, however, nothing is so simple. Many countries offer special incentives to companies that invest in capital assets and give them tax relief and allowances that are much more generous than the accounting charges made for their use in the owning company's published reports. This relief can be exploited when combined with asset leasing arrangements.

Some countries, for instance, provide tax relief on the cost of assets that are leased to the legal owner, the lessor. Others provide relief to the lessee

---

Box 2.2 Tax havens and criminality

Meyer Lansky, reputedly the treasurer of the U.S. mob and the model for the Hyman Roth character played by the actor Lee Strasberg in *The Godfather II*, was a legendary figure who forged links from the 1930s between Switzerland, the Bahamas, and criminal groups. There is some debate about how precisely Lansky and Co. used tax havens, whether only for money laundering purposes (Maillard 1998) or for general financial criminal activities (Blum 1984; Dupuis-Danon 2004; Naím 2005; Naylor 2002). There is agreement, however, that organized crime is strongly represented in some tax havens.

Maingot maintains that "some 75% of all sophisticated drug trafficking operations use offshore secrecy havens" (2005, 181). He also believes that drug money, and not the Euromarket, was the principal cause for the phenomenal growth of the Caribbean havens in the 1970s and 1980s (see also Naylor 2002). "It is evident to all who have studied the offshore banking business," he writes, "that its growth has been fuelled by the phenomenal increase in cash from the US drug trade" (Maingot 2005, 181). Of the criminal cases identified in IRS investigations from 1978 to 1983 that occurred in the Caribbean, 45% involved illegal transactions derived from legal income (i.e., tax evasion on otherwise legitimate trade). In the other 55%, illegal income was involved, 161 of cases dealt with drug traffic. Of these, 29% involved the Cayman Islands, 28% involved Panama, 22% the Bahamas, and 11% the Netherlands Antilles. These four offshore sites alone accounted for 85% of the cases involving transactions of illegal income (Maingot 2005, 180).

Organized crime tends to use the techniques of concealment in tax havens and the professional services that are used by individuals and corporations. In late 2005, Callum McCarthy, head of the UK's Financial Services Authority (FSA), publicly declared that he had information showing that organized crime groups have infiltrated some of London's best-known financial institutions. They did so to learn logistics and mechanisms and techniques to avoid detection.

who leases the asset. There are many such rules, and they change from one country to another. Companies can decide to exploit these rules for their benefit. They do so through a process called "tax arbitrage," where they choose to locate transactions so that they get maximum tax benefit by trading off the rules of one country against the rules of the country that taxes the other side of the arrangement. Tax arbitrage can also be used to create double dipping, where two sets of tax relief are generated on one expense.

Money Laundering and Capital Flight

Money laundering and capital flight are not the same thing, although capital flight often involves laundered money. Capital flight is the deliberate and illicit expatriation of money by those resident or taxable within the country of origin.[2] We discuss capital flight in chapter eight. The best available estimates of cross-border illicit money flows are on the order of $1 trillion to $1.6 trillion annually (Baker 2005).

Under the U.S. Foreign Assistance Act a money laundering country is a country "whose financial institutions engage in currency transactions involving significant amount of proceeds from international narcotics trafficking" (INCSR 2008, 3). The IMF estimates the magnitude of money laundering worldwide at 3–5% of the world's GDP, thus giving us $2.17–$3.61 trillion laundered per annum (INCSR 2008, 5)—a figure that is larger than the U.S. federal budget! The figure of 3–5% of the world's GDP has been cited on various occasions by, among others, Michel Camdessus, former director general of the IMF. However, Camdessus did not cite any specific research to back up his claim. Tom Naylor (2002) stresses the difficulties with these estimates, which are based on assumptions of a certain ratio between discovered cases and all cases of money laundering. To build reliable estimates of money laundering we need to know the overall turnover of criminal businesses, their average rate of profit, rate of saving, and accumulated savings—all of which are impossible to discover. The truth is that nobody knows how much money is laundered through tax havens.

Not all money laundering operates through tax havens. Tax havens are, in fact, a minority of the countries that appear on the list of jurisdictions defined by INCSR as "major money laundering countries" (2008, 58; See table 2.8). The principal international institution dealing with money

2. The concept of capital flight is overly complicated. It is very difficult, for instance, to differentiate between capital flight and mere capital outflow (see Beja 2005).

Table 2.8 Money laundering, jurisdictions of primary concern

Jurisdiction	Tax haven status	Jurisdiction	Tax haven status
Afghanistan	no	Italy	no
Antigua	yes	Japan	no
Australia	no	Jersey	yes
Austria	no	Kenya	no
Bahamas	yes	Latvia	yes
Belize	yes	Lebanon	yes
Brazil	no	Liechtenstein	yes
Burma	no	Luxembourg	yes
Cambodia	no	Macau	no
Canada	no	Mexico	no
Cayman Is.	yes	Netherlands	yes
China	no	Nigeria	no
Colombia	no	Pakistan	no
Costa Rica	yes	Panama	yes
Cyprus	yes	Paraguay	no
Dominican rep	yes	Philippines	no
France	no	Russia	no
Germany	no	Singapore	yes
Greece	no	Spain	no
Guatemala	no	Switzerland	yes
Guernsey	yes	Taiwan	no
Haiti	no	Thailand	no
Hong Kong	yes	Turkey	no
India	no	Ukraine	no
Indonesia	no	UAE	no
Iran	no	U.S.	no
Isle of Man	yes	Uruguay	yes
Israel	no	Venezuela	no

Source: INCSR 2008.

laundering is the Financial Action Task Force on Money Laundering (FATF), to which we return in chapter 9. Of the fifteen jurisdictions listed by the FATF (2000a) on its initial list of non-cooperative countries and territories—a list that confirms the common perception of a link between tax havens and money laundering—only two are not considered tax havens.

In February 2001, U.S. Senator Carl Levin submitted an explosive report to Congress on the participation of U.S. banks in money-laundering rackets. Most major financial institutions are listed in the report, including Citigroup, Bank of New York, Bank of America, and JP Morgan Chase.

As every major bank works with correspondent banks internationally, the Levin report suggests that virtually the entire international financial industry is heavily involved in money laundering. Of all the services provided by offshore banks, the report singled out access to electronic networks of international transfers of funds and securities as the most significant instrument of money laundering. Launderers often protect themselves by setting up subsidiaries in tax havens that serve as clients of a bigger bank, itself linked to a correspondent bank in a major financial center. Levin's report showed that the major U.S. banks were aware of these practices but have done nothing to stop it, not wishing to jeopardize a lucrative business.

The European Parliament has launched its own investigation into these practices. Its report is unlikely to prove as powerful as the Levin report, but is very likely to reach similar conclusions regarding practices on that side of the Atlantic.

Tax havens claim to have tightened their regulations in response to various campaigns that have targeted them (discussed in chapters 9 and 10). They claim that money laundering is more difficult now, and certainly the handling of cash in these locations is much less likely than the 1980s. Some tax havens have taken the issue of money laundering very seriously. Luxembourg, for instance, has been particularly vigilant in the past few years in practicing stringent "know your client" procedures, imposed and audited by the Luxembourgeois authority. Sharman and Mistry (2008) report that Barbados and Vanuatu have tightened their regulations. Others, among them some British overseas territories, have not. The NAO (2007) report for the UK government found similar lapses in money laundering procedures in all the major UK dependent tax havens. At the same time, traffickers may have simply become more sophisticated, aided, and abetted by the ease of electronic transfers. The INCSR's 2008 report declares: "We can say with certainty that the use of offshore financial centers [i.e., tax havens], casinos, and the Internet is demonstrably growing at an alarming rate" (2008, 4).

Rawlings and Unger (2005) argue that some tax havens specifically target criminal money as a developmental strategy. In 1995, the Seychelles government passed the Economic Development Act (EDA), which created a board that could give specified concessions and incentives to foreign investors. They note that "One of these incentives was complete immunity from prosecution in criminal proceedings and the protection of assets from forfeiture even if investment were earned as a result of crimes committed outside the Seychelles" (Rawlings and Unger 2005, 5). To obtain this immunity an individual had to invest a minimum of $10 million in the Seychelles. The EDA was strongly condemned and the provision was repealed in 2000, but by then the funds were already in the Seychelles.

Box 2.3 Money laundering, Pacific Islands style[1]

Pacific Island tax havens are strongly associated with money laundering schemes. Nauru, a small Pacific atoll, was involved in the largest money laundering case in history, the so-called Russiagate scandal of the late 1990s, which involved the Bank of New York. U.S. law enforcement agencies contended that the bank facilitated at least 87,000 electronic transfers through Nauru accounts, totaling $15 billion in value. Some transfers, it was suggested, were for capital flight, some for tax evasion, but some derived from criminal activities such as contract murder, narcotics trafficking, and prostitution.

Nauru's Sinex Bank, owned by DKB, a Russian parent, was reported to have deposited $3 billion at the Bank of New York. Sinex had a questionable client base; Lucy Edwards, the Bank of New York vice president who entered a guilty plea to charges of money laundering, conceded: "I was aware that personnel from DKB were on occasion . . . afraid to leave the bank because they said customers with machine guns were waiting for them" (quoted in Van Fossen 2003, 244).

Victor Melnikov, deputy chair of the Russian Central Bank, stated that $70 billion had been transferred to Nauru from Russia in 1998, compared to total Russian exports of $74 billion. This is a figure remarkably close to the amount of IMF credit advanced to Russia in July 1998 in response to the financial crisis engulfing in the country that year. It suggests that much of the IMF money may have disappeared into offshore accounts without trace, and some of it through Nauru. In March 1999 Alexander Pochinok, head of the Russian Finance Department, claimed that 90% of Russian banks maintained 6,600 offshore banking accounts in Nauru, which was receiving $10 billion of Russian flight capital each month.

Not to be outdone, the neighboring islands of Palau and Vanuatu were implicated in capital flight from the former Soviet Union as well. As a result in December 1999, the Bank of New York, the Republic Bank of New York, Deutsche Bank, and its newly acquired subsidiary Bankers Trust, suspended all U.S. dollar transactions with Nauru, Palau, and Vanuatu, making it very difficult to move any funds into and out of these locations unless routed through Australia. But this does not seem to have ended tax evasion. In January 2001, JP Morgan Chase and the Bank of New York refused to have financial dealings with Nauru. In 2008, a major money laundering scandal broke in Vanuatu relating to the local branch of international accountants PKF. In response, the Vanuatu government has said it is planning to close down its tax haven activities. It is not yet clear what this means.

A German version of the Bank of New York scandal emerged in the media in 2001, with reports that Russian companies in 1999 used the United Global Bank in Samoa to transfer DM1.2 billion to the West Deutsche Landesbank as part of DM7 billion that Russians had deposited there. In February 2001 the Ukrainian tax police accused the country's former deputy prime minister and later opposition politician Yulia Tymoshenko of arranging the illegal transfer, via Latvia, of about $1 billion from United Energy Systems of Ukraine to the Nauru-based First Trading Bank controlled by Ukraine's former prime minister Pavlo Lazarenko, when she was the head of United Energy during 1996–97. The $1 billion transfer was to have purchased Russian gas. The tax police charged that the gas funds had been transferred to the private accounts of Tymoshenko, Lazarenko, and others, all of whom denied charges that were, they claimed, politically motivated.

Numerous reports of other multimillion-dollar frauds linked to Nauru offshore banks (but not necessarily connected with the former USSR) have appeared in newspapers around the world since 1999.

1. This box draws heavily on the work of Van Fossen 2003.

Embezzlement

It is worrisome that all the financial scandals of recent years involved offshore subsidiaries of at least one of the world's premier banking groups (Citigroup with Parmalat and Enron, Chase Manhattan with Enron, Société Generale with Vivendi). Yet this is only a small portion of tax haven activity.

The World Bank estimated in 2004 that over a trillion dollars are paid in bribes each year worldwide—and this does not include embezzlement of public funds or theft of public assets. Most of the data cannot be deduced from looking at "errors and omissions" entries or GDP measures in national accounts—such activity simply goes unrecorded in national statistics.

Offshore subsidiaries of the world's premier banks are heavily implicated in embezzlement and money laundering. Oxfam estimates that from 1993 to 1998, during the reign of Nigeria's dictator Sani Abacha, about $5 billion disappeared from state coffers, of which $2.5 billion was embezzled by the dictator and his family alone (Hodess 2004, 5). The Swiss Federal Banking Commission released the names of the banks involved in management of the money embezzled by the former Nigerian dictator in September 2000. The list contains the names of some of the best-known international banks, such as Credit Suisse, Credit Agricole Indosuez, BNP, and Baring Brothers. Subsequently the Nigerian administration has sought to recover the money, with a modicum of success. By November 2005 Switzerland had repatriated $505.5 million to Nigeria (World Bank 2006). Jersey also repatriated funds, but so far, the UK has refused to do so. The UK regulator, the FSA, launched its own investigation into twenty-three banks involved in the Nigerian racket. Fifteen banks showed "significant weaknesses" in their anti-money laundering, and the report provided a long list of these weaknesses. The report did not name any specific bank. However, the less prudent specialist press did name the recalcitrant banks, and they included the very cream of London: Barclays, HSBC, Standard Chartered, and Merrill Lynch. No prosecutions for handling these funds followed the disclosures.

If there is one odd thing in this episode, it is the sudden urge for transparency demonstrated by the Swiss. Why has Switzerland changed its tune? Switzerland, it seems, has had enough of being singled out and wanted to demonstrate that it was only a minor player in the international dirty money game, in effect a mere servant to the City of London. Of the $4 billion diverted to Switzerland, 59% came from London and 42% subsequently returned to London.

Tax havens undoubtedly facilitate tax evasion, tax avoidance, money laundering, and corruption, but no one is able to estimate the sums involved with any degree of accuracy. Consequently no one is able to address the corruption that underpins this market.

Conclusion

Quantitative research on the tax haven phenomenon has improved tremendously in the past few years, due to the efforts of some accountants and economists. The available data, however, are still no more than rough estimates based on creative manipulation of existing national and, at times, business statistics. Yet even such rough estimates lead us to the unavoidable conclusion that tax havens are not marginal. They must be understood as a core component of a modern, globalized economy.

These estimates show that criminal money does flow through tax havens, as is often thought, but it is only a small part of the problem. Rich people are spreading their savings around the world in an opaque manner that contributes to an important tax gap for the government. Moreover, the heavy use of tax havens by multinational banks and firms renders them an integral part of contemporary globalization.

Chapter 3

The Instruments of Tax Havens

Despite the secrecy that surrounds tax havens, we have considerable knowledge of their role and function in globalization. What are the instruments through which this "bright guilty world," to quote Orson Welles, lives its daily life?

Two groups use tax havens: individuals and companies. Both use similar techniques of tax avoidance, such as offshore companies and offshore trusts, but they do so with differing intent. We begin this chapter by describing the principle of avoidance, then go on to describe the various instruments used for avoidance and the professionals who help set up such schemes. Throughout the discussion we bear in mind that the dividing line between tax avoidance and tax evasion is not always as clear as professional accountants would have us believe. Given the complexity of international taxation, it is often the case that individuals or even companies using these arrangements have little idea on which side of the fine dividing line between evasion and avoidance they might be.

Sovereignty, Territoriality, and Tax: Basic Principles

The structural conditions that gave rise to the offshore world go back to the fundamental building blocks of global governance: sovereignty and territoriality. Typically sovereignty and territoriality are treated as political concepts, but they are also important to our understanding of economics.

The evolutionary economist John R. Commons ([1924] 1959) introduced an important idea that explains the links among sovereignty, territoriality, and the market. Commons argued that economic transactions take place within two spheres simultaneously—the "physical" sphere of exchanges of goods, services, and financial products, and the legal sphere where the exchange of property titles takes place. Conventional economics tended to study the first sphere in isolation, whereas lawyers and accountants focus on the second. Economists, Commons argued, must combine the two spheres. We believe his argument has considerable merit.

Every exchange is a transfer of property title, which requires an explicit or implicit contractual agreement among two or more parties. Consequently, the legal sphere of economic life functions well when a recognized political authority is able to define the generally acceptable "rules of the game" under which such agreements take place. Such an authority defines the nature, rights, and duties of the contracting parties as well as the rules of contract. The authority must also be in a position to enforce these agreements, ensuring that once signed and sealed they are fulfilled or if not fulfilled the aggrieved party has recourse for compensation. An authority, what political scientists call a "governance structure," is indispensable, ensuring the very functioning of a market economy.

In principle, different types of authorities can regulate market relationships. In the modern world, however, the state has emerged as the main, but by no means the sole, source of governance. State authority is territorially circumscribed, meaning each sovereign space or territory is regulated, at least in theory, by a sovereign state. The state writes laws within a given territory, including the territory's contract law. The state "charges" for the various services it provides, and taxes are typically the main source of its revenues.

This scenario works if we assume the world is divided neatly into nation-states. The reality, of course, is different. As a growing portion of economic life takes place between contracting parties located in different countries, a functioning world market requires an international extension of the legal sphere. As a growing number of states—crucially the majority of the economically advanced states—supported the development of cross-border trade and investment, they moved to internationalize the rules and laws that govern economic transactions as well. The debate whether the world economy is now global or not bears testimony to the many agreements on cross-border transactions both reached and normalized. In fact the methods by which such agreements were reached gave rise to tax havens. Why is that?

As the vast majority of the world's governments have come to accept the merits of an open market economy, they face a dilemma. The efficient and perhaps logical method for extending the legal sphere of contractual relationships internationally, resulting in a universally agreed set of international rules and laws of contracts, would have been to create a coordinated structure of global governance. It could have taken the form of an international organization with a measure of sovereign powers, including coercive and judicial powers, and could have harmonized contract law across the globe, providing the legal, political, and coercive mechanisms to sustain cross-border market transactions. But this hypothetical organization would have required the transfer of a portion of state sovereignty to a supranational agency—in effect, the establishment of a global state. The League of Nations and subsequently the United Nations were created for precisely such a purpose, but the vast majority of states were not prepared to transfer sovereignty to these organizations.

Consequently, a different method of governance has evolved. The idea was simple: legal personalities, whether an individual or a corporate entity, and every item of exchange, including services and financial products, are bound by the rules of the sovereign territory in which they are located. When personalities or items move to a different territory, they are bound (primarily) by the rules of that second territory. With this simple yet ingenious solution, the world market can function in a fragmented political system.

Economic transactions, however, take place simultaneously in the spatio-temporal and the legal spheres. The location of goods or legal personalities in the spatio-temporal world is not an issue, but the location of such items in the legal sphere is. It follows that every economic transaction is "marked" in the legal sphere by a sovereign stamp. Hence a new system of marking legal personalities and transactions has evolved since the early nineteenth century. Individuals are required to possess some recognizable identity, such as citizenship, national identity cards, passports, national security numbers; companies, banks, and other financial institutions must apply for permission to be incorporated and are licensed by a sovereign state. Mobile items such as vehicles, airplanes, and ships must have a license issued by a national authority and must display that license wherever they go. In theory, every single item exchanged, including services and financial products, must also have a sovereign home. Goods are marked as "made in" this or that country. Indeed, every valid contract must specify the sovereign location that governs its conduct—even though in many cases, the sovereign state may be entirely unaware that its laws have been chosen to adjudicate disputes.

The marking of legal personalities, goods, and services by territorial states places the marked individuals, goods, and services under the tax rules of these territories. As individuals, goods, and service are becoming increasingly mobile, the question which territory is entitled to which portion of taxation becomes acute (Rixen 2008). Simply stated, international economic activities generate overlapping tax claims, and taxation becomes a barrier to the internationalization of economic activities.

This problem of overlap has obvious solutions. Either income or profits that result from international activities can be taxed where the income is earned, in other words in the *source* country, or where the recipient is normally based, that is in the country of *residence*. As we will see, there problems are associated with each solution, for each offers opportunities for avoidance and evasion. Not surprising, there is considerable discussion of the two principles among tax haven experts. At heart, however, the tax haven strategy hinges on neither one.

Sovereignty and the Location of Taxable Events

Because individuals can move from one place to another and capital is mobile as well, the location of each "taxable event" must be formally established in the legal sphere. In the jargon of tax planning,

> For a tax liability to arise there has to be something called a "connecting factor" between a taxing jurisdiction on the one hand and a taxpayer or taxable event on the other. (Schmidt report 1999)

A state has the sovereign right to insist on the rules that establish the nature of the connecting factor to its taxpayers, and it is universally accepted that one state cannot dictate to another on such rules. The problem, however, is that the very principle that establishes a connecting factor between taxing jurisdiction and the taxpayer or taxable event opens up the possibility of disassociation of the physical from the legal location of a transaction. As a result, a transaction can take place physically in one country but can be legally registered or marked in another.

The proliferation of sovereign states in the nineteenth and twentieth centuries brought with it a proliferation in the rules for establishing such links and, as a result, to the development of unintentional cracks and loopholes in regulatory and taxing regimes. Such cracks and loopholes are opportunities for what is called, euphemistically, "international tax planning," which aims to reduce taxation on worldwide earnings. One favored technique involves choosing among the rules that link jurisdictions, taxpayers, and taxable events, with the aim of shifting profits into low-tax countries and costs to high-tax countries. This "tax arbitrage" is not an exact science, but often a matter of interpretation of the rules and regulations of different countries. It has the enormous benefit of adding further uncertainty for those who act in the gray area between tax compliance and tax evasion. Not only can knowledgeable practitioners exploit uncertainty within one state as to the meaning of tax law, but they can also exploit the uncertainty that the interaction of the law of two or more countries provides. International tax planning has emerged as an extremely lucrative business run by some of the best-paid professionals in the world.

More problematic, some states create rules establishing a relationship to taxable events that are aimed, or so it appears, at luring taxpayers and taxable events to their domains from wherever the real events actually occur. Some countries have even innovated legal conditions under which taxable events can be represented or registered as if they take place there, while they simultaneously deem those events as taking place elsewhere (the beauty of the invention being that the "elsewhere" is never specified and as we will see, it is often nowhere). In such cases, the taxpayer ends up in the paradoxical but highly lucrative position of being in a no-man's-land in tax terms, which means paying no tax at all. The taxpayer may also avoid regulation in this way. Countries have invented, as we show below, a whole series of exemptions, such as the appropriately titled exempt company, which allow taxpayers to inhabit such legal deserts. They are legal, because each sovereign state is entitled to write the rules of legal residence as it wishes.

We can now refine our definition of tax havens. The tax haven boils down to a very simple idea: the state creates legal instruments by which individuals and companies can reduce, or completely sever, their "connecting factor" to their country of origin. They do so knowing that individuals and companies have an incentive to sever their connecting factor: to avoid taxation. State authorities may challenge the assertion that a connecting factor has been severed (and they do so, often), or may demand taxation based on either source or residence basis notwithstanding the claimed connection to a tax haven. In response, tax havens have invented other instruments to ensure opacity and secrecy, so that the original authority may not even know that a taxpayer has severed a connecting factor. Not surprising, many states consider such behavior parasitic and harmful (Palan and Abbott 1996; Slemrod and Wilson 2006).

The Simplest Technique of Tax Planning: Relocate to Low-Tax Jurisdiction

The simplest method of removing a connecting factor between taxpayer and his or her country of origin is by moving to a low-tax country. Some tax havens, including Monaco, San Marino, Switzerland, the UK, the Bahamas, and Dubai, have specialized in providing real or virtual residence for wealthy individuals.

One of the most popular spots for relocation for tax purposes is Monaco, which has two clear advantages. Monaco is a beautiful 0.76 square mile principality located on the French Riviera, not far from the airports at Turin and Nice. Moreover, Monaco imposes no personal taxation at. These advantages have attracted scores of highly paid sports and other celebrities, such as Boris Becker and Jason Button, as well as entrepreneurs such as the wife of Sir Philip Green, owner of many UK high street stores.

Switzerland offers deals that are slightly more complicated. It levies federal, cantonal, and municipal taxation, and in this respect does not appear to be a tax haven. Swiss cantons are very pragmatic and strike special deals with wealthy foreigners (but not with Swiss citizens) to help them reduce their overall tax burden. For example, Formula 1 driver Michael Schumacher relocated in 1996 to the Domaine de la Chenaie, in Vufflens-le-Château, near Nyon. Schumacher received some very special tax benefits, classifying him as a foreigner without income. He is allowed to pay tax in Switzerland based on his expenses, such as rent, rather than on his income. Lewis Hamilton is the latest Formula 1 driver to locate in Switzerland, along with musicians and film stars such as David Bowie, Phil Collins, Tina Turner, Alain Delon, and Isabelle Adjani.

The UK offers a similar facility to non-domiciled people and so has attracted scores of the world's rich. Dubai has embarked on an ambitious plan, combining a tax haven with a duty-free zone (the Emirates Free Zone). Using modern marketing techniques, such as establishing the first so-called seven star hotel in the world, a set of artificial islands shaped as palm trees, and links to celebrities such as David Beckham, Dubai markets itself as a playground for the rich. Dubai never fails to mention that it imposes no personal taxation whatsoever.

Relocating to a tax haven is a drastic move for an individual to undertake. There are other more sophisticated ways to avoid paying tax and escape regulations.

The Permanent Tourist

Conflicting rules of residency for tax purposes have created a new term in tax avoidance. PTs or permanent tourists are a nomadic tribe of wealthy individuals who reside nowhere but are catered to by scores of professionals. As Bill Maurer explains:

> In a nutshell, the PT merely arranges his or her "paperwork" in such a way that all governments consider him a tourist—a person who is just "passing through." The advantage is that by being thought of by government officials as a person who is merely "parked temporarily," a PT is not

subject to taxes, military service, lawsuits, or persecution for taking part in innocent but forbidden pursuits or pleasures. (Maurer 1998, 505)

Permanent tourism is a big business. Thousands of publications, websites, and professional outfits cater to the world's PTs. There are, however, no reliable estimates of the number of PTs. Current estimates of tax evasion and avoidance noted in chapter 2 only partially take into account the PT phenomenon. The PTs move about below the radar.

How Individuals Move Capital to Tax Havens

Not everyone can be a PT. One alternative favored by wealthy individuals is to move mobile capital into one of the various instrument of offshore avoidance discussed in the next section, such as a company, foundation, or trust. Income from capital, such as interest or dividends, is typically not declared in the place of residence. Such avoidance can be illegal, so tax havens are carefully vetted to ensure that they have no duty to provide information to the tax authorities of the country in which taxpayer is based.

To maintain secrecy, the offshore banking industry helps individuals to gain access to their money through an offshore debit or credit card. The cards are used "onshore" (usually where the person lives) but are settled from a bank account located in the offshore territory in which the taxpayer is holding funds to avoid tax. The debit or credit card need not be held in the name of the person actually using it; indeed, it is relatively easy to obtain anonymous cards.

Not surprising, offshore credit and debit cards have attracted the attention of tax authorities. Barclays Bank, a large British high street bank, was ordered to disclose details of many offshore credit cards that it ran for UK residents in 2006. (A sample survey had shown that only 19% of Barclay's customers with UK addresses and cards linked to international accounts were filing tax returns in the UK. In other words, 81% of Barclays offshore credit cardholders in the UK claimed to have no taxable investment income in the UK. HM Revenue & Customs expected to recover at least US$2.85 billion through this inquiry [Gutcher 2006].)

The Instruments of Tax Havens

Relocation to tax haven may be a drastic move for an individual to undertake, but companies can relocate by the simple expedient of creating new subsidiaries in tax havens. Their presence is easily disguised, first by the secrecy to which we have referred elsewhere, and second because corporations are allowed to present one set of accounts. These accounts are, however, prepared on a consolidated basis. "Consolidated" means that all transactions between different parts of the corporation are eliminated from the accounts. There may be hundreds or even thousands of such constituent companies, which can be hidden from the public eye because of this accounting convention.

The convention has some other benefits. The accounts presented to a stock exchange and to shareholders might make it look as if there is a single multinational entity but in reality, when it comes to taxation, there is no such thing as an MNE. Companies can legally maintain economic ties between their subsidiaries, but every single subsidiary is deemed a separate entity when it comes to taxation. Consequently, multinational corporation is an economic but not a legal concept (Robé 1997). A parent company usually owns all or most of the other entities in a group, and controls them all because ownership of a company's shares provides that right under company law. However, the companies remain legally distinct and entirely separate for tax purposes.

This corporate structure creates both problems for taxing authorities and opportunities for the companies. As many companies are trading internationally, they can be taxed, like individuals, either at the place where they make profits or at the place of residence of the company or its subsidiaries. According to the source principle, a state can impose corporate profits on all companies generating profits in its territory, whether domestic or foreign. For instance, the United States taxes Toyota, a Japanese company, on all its profits accrued in the United States. According to the residence principle, businesses are taxed depending on the jurisdiction where they are registered, irrespective of where they actually make profits. So the United States taxes Toyota US (but not Toyota Japan) on its profits irrespective of where they are earned.

Both systems are problematic, but the difficulty of determining the share of an MNE's profits assignable to a particular territory using the source principle (how much of Toyota's global profits can be assigned to its U.S. operations?) has resulted in use of the residence principle as the most common basis for corporate taxes. Based on this principle, firms and their subsidiaries are taxed at the place of their registration, with allowance being made for tax paid elsewhere.

Companies are taxed on profits and not on turnover, and MNEs consist of legally separate companies, without having to relocate. They do not have to move to tax havens to take advantage of low taxation and secrecy; they need only shift profits and taxable events to their resident subsidiaries in tax havens. Their consolidated accounts hide such shifts and instead give the impression that the company floats above mere national spaces.

Tax havens have developed a whole range of opaque corporate structures that help companies move capital and shift profits from high- to low-tax countries. In a bizarre twist, wealthy individuals can set themselves up as companies in tax havens and avoid taxes as well. Below we discuss the favorite methods of "relocating" to low-tax countries?

The International Business Corporation (IBC)

The basic method of relocation requires the setting up of a subsidiary, affiliate, or company in a tax haven. Tax havens have responded to the demand for such entities by creating the perfect instrument, the IBC.

IBCs are highly versatile, limited liability companies that are set up in tax havens either as subsidiaries of onshore companies or as independent companies. Their principal purpose is to shift the profitable portion of a business to a low-tax jurisdiction. IBCs can operate businesses offshore and raise capital by issuing shares, bonds, and other instruments. They are also used for the legal possession of property rights, the organization of trading on financial markets, managing investment funds, and as part of complex financial structures.

A limited company is a corporation whose liability is limited by law. Typically, in an onshore setting, a limited liability company is regulated by a Memorandum of Association (or its equivalent in other legal systems), which says what the company may do, and by Articles of Association, which says how it will manage its business. The company is actually run by a director or board of directors, and its legal affairs are managed by the company secretary. Most countries have introduced regulations that are intended to protect shareholders and traders from abuse. Such safeguards require: maintaining a public register of companies, listing all those in existence; having a registered place of business at which a company may be contacted; making known details of a company's issued share capital and the names and addresses of those owning and providing that capital; placing on record full information on its directors and secretary; and filing annual accounts for public inspection. Tax havens provide almost none of these safeguards. The typical offshore IBC has the following characteristics:

Secrecy of ownership. There are as many rules and regulations for setting up IBCs in tax havens as there are tax havens. The principle, however, is always the same: if owners wish to conceal their identity, they can do so very effectively. The information normally placed on the public record to protect those dealing with the company can be kept secret in a tax haven, or a nominee name can be used to hide the true identity of the owners. In many cases, IBCs may have only one director (i.e., it can be, in effect, a company of one person, which may appeal to individuals seeking to take advantage of limited liability rules). In others, residents of the host country may act as nominee directors. In a further arrangement, bearer share certificates can be used so that practical ownership is not recorded (such activity is becoming less common) or registered share certificates can be used, but no public registry of shareholders is maintained.

No filing requirements. IBCs typically have no requirement to file accounts on the public record. In some locations, they are not even required to keep books and records. In addition, it is rare for Memorandums and Articles of Association to be on public record. If officers must be named, they will be local nominees. This practice provides a lucrative source of income to local professionals and serves as a hidden source of revenue to the tax haven. If a registered office is required, often it is simply a "brass plaque" address and has no bearing upon the real location of the entity. Many tax havens, however, have no requirement to maintain local officers. Some tax havens prohibit IBCs owned by local people to prevent their citizens from avoiding tax.

In most tax havens, companies need not send accounts to any regulatory authority, not even to those responsible for tax (because no tax is due). As such, local authorities have almost no oversight over the actions of limited companies, for they have ensured that they have no information to appraise. It is, therefore, extremely difficult to find any reliable information on an IBC.

Protection from creditors. In most tax havens, shareholders may acquire one or more shares in the company. As long as they have paid the full subscription price for their share, which rarely exceeds one U.S. dollar, one euro, or one pound sterling, they have no further liability for its debts. This remains true when a company becomes insolvent and is unable to pay its creditors.

Low incorporation costs. The costs of setting up IBCs are minimal, usually in a range between $100 and $500. IBCs are generally exempt from all taxes, although they pay a minimal annual "license fee" to the tax haven. Many tax havens even permit the creation of "off the shelf" companies. Scores of companies are set up in advance by tax professionals, who then advertise them or sell to any client who wants an offshore IBC. In this way an IBC can be set up overnight. IBCs also have unlimited powers to trade without regulation.

Considering the above, it is no surprise that the IBC has proved immensely popular. There are believed to be in excess of two million IBCs in tax havens, and their number increases 10% to 15% per annum. Table 2.3 provides the latest available comprehensive survey of the world's IBCs.

Exempt Corporations

A specialized technique allowed in several tax havens is the exempt corporation. The tax authorities know, of course, that many IBCs are merely sham operations, and they now demand evidence of real activity by the IBC. If such evidence is lacking, they are likely to treat the IBC as if it is operating in their territory and tax it accordingly, using Controlled Foreign Company (CFC) rules.

The more agile tax havens, such as the Cayman Islands, have responded by demanding that every IBC maintain some presence on the Island—an important component of Cayman's purportedly regulated financial environment. Yet tax havens, including Caymans, have innovated schemes for avoiding these rules as well, including rules to which they have subscribed. A mechanism was needed that allowed a tax haven company owned by people not resident in that location to appear to have a local economic presence while remaining untaxed. At the same time, the tax haven needed to tax companies operating locally and owned by local people. How can both needs be accommodated?

The Island of Jersey provides one solution to the dilemma. On the face of it, Jersey adopts the conventional method of company incorporation and apparently does not allow for sham incorporation. Section 123 (1) of Jersey's tax laws states that a company is resident in Jersey if "its business is managed and controlled in the Island." However, section 123 (A) (9) of the same law states: "the office of director of an exempt company shall be deemed not to be an office exercised within the Island." This provision allows a company to be managed and controlled from Jersey, but "deemed," by the Jersey authorities, to be managed and controlled elsewhere and hence not subject to Jersey's taxation. Yet because the company shows real "presence" in Jersey, as far as other countries are concerned, it is managed from Jersey and hence is not subject to taxation elsewhere. Jersey chooses not to ask the obvious follow-on question: if the company is not located in Jersey, where is it? Jersey's authorities know that the answer is "nowhere," and the fiction of "deeming" a company to be elsewhere creates a tax advantage to the corporation. This particular structure is now disappearing from Jersey under pressure from EU regulation, but the practice remains common elsewhere.

Redomiciliation

The scope for abuse was expanded by an innovation of the last decade—redomiciliation, a response to the increase in offshore regulation. The legal basis for redomiciliation was adapted from a State of Delaware law (discussed in chapter 4)—a point that tax haven authorities never fail to mention. It involves relocating the legal domain in which a company is registered from one territory with the power to register companies to another. For example, a company registered in Gibraltar might be redomiciled to the Isle of Man. The original date of incorporation and company existence remain the same and are unaffected by the change, but the statute under which they are registered, the law that governs their regulation, the regulator with responsibility for them, and the place of their registered office (invariably required to be in the domain of registration) will all have changed.

Most tax havens now allow this process. The advantages to tax evaders are obvious. At the first hint of an inquiry, they can apply to have their company redomiciled to another location. It then legally ceases to exist in the place where the inquiry has arisen and now exists somewhere else. The agency making the inquiry now has to (expensively and laboriously) begin the process in another place. Redomiciliation can happen repeatedly, destroying any chance of securing effective information exchange from a persistent abuser. The havens of the world deliberately created this opportunity to facilitate tax evasion. There is no other logical reason for redomiciliation.

The Limited Liability Partnership (LLP)
LLP is another limited liability entity developed in the last decade to promote secrecy and to protect tax-haven–registered companies from claims. LLPs add another layer of confusion regarding ownership of assets. Yet the Big Four accountancy firms—Deloitte Touche Tohmatsu, PricewaterhouseCoopers, Ernst & Young, and KPMG—have lobbied hard for and promoted legislation to create such entitles in Jersey, and even threatened to leave the UK if it did not provide similar opportunities (Select Committee on Trade and Industry 1998). These entities, or variations upon them, are now widely available in tax havens.

LLPs have a particular role in the tax planning of major corporations because they are considered "tax transparent." Although they legally exist in a tax haven, they have no tax residence in those havens. Instead, members of these entities are taxed as if they undertook the transactions of an LLP. This allows the separation of legal ownership of assets from the location of income arising from them. Tax is divided between countries—an opportunity, of course, for complex tax planning schemes. Much of the recent anti-avoidance legislation in the UK, including some in the Finance Act 2008 with regard to both stamp duty avoidance and the loss of corporation tax, is aimed at combating these abuses.

Protected Cell Company (PCC)

An even more complex form of company is the PCC, first provided by the Island of Guernsey in 1997. However, Guernsey is no longer alone in supplying such companies. Malta, the Netherlands Antilles, many of the Caribbean havens, and the Isle of Man allow these arrangements as well, as do some Swiss cantons.

A PCC operates as if it were a group of separate companies except all are part of the same legal entity. There is a "parent level," which provides management services for the company as a whole, and there are several segregated parts called cells. Each cell is legally independent and separate from the others, as well as from the "parent level." Each cell has a unique name and the assets, and the liabilities and activities of each cell are ring-fenced from the others. Due to a lack of transparency, it is often difficult to tell that a company is a protected cell of another company, or that there is even a relationship between different companies, which bear different names.

Protected Cell Companies are generally used for insuring different classes of risk or for collective investment schemes that incorporate different types of funds. Such arrangements provide the low transaction fees associated with moving assets within a single company (transferring assets between cells) with the legal protection of a multi-company structure (limiting the risk to the whole entity if one cell goes bust or is sued) (Sharman 2006). The use of PCCs even in this apparently legitimate way is particularly worrying within the insurance sector. No one insuring with such an entity can be sure what assets might be used to cover his or her risk.

Of even greater concern, PCCs help construct an impenetrable wall against creditors and prying eyes. The advantage of the arrangement, if "advantage" is the right word, is that if one cell becomes insolvent, creditors have recourse only to the assets of that particular cell and not to any other. But creditors may not know until it is too late that they have invested in a PCC. PCCs were originally created for use in reinsurance activity, but the only realistic use of such entities now is to evade obligations arising under the laws of other countries. The dangers are obvious. Capital flight becomes corporate flight with a world populated by roving, unaccountable companies.

Foundations, Trusts, and the Anstalt

The other popular technique of tax avoidance and evasion are offshore trusts and foundations. Trusts can be dated as far back as the Crusaders: when English knights left on long expeditions to the Holy Land, they left others to manage their affairs under what became known as trust

---

Box 3.1 IBCs and tax avoidance

IBCs can be used in a variety of ways to shift profits from high-tax countries to tax havens. Here are a few of the better-known methods.

One popular technique is to set up an IBC as an "intermediate holding company" in a tax haven. Such holding companies are owned by parent companies and in turn own operating subsidiaries. Typically, little or nothing happens in the intermediate locations, except that they collect dividend income from the subsidiaries they own and then usually loan, but do not pay as dividends, the resulting cash to the parent company in London, New York, or wherever.

Some companies go a step further and install the parent company in a tax haven. This practice is called "inversion." The domestic company establishes a subsidiary—perhaps little more than a mailbox—in a tax haven and subsequently inverts corporate ownership by turning the subsidiary into the parent company. This tactic was very popular in the United States for two or three years after 2000, the usual inversion destination being Bermuda (whence the extraordinary FDI figures for Bermuda noted in chapter 2). The most widely cited reason for corporate inversion was to circumvent CFC rules (discussed in chapter 9). Patriotic sentiments in the United States were used to block such moves (Olson 2002). The process reemerged in the UK in 2008 with UK stock exchange-quoted companies registering new parent entities in Jersey that are tax-resident in Ireland.

IBC subsidiaries are used for other purposes. Some products are recorded as being sold from almost anywhere, and it is hard to prove that the claim is untrue. This is particularly the case with software and other products sold on line. In such cases the company sells items through its tax haven subsidiary and pays little or no tax as a result.

The majority of MNE-owned IBCs are used for transfer pricing. One popular technique is to place the rights for intellectual property in the hands of an offshore subsidiary. "Intellectual property" comprises patents (on which royalties are paid) and copyrights (on which license fees are paid). Any company can decide where it wishes to locate ownership of its patents and copyrights, and it need not be the country of creation. There is usually little or no tax penalty on relocating them to a low-tax country. The same is true of material such as logos. Substantial charges can be levied on associated group companies in states with much higher tax rates, payments being made to a tax haven subsidiary, where little or no tax is paid. This is now a major threat to the taxation revenues of many developed countries.

An example is to be found within the Virgin Corporation, which is widely reported to license the use of its Virgin logo to all Virgin operations from the British Virgin Islands. Profits presumably accrue in the zero-taxed BVI.

Microsoft holds copyright in most of its products for sale outside the United States in Ireland, a low-tax state. As a result Microsoft appears to be the largest company in Ireland, though the vast majority of its income in that country has little or nothing to do with its activities there (see box 5.2. for discussion). This was certainly profitable for Ireland. Between 2001 and 2004 Microsoft paid the equivalent of $1 billion in taxes to the Irish tax authorities, at the local rate of 12.5%—which is quite low when compared to the 35% tax that Microsoft pays in the United States.

Group financing can also take place offshore. All business activities require finance to establish a physical presence and to fund the day-to-day activities of the business. This money can be provided in two ways: share capital or loan capital. Share capital earns dividends payable from profits. Loan capital pays interest regardless of whether or not profits are generated. Loan capital can be supplied by an external source such as a bank or venture capital group or from an internal finance company. Internal finance companies and/or IBCs are often set up offshore in locations such as the Netherlands and Ireland, which have deliberately created tax structures to attract such "businesses."

Interest payments are deducted in most states from the paying company's profit and so reduce its tax bill. Interest is much more favorably treated for tax purposes than dividends. An MNE can often arrange to receive interest in a low-tax area but secure tax relief for that interest in a high-tax area, thus creating a permanent tax saving. This is harder to achieve for dividends, especially where there is tax withholding before they are paid. The outcome of this different treatment is predictable: companies prefer to lend capital.

Abuse is often complex. For example, third party funds are borrowed in territories with relatively high tax rates and efficient capital markets, where there are no restrictions on the use of those funds with regard to tax relief. The UK is such a location. Funds are then lent with very low margins earned to a financial center such as Dublin. From there they are lent on to foreign subsidiaries and the charges are inflated, especially if that subsidiary is located in a high-risk area. In effect, this is another form of transfer pricing, but this time financial products were created specifically for the purpose.

The offshore operations of many MNEs are a charade. It seems logical that a company would employ its staff where they work or where they live. However, in the United States payroll and other taxes would be due on U.S.-based staff working overseas. Such taxes can be avoided if it is claimed that the staff in question are employed through a tax haven company. The United States moved to block such arrangements in 2008, but they remain commonplace elsewhere.

IBCs can be set up by individuals. People with very high incomes, such as professional athletes, inventors, and top corporate management, set up an IBC in a tax haven into which their salaries are paid. They become, in turn, employees of their companies but receive only nominal remuneration from these companies when they repatriate income and bring it onshore.

Individuals use IBCs for other purposes as well. IBCs and offshore trusts allow taxpayers to recategorize income as having a different form and hence subject to a different tax or to no tax at all. Income can be recategorized as capital gains, for capital gains tax is usually charged at a lower rate than income tax. Alternatively, income derived from labor is recategorized as investment income by way of payment of dividends to owners instead of the payment of wages to the same people. Social security charges can be either avoided or evaded by such schemes.

arrangements. Such arrangements remain peculiar to Anglo-Saxon (English) law.

In trusts a person or entity (the trustee) holds legal title to certain property (the trust property) but has a fiduciary duty to exercise legal control for the benefit of one or more individuals or organizations (the beneficiary), who hold "beneficial" or "equitable" title. To put it another way, a trust arises when "there is a gift by a person (known as a settlor) of property to trustees for them to manage for the benefit of others (known as beneficiaries)" (Schmidt Report 1999).

Trusts are contractual agreements between two private individuals that create a barrier between the legal owner of an asset and its beneficiary. The instrument enables the transfer of legal ownership of property or financial assets to another person on behalf of third parties. Trusts provide secrecy because they do not require any form of registration in most jurisdictions, and even where registration is required (as in the UK, but only for taxation purposes), it is not placed on public record. Nor is the trust deed that regulates management of the trust a matter of public record—in fact, it is still possible for a valid trust to be created verbally.

Trusts have been used offshore since the 1920s in the Channel Islands and Switzerland (although Switzerland is a civil law country and, strictly speaking, does not recognize this facility), but they have become much more widespread since the 1960s. They are commonplace nowadays in the offshore world, and some jurisdictions, such as Jersey, Cayman, and the BVI, specialize in supplying them. Almost no tax haven is without trust law, however.

To be even vaguely legal, a trust arrangement usually requires the person creating the trust to forego entirely any interest in the income arising from it. In practice, the offshore finance industry deliberately ignores this requirement and assists individuals to evade their tax obligations by creating sham arrangements that have the appearance of trusts. They look as though the individual has foregone an interest, but in fact the trust is often run by "nominee" trustees who are residents of a tax haven. Even these arrangements are not necessary, however, because once assets are transferred to an offshore trust it is usually very difficult to trace them back to their owners. The absence of registration procedures compounds this difficulty. In addition, the settlor is frequently not named in trust deeds, or a nominee is used to disguise the relationship between settlor and property.

The trustees are liable to tax on the income that they receive from trust assets unless that income must, under the terms of the trust, be paid to another person. Because offshore trusts are "discretionary," where at least notionally the trustees can allocate the income to almost anyone they wish, it is almost invariably the trustees who are taxable. In the case of an offshore trust the trustees are usually professional people (accountants, lawyers, trust company officials, or even trust companies), ensuring that the trust earns and accumulates its income tax-free. In addition, because the trust is located offshore, it does not have to declare to tax authorities the payment of income to any beneficiary who does not live in the tax haven in which the trust is located—and there is no reason why beneficiaries should live there. Income is paid into the beneficiary's offshore bank account without anyone in his or her home jurisdiction knowing. This procedure makes tax evasion relatively simple.

It has been made even easier by legislation over the last few years in locations such as Cayman (Star trusts), the BVI (Vista trusts), and Jersey (trusts with reservation of powers). These trust arrangements, all apparently inspired by members of the Society of Trust and Estate Practitioners (a professional body based in London), considerably distort the concept of a trust (Gray 2005). In all these cases, the settlor of the trust retains considerable power over the trust arrangement after its creation, including power to direct its investment decisions, payment to beneficiaries (the settlor may be a beneficiary of the trust), and even the power to dissolve the trust. These arrangements are hardly trusts at all but are instead means to disguise the ownership of assets. They provide considerable benefit to those wishing to evade taxes.

It is important to note that trusts are not set up only for tax reasons. Individuals may wish to hide assets from their spouses; family or business partners may use the trust facility as well. Trusts may also be used to avoid inheritance laws. Some users may be seeking to avoid regulation, for example on controlling too large a part of an industry. Tax is, however, a common motivation. In all cases, the trust is likely a charade or sham, especially when instructions to trustees given in side letters are taken into account. According to one estimate, in 2004 there were at least 1,000 offshore trusts managing approximately 350,000 accounts with assets between $3 and $8 trillion (STEP 2004). A STEP magazine survey found that among the thirty-one offshore territories most involved in this market, trusts are used primarily as a tool for wealth management (35% of respondents) and as a tool for tax reduction (25%).

Foundations are another method to conceal assets. Foundations are a form of trust that is recognized as having separate legal existence akin to a limited company. The foundation's success arises from its combination of secrecy with a legal existence separating it from the lawyer who manages it and from the settlor and its non-taxable status.

Foundations have no owners or shareholders. They are set up to manage assets whose income must serve a specified goal. Among the leading tax havens, the Netherlands Antilles, Austria, Denmark, Panama, the Netherlands, Liechtenstein, and Switzerland allow the creation of private foundations. Again, many tax havens demand only minimal disclosure from foundations. In one extreme case, Panama, no approval is needed to create a foundation.

Another well-known method of concealment is the Anstalt, a specialty of Liechtenstein. The Anstalt is a complex hybrid between the foundation and the trust. Invented in the 1920s, it is a privileged instrument used particularly by wealthy families as a method for avoiding inheritance taxes. There is almost no official record of the activities of an Anstalt so long as it is set up for personal or family use, usually by a non-Liechtenstein resident. The name of the person creating the foundation is not recorded. The foundation must have a constitution or a deed, but many of the foundations used to evade taxes do not require any form of registration at all. Their existence is known only to the lawyers and bankers who supply services to them and who are legally bound by absolute secrecy. Even if registration is required (for example, because the foundation is charitable), no information of any sort concerning the foundation, not even its name, is available to the public.

Foundations and Anstalts that do not trade in Liechtenstein do not need to keep accounting records if they do not wish to do so. In fact, no accounts have to be sent to any authority. A tax charge of between 0.5% and 1% of the value of the foundation's capital assets is paid annually, although without records such charges presumably cannot be policed. Nevertheless, 30% of Liechtenstein's state income comes from this source. Anstalts plus some of the strictest banking secrecy laws in the world mean that Liechtenstein offers no transparency at all. The Anstalts have been a great success, though their number is unknown. Peillon and Montebourg (2000) estimate 13,000, but 2008 reports in the media suggest a much higher number, approaching 80,000, which—given the size of the financial services market in Liechtenstein—seems more likely. Envious of Liechtenstein's success, Jersey in 2008 proposed its own foundation laws.

Offshore Banking Licenses and Other Financial Institutions

Banks

In the past, tax havens supplied cheap banking licenses and boasted a great number of banks in their territories. Offshore banking licenses are the banking equivalent of IBCs, although the latter are sufficiently versatile to serve as financial institutions as well. The attractions of OFC banks are obvious: no capital tax, no withholding tax on dividends or interest, no tax on transfers, no corporation tax, no capital gains tax, no exchange

controls, light regulation and supervision, less stringent reporting requirements, and less stringent trading restrictions. Not surprising, all of
the world's premier and middle ranking banks and the vast majority of the
world's small banks maintain at least one subsidiary in tax havens, and
most maintain many such subsidiaries.

The result has been an extraordinary proliferation of banks. The Bahamas has claimed to have 4,300 banks licensed in its territory. Cayman,
with a population of 51,000, boasted 427 banks in 2007, one for every 120
residents (Ridley 2007).

Tax havens are used by three types of financial institutions. First, the
majority of tax-haven banks are empty shells. They have either no or
minimal physical presence in the jurisdiction. These institutions are over-
whelmingly involved in criminal financial activities (BIS 2003a), particularly those registered in countries that fail to cooperate with the FATF and
the FSF. Some experts believe that 40% of all the financial activities of
such institutions are of criminal or at the very least illegal nature (Dupuis-
Danon 2004). There have been serious attempts to close this type of banks,
so far with only partial success.

The Basel Committee on Banking Supervision identifies a second type
of offshore bank that serves as a subsidiary of large onshore banks. Many
of these subsidiaries are owned by well-known retail banks, are managed
by them, and may share their names (e.g., Barclays Jersey). Yet legally,
they are separate entities. Banks use their tax haven subsidiaries for both
legal and illegal activities. Legally, or quasi legally, offshore subsidies are
used to evade either taxes or regulations (BIS 2003b). The UK tax amnesty
in 2007, which focused solely on the customers of the UK's major retail
banks, proved how extensively these subsidiaries were being used for tax
evasion purposes. Multinational corporations set up offshore banks for
the same purpose, to finance their own activities.

Finally, there are genuine offshore banks located in properly regulated
jurisdictions. According to one estimate, by late 1998 there were approximately 4,000 such banks, spread over sixty territories, nearly half of which
were located in Latin America and the Caribbean. These banks managed
about $5 trillion in assets. Of course, it is exceptionally difficult to tell
which bank is in which category, because of the secretive nature of offshore and of corporate reporting.

Insurance Companies

Tax havens have become the venue for the proliferation of the so-called
captive insurance companies. These are subsidiaries created by a multinational company in an OFC to manage risk and minimize taxes. Practically
all the onshore insurance companies establish subsidiaries in OFCs to

Table 3.1 Captive growth, 1989–2007

Year	Number of captives
1989	2,535
1992	2,896
1995	3,199
1997	3,361
1998	3,418
2005	4,772
2006	4,951
2007	5,119

Source: Insurance Information Institute, based on Business Insurance and Conning Research data.

reinsure certain risks underwritten by the parent and reduce overall reserve and capital requirements. An onshore reinsurance company incorporates a subsidiary in an OFC to reinsure against catastrophic risk. The attractions of an OFC in these circumstances include favorable income/withholding and capital tax regimes, as well as low or weakly enforced actuarial reserve requirements and capital standards.

The first such insurers emerged in Europe in the 1920s and 1930s at the instigation of oil majors like BP and ICI. They have done well financially, for they proved more adept at weighing the risk of their operations than were traditional insurance companies. The last three decades have seen a tremendous growth in the number of captive insurance companies. Their number is estimated at a little more than 5,000 worldwide, affecting about $20 billion in premiums and managing a total of more than $50 billion in assets (www.captive.com).

The offshore center that first specialized in captives was Bermuda. Spiraling costs of litigation in the United States in the 1980s, associated with health risks and particularly asbestos, offered an opportunity that Bermuda was quick to grasp. As industrial enterprises have seen their insurance premiums soar, the big U.S. insurer Marsh & McLennan begun to develop captive insurance companies in Bermuda (Evans 2002). Bermuda has since continued to innovate and since the mid-2000s has become one of the leading places for reinsurance (Munich Re and Swiss Re are leading providers). Guernsey and the Cayman Islands have joined this activity, and Luxembourg, Dublin, and Gibraltar are also active in the reinsurance market. Coming late to the game, BVI tends to specialize in smaller captives. The Isle of Man, Bermuda, and the Caymans tend to attract U.S. multinationals, whereas European companies choose Guernsey.

Table 3.2   Leading captive domiciles, 2007

Rank	Location	Number of captives	
		2006	*2007*
1	Bermuda	989	958
2	Cayman Islands	740	765
3	Vermont	563	567
4	British Virgin Islands	400[1]	409[1]
5	Guernsey	381	368
6	Barbados	235	256
7	Luxembourg	208	210
8	Turks and Caicos Islands	169[2]	173[1]
9	Hawaii	160	163
10	South Carolina	146	158
11	Isle of Man	161	155
12	Dublin	154[3]	131
13	Nevada	95	115
14	Arizona	83[3]	108
15	Utah	30	92
16	D.C.	70	77
17	Singapore	60	62
18	Switzerland	48	48
19	New York	39	44
20	Labuan	26[1]	31
	Total top 20	**4,757**	**4,890**
	Total worldwide	**4,951**	**5,119**

Source: *Business Insurance,* March 3, 2008.
[1] *Business Insurance* estimate.
[2] Excludes credit life insurers.
[3] Restated.

The British Isles, including the Isle of Man, have developed another segment of the insurance market: the laundering of drug money through life insurance contracts. Many insurance companies have been involved in laundering circuits. Other tax havens have learned to establish insurance companies for the sole purpose of avoidance, a U.S. law tax-exempts those insurance companies that collect less than $350,000 in premiums exploited for this purpose. A small insurance company may be created with little income, not even enough to pay one employee, but it will put aside extremely high reserves to cope with a future crisis—and the reserves will be placed where they are not taxed. Very often, such companies have only one or two "clients."

In all cases, securing a double tax advantage is an attraction for reinsurance. The offshore premium is not taxed on receipt in that location, but it is subject to tax relief in a country with a higher tax rate. This provides an effective form of tax subsidy for these operations.

Investment Funds and Derivative Trading

Tax havens attract considerable numbers of new financial institution, which flock there to take advantage of tax incentives or undertake risky investments that are difficult to implement under onshore regulation.

Among the best known of these investment vehicles are the hedge funds, which we discuss in chapter 7. The figures for the offshore hedge fund industry are in dispute—a debate that raises the perennial question of regulation and oversight. The International Financial Services, London (IFSL) believes that in 2003 offshore locations accounted for 40% of the number of funds and 49% of assets under management. By January 2006, 55% of hedge funds were registered offshore. The most popular offshore location was the Cayman Islands (63% by number of offshore funds), followed by the British Virgin Islands (13%), and Bermuda (11%). The United States was the most popular onshore location (with most funds registered in Delaware), accounting for 48% of the number of onshore funds, followed by Ireland with 7% (IFSL 2007). The absolute value of funds had also risen by this date to about $1.5 trillion, meaning that by 2006 there were more offshore hedge fund assets than there were total hedge fund assets in 2003.

Predictably, offshore is not where hedge fund management actually takes place. In 2006 around 36% of global hedge fund assets were managed in New York, down from 45% in 2002. London is the second largest global center for hedge funds managers—although formally the UK's legal system does not recognize a facility called hedge fund (Clark 2008). Its share of the global hedge fund industry more than doubled between 2002 and 2006, to 21% (IFSL 2007). The tax haven activity is probably little more than a "booking operation" for transactions that take place elsewhere.

The latest offshore fashion is private equity funds. A substantial part of the private equity sector is offshore. The *Observer* has estimated that 80% of the main UK private equity earners are domiciled outside the UK. The private equity funds to which they are linked are all located offshore to ensure that they do not pay UK capital gains tax (Sunderland and Mathiason 2007). Jersey-based lawyers advertise their private equity client base on the Web. They include CVC Capital Partners, Alpha Group, AXA Private Equity, Terra Firma, Carlyle Group, Investindustrial, and Mercapital. Major private equity groups such as Permira, owners of the Automobile Association in the UK, are based offshore. The first company quoted on the London Stock Exchange's Specialist Fund Market on May 29, 2008 was the Da Vinci CIS Private Sector Growth Fund Limited, based in Guernsey. The Specialist Fund Market was launched by the London Stock Exchange in November 2007 as a regulated market for highly specialized investment entities. Its lighter regulations are aimed at attracting hedge

---

Box 3.2 Mix and match—recipes to suit the client's need:
Special purpose vehicles

One of the most rapidly growing uses of OFCs is special purpose vehicles (SPVs) or special purpose entities (SPEs). These arrangements rose to prominence when it was discovered that Enron had been using about 3,000 such financial vehicles, 800 of them parked in different tax havens. Parmalat, World-Com, and other well-known corporate failures used SPVs as instruments of false accounting. What are these SPVs?

SPVs are asset holding vehicles used to isolate high-risk assets. They are subsidiaries or affiliates of large companies, normally established to manage risk as when financing large projects. They are used primarily, or so it is argued, to reduce the cost of bankruptcy (Gorton and Souleles 2005), but due to weaknesses and ambiguity in accounting rules they can be used for other purposes as well. Financial institutions make use of SPVs to take advantage of less restrictive regulations. Banks, in particular, use them to raise Tier I capital in the low-tax environments of tax havens. Non-bank financial institutions set up SPVs to take advantage of more liberal rules, thereby reducing capital requirements.

Little appreciated until recently was the commonplace practice among SPVs of issuing complex financial instruments owned by charitable trusts (see the discussion in chapter 7). This arrangement ensures that the entity promoting the SPV can claim that it neither owns nor controls the resulting company and as such can keep it off the balance sheet. The objective is clear: the company creating the structure wants to hide the true nature of its financial position. The charitable trust is supposedly controlled by professional trustees, but in practice the whole arrangement is managed and controlled by the entity whose debt the SPV issues. A structure of this sort contributed to the biggest banking failure in the UK for over a century when Northern Rock failed in 2007.

---

funds and private equity funds, but implicit is the understanding that taxes are saved by choice of location as well.

Emulating Onshore Regulation for Offshore Purpose:
How the Veneer of Respectability Pays

In addition to the instruments already described, tax havens and the professionals that use them have another set of tricks up their sleeves. A great variety of ingenious techniques emulate onshore regulation for offshore purposes. The sheer number and variety of such techniques prevent a thorough account. One scheme reported in the British press, using Jersey's stock market to avoid tax, offers some insight into these methods.

A top London accountancy firm devised a sophisticated scheme to exploit Treasury concessions on charitable donations. Vantis, the firm in question, floated four companies on the Jersey Stock Exchange. The prices of these companies mysteriously rose immediately after flotation—not just a bit but phenomenally. After the increase, the investors who had subscribed before the flotation gave their shares to UK-based charities and claimed tax relief on the gift, generating substantial tax refunds for themselves. The stock value then, equally mysteriously, dropped. The charities in question had to write off the value of the donated shares as a cost in their accounts, because they could not be resold. The *Sunday Times* suggests almost 400 people used the scheme. Suspecting fraud, the British revenue service is now investigating whether the price of the shares was manipulated for tax purposes.

The Professionals at the Heart of the Offshore World

A great deal of evidence suggests that the complicated rules that create and regulate the offshore no-man's-land did not emerge spontaneously. Rather they were devised by the very professionals who are advising their clients to take advantage of them.

Consider the complexity and variety of techniques, and the fact that many of the techniques we have described are at best on the very margins of the law, if not outright illegal. They have to be designed by specialized professionals. Dubious tax shelter sales are no longer the province of shady, fly by night companies with limited resources. They have become big business, assigned to talented professionals and drawing on the vast resources and high reputations of the largest accounting firms, law firms, investment advisory firms, and banks.

Many household name MNEs have created specialized departments to deal with their tax affairs. These departments are considered profit centers and value creators, and staff are remunerated on their ability to produce tax savings for the company (Slemrod 2004, 11). In a 2000 survey conducted by *Fortune* magazine of 1,000 directors of tax services of large corporations, 46% reported that their work was remunerated on their ability to reduce the effective tax rate for the company and 16% responded that their primary objective was to search for legal compliance regarding tax practices. These are the professionals at the heart of the tax havens businesses.

Professionals and the Law

Accountants frequently say that tax planning falls into one of two categories. The first is tax evasion, which is illegal. The second is tax avoidance, which is legal. They say that the distinction between the two categories is clear and unambiguous, and as long as they are avoiding and not evading what they do is legal. The precedents vary from jurisdiction to jurisdiction, but many countries in the world (and a majority of the significant tax havens) use English law as the basis for their tax decision making.

One legal basis for this view is that of Lord Clyde, who said in 1929 in the House of Lords, "No man in this country is under the smallest obligation, moral or other, so to arrange his legal relations to his business or to his property as to enable the Inland Revenue to put the largest possible shovel into his stores." Not everyone agrees. Lord Templeman said, also in the House of Lords but in 1993: "In common with my predecessors I regard tax avoidance schemes of the kind invented and implemented [in the present case] as no better than attempts to cheat the Revenue."

Most accountants reject Templeman's view. The prevalent opinion may be that of David Clegg, a tax partner in Ernst & Young South Africa, who said on behalf of his firm: "It is my view that morality has no place in the application of tax law since morality is largely subjective. Where it has a place, it is in the writing of tax law in such a way that it is both clear and equitable, within the context of its tax raising purpose" (Clegg 2006). This attitude explains why accountants and other tax intermediaries use any loophole available to reduce tax, disregarding ethical constraint others might think applicable. They are pressured to do so by their insurers, for failure might expose them to legal claims for failing to minimize their clients' tax liability.

We believe that the situation is actually more complicated than any of these views suggest. The law in any country is built out of words, and words are always open to interpretation. Tax avoidance (sometimes called "aggressive" tax avoidance to differentiate it from tax compliance) seeks to exploit this uncertainty of interpretation. Following the UK budget in March 2005, a spokesperson for Moore Stephens, an international firm of accountants, was quoted in the *Guardian*: "No matter what legislation is in place, the accountants and lawyers will find a way around it. Rules are rules, but rules are meant to be broken." The firm subsequently issued a statement suggesting that he had been misquoted and that he would never countenance breaking the law. The spokesperson, however, had captured the mores of the "service" industry that has grown up around tax havens.

Some tax authorities, including those in the United States and UK, have responded by requiring the registration of tax planning schemes. However, as the UK has found, some tax advisers refuse to cooperate even if required to do so by law (Neveling 2007a).

The "Big Four" International Accountant Firms

Undoubtedly, the most significant players in the tax avoidance/evasion game are the so-called Big Four international accounting firms: KPMG, Ernst & Young, PricewaterhouseCoopers, and Deloitte Touche Tohmatsu.

The Big Four are powerful actors in the global economy, and they are often key to the success of offshore financial centers where they work. John Christensen and Mark Hampton (1999) have shown from the case of Jersey how several tax havens have in effect been "captured" by these private interests, which literally draft local laws to suit their interests. The failure of what was their peer when the firms were a Big Five—Big Four plus Arthur Andersen—indicates the risk they take in pursuing their offshore activities.

The postwar dominance of the world economy by U.S. companies, combined with the preeminence of the City of London and Wall Street, placed Anglo-Saxon consultant firms in the driving seat. English and U.S. common law, and the willingness of regulatory authorities to leave the task of defining "acceptable business practices" to the professionals, encouraged these firms to promote vague rules of conduct, allowing them to do just about whatever they want. Conflicts of interest are bound to arise when the same consultant is adviser on tax avoidance and auditor of accounts (Strange 1988). As we have seen repeatedly, and the recent subprime crisis is only the latest of many incidents, the Big Four seem less interested in ensuring the safety of global capitalism by verifying that business practices are sound than in protecting private wealth at all costs.

The Big Four serve as advisers and auditors to the world's largest companies. They each operate in about 140 countries. When challenged about his firm's activities in tax havens by one of the authors of this book, Loughlin Hickey, head of tax worldwide at KPMG (voted in December 2005 the most influential man in the world on taxation policy by *Business Tax*) declared: "I am proud that KPMG is in those territories. KPMG's role is to contribute to the efficient working of the system, both regulatory and tax. Quite frankly if principled firms like ourselves are not in these territories we don't aid them." Curiously, benefit to development is not a view shared by the U.S. tax authorities, with whom KPMG entered an amicable arrangement in August 2005, paying $456 million in fines after an investigation discovered that the firm sold tax evasion products to several hundred people and so helped them avoid payment of approximately $1.4 billion in taxes. In return KPMG had received commissions totaling $124 million, an average of nearly 9%. Cono Namorato, chief administrative officer of the UK's revenue service, opined that "KPMG has chosen profits at the expense of professionalism." Indeed, KPMG revenues grew 16.7% in 2005 to reach $15.69 billion, "an exceptional year" in the words of its director Sir Mike Rake (KPMG 2005).

What is beyond dispute is that tax is a basic tool in the commercial strategies of these firms (Strange 1998). In the late 1990s Deloitte Touche Tohmatsu offered prospective clients a straightforward deal: they would retain a 30% cut of any tax they manage to save for the client. Deloitte Touche Tohmatsu pledged to defend their strategy before the U.S. tax authorities but not before a law court (Novack and Saunders 1998). In 2005 the European Court of Justice offered an opinion on a KPMG-promoted

---

Box 3.3 Congressional subcommittee chaired by Senator Carl Levin

---

The Levin Subcommittee has focused its investigation on generic abusive tax shelters sold to multiple clients as opposed to a custom-tailored tax strategy sold to a single client. It noted that numerous respected members of the U.S. business community were heavily involved in the development, marketing, and implementation of generic tax products whose principal objective was to reduce or eliminate a client's U.S. tax liability.

In an earlier report to the U.S. Senate, the Subcommittee had noted that just four artificial schemes marketed by international accountants KPMG might have cost the U.S. Treasury at least $7.2 billion (U.S. Senate 2003). Senator Carl Levin said of this activity that "most are so complex that they are MEGOs, 'My Eyes Glaze Over' type of schemes. Those who cook up these concoctions count on their complexity to escape scrutiny and public ire" (Levin 2003).

Levin also made clear that tax shelters are complex transactions with no economic substance other than to provide large tax benefits unintended by the tax code. Levin (2003) discusses the operating methods of one of the big accountant firms, KPMG. He described a four-step move:

Step one: innovation. KPMG set up a Tax Innovation Center in 1997. The center's role was to invent new financial products that could avoid taxes.

Step two: validation. Once developed, these products move into the hands of the internal control department of KPMG for an opinion on their legality.

Step three: marketing. To support the marketing operation tax advisers provided "letters of opinion"—legal documents signed by lawyers and selling for between $50,000 and $75,000, stating that the proposed product did not violate the tax code. The taxpayer could then negotiate "in good faith" with the tax authorities, and mitigate penalties if the arrangement was challenged.

Step four: implementation. Once the customer is hooked, the organization gets going, setting the arrangements, some of them offshore.

These kinds of services were provided by all the major international accountants.

Senator Levin was joined by senators Norm Coleman and Barack Obama in February 2007, in tabling the Stop Tax Haven Abuse Act (Levin 2007). If enacted the legislation will signal a fundamental shift in U.S. policy toward tax havens.

scheme for avoiding the UK's sales tax or VAT. In their promotional literature for the scheme, KPMG admitted that they knew the UK taxation authorities would consider the scheme to be "unacceptable tax avoidance." They nonetheless promoted it as a tax product to people who were not already clients of their firm. The court opinion concluded that KPMG's tax shelter was an improper attempt to avoid VAT—which apparently had not troubled the firm at the time of sale.

Conclusion

Throughout the years, tax havens have developed a great variety of organizations and legal instruments with the sole aim of facilitating avoidance and evasion by nonresidents. Many of these instruments provide a de facto (if not always de jure) impenetrable barrier of secrecy for their true owners. The battle against tax avoidance and evasion, which began in earnest in the late 1990s, has so far provoked ever more obscure, complex, and sophisticated instruments of avoidance. The variety and rapid development of new legal instruments tells us that tax havens are jurisdictions that use their sovereign prerogative to write law in order to create instruments of avoidance, ably assisted by the expatriate communities hosted within them. The complexity of the vehicles of avoidance, in turn, proved a great boon to hordes of professional institutions, led by the Big Four international accounting firms, without which all this would be impossible. These professionals are the very heart of the gigantic offshore world. The extent and impact of offshore is hard to assess, but its ramifications became clear as the economic crisis of 2008/9 unfolded.

Part II

The Evolution of Tax Havens

Chapter 4

Origins of the Tax Havens

The history of tax havens is riddled with myths and legends. The hideouts of pirates and robbers have added new layers of mystery and glamour to their names through association with shady deals, mafias, and the secret services. There are many conflicting accounts of the origins of tax havens, few of them backed by hard evidence. Some of the best-known myths of origin can be dismissed outright.

The first myth holds that Swiss bankers invented secret bank accounts to protect Jewish assets from the Nazis. In reality, secret bank accounts were invented to protect Swiss bankers from prosecution by other states. The second common myth, propounded by liberal economists as well as the IMF (Cassard 1994) and the OECD (1998), is that tax havens emerged in response to rising tax burdens during the 1960s. This simply cannot be true: Switzerland was known as a tax haven in the 1920s, Liechtenstein introduced the Anstalt in 1926, Luxembourg established its holding company rules in 1929, and Bermuda was known as a tax haven since around 1935. The third common myth, perpetrated by the tax havens themselves, is that they were innocent bystanders exploited by mobile capital. Such claims conveniently overlook the efforts that tax havens make to attract foreign capital.

The origins of avoidance, concealment, and tax evasion can be traced to a very distant past. Greek and Roman citizens were adept at concealing their financial assets from the authorities (Doggart 2002). Not to be outdone, medieval lenders invented a whole host of techniques to conceal the interest payments they were receiving on their loans despite religious interdiction. Dutch, English, and French merchants used the practice of "warehousing," in which traders deferred taxes on stored goods until they were sold. Concealment may have a long history, but tax havens are a more recent development. In 1869, Prince Charles III of Monaco authorized the establishment of the principality's famous casino. Income generated by the casino allowed him to abolish all forms of income tax in Monaco, creating— perhaps unintentionally—the first genuine modern tax haven.

Broadly, we distinguish three stages in tax havens' development. The first stage, roughly from the late nineteenth century to the 1920s, witnessed the emergence of most of the familiar instruments of tax havens. During the second stage, following the end of World War I through the early 1970s, a small number of states led by Switzerland began to develop tax haven regimes as an intentional developmental strategy. In the third stage, from the early 1970s and through the late 1990s, the number of tax havens rose dramatically, as did the scope, planning, and sheer volume of financial assets passed through them. These were the "golden years" of tax havens.

The Incorporation Game in Late-Nineteenth-Century United States

"Where did it come from, this collectivity knows as the corporation? Perhaps no one really knows," writes Adolf Berle (1950, 189). Some historians date the beginning of the modern corporation to the first two joint stock companies—Russia and Guinea—established in 1553 in England. Others trace the birth of the modern corporation to 1601, when Queen Elizabeth I created the East India Trading Company. Whichever is right, the concept of the corporation was dealt a serious blow by a wave of speculation and fraudulent promotions in the beginning of the eighteenth century, known collectively as the South Sea Bubble. The Bubble Act of 1720, passed by Parliament, "stipulated that only firms incorporated by royal charter or act of Parliament were permitted to issue transferable shares" (Pearson 2006, xvii). The United States inherited the British attitude toward corporations. Until the 1830s, corporateness could be conferred in the United States only by a special act of the legislature (Epstein 1969, 23).

Corporations were few and far between, requiring a Royal Charter, Act of Congress, or Act of Parliament. Corporation law evolved slowly and hesitantly in the nineteenth century, with the United States taking the lead. The first general corporations law is credited to the State of New York in 1823 (Lindholm 1944), although that law was applicable only to manufacturing corporations. In the 1830s, despite opposition, general acts of incorporation were adopted in many U.S. states. England passed the Companies Registration and Companies Clauses Consolidation acts in 1844, followed by similar legislation for Scotland in 1845. Other laws in 1844 and 1862 created a more permissive environment in Britain, removing important limitations on the growth and ultimate size of companies (Payne 1967).

In an 1886 important ruling, in *Santa Clara v. Southern Pacific Railroad*, the U.S. Supreme Court provided constitutional protection to corporate efforts to escape state regulation by declaring that corporations were "persons," thus coming under the purview of the Fourteenth Amendment. The rights and duties accorded to individuals were henceforth extended to corporations as well. By the last quarter of the nineteenth century, British courts were also beginning to recognize the concept of "corporate personality" (Couzin 2002, 12).

Another significant date in the development of the corporation was 1875, when the state of New Jersey passed the prototype of the modern law of corporation (Berle 1950). Britain took longer to adopt the new form of corporation. Although de facto private companies existed in Britain by the turn of the nineteenth century, the legal distinction between "private" and "public" was not made until the Companies Act of 1907 (Gourvish 1987).

With incorporation came corporate taxation, with the State of Massachusetts pioneering the field. Corporate taxation was problematic because the individual owners of the corporation were already paying tax, thus raising the issue of "double taxation." As early as 1813, the Supreme Court had decided that corporations could be taxed only for real estate and for personal property (Lindholm 1944, 55), although banks had been paying tax since 1812.

The principle of taxing corporations as entities separate from their owners was established in the United States by the Revenue Act of 1894. The act was later ruled unconstitutional, but when a constitutionally acceptable way to tax corporate income was enacted in 1909, the principle prevailed. Federal tax remained, however, very low in today's terms: in 1909, the rate of corporate taxation was 1% on taxable events of over $5,000, rising in 1918 to 12% on events over $2,000. Corporate tax rates remained more or less at that level until 1940, when the top bracket of income above $32,000 was taxed at 38%. Today the top rate in the United States is 39%. In Britain corporation tax was a variant of income tax until 1965, when corporation tax was separated. In France, the revolution established the "patente," which was to be paid by corporations in proportion to their turnover.

New Jersey and Delaware

In some of their earliest forms, tax havens emerged as a reaction more to regulation than to taxation as such. Indeed, among the three pillars of tax havens we discussed in chapter 1, ease of incorporation and loose regulation emerged first as a competitive state strategy. The origins of the incorporation game—associated today with Belgium's coordination centers, "Irish doc" companies, and more broadly with the millions of International Business Corporations (IBCs) spread around different tax havens—can be traced back to late nineteenth century United States. It developed among the states, not necessarily in lowering corporate taxation—which in any case was quite low—but in offering a more permissive environment for corporations.

The state of New Jersey passed the prototype of the modern law of corporation in 1875. New Jersey's liberal attitudes attracted the attention of its wealthier neighbors. By the 1880s, the states of New York and Massachusetts had the highest concentration of company headquarters in the country. The first person to hit on the idea that more permissive corporate law might lure away some of New York's companies was a New York corporate lawyer, James Dill. Dill maintained a house in East Orange, New Jersey. When he was consulted by New Jersey governor Leon Abbett as to the best way to increase the financial resources of the state, Dill suggested liberalizing of the corporation law (Lindholm 1944, 56). Dill was then asked to draft New Jersey's corporation statute of 1889. In 1896, New Jersey passed another law, the General Revision Act, permitting unlimited size and market share, removing all time limits on corporate charters, reducing shareholder powers, and allowing all kinds of mergers, acquisitions, and purchases.

In 1899 New Jersey passed another act, which permitted corporations to own equity in other companies—therefore luring the Standard Oil Trust, based in New York, to legal rebirth as a holding company, the Standard Oil Company of New Jersey (SOCNJ). The act introduced the idea of incorporation within incorporation, or a group of companies linked together by economic ties—and with it came the possibility of transfer pricing. Similar notions can be traced to an earlier innovation, the holding company, in 1893 in the Netherlands. The Dutch exempted from tax all income earned by foreign subsidiaries of local companies in an attempt to help Dutch firms expand in Asia. Over time the Dutch holding company evolved into a very lucrative tax avoidance scheme. Very soon thereafter, the principle of the company group developed in Britain as a response to the threat from U.S. corporations. As U.S. Tobacco and Co. began to invade the British market, C. Wills led the response by creating the Imperial Tobacco Co. of Great Britain in 1901.

New Jersey's measure met with some success. Soon another U.S. state suffering from budgetary problems, Delaware, decided to emulate New Jersey's example. Again, a group of lawyers in New York played a vital role behind the scenes in drafting an even more liberal law. Delaware law of 1898 set the standard to be followed by tax havens worldwide, by allowing corporations to write their own rules of governance. New Jersey's law sparked what was seen at the time as a "race to the bottom," with states all over the country gutting corporate law to become more business-friendly. By 1902, there were 1,407 companies registered in tiny Delaware; 4,776 in 1919. The actions of New Jersey and Delaware stimulated a new "incorporation game," as other small states such as Vermont and Nevada learned to compete with more prosperous states by offering tax breaks and liberal incorporation laws. Today, approximately 60% of all U.S. Fortune 500 companies are incorporated in Delaware. New Jersey remains the U.S. "home of the trusts" (Lindhom 1944, 56).

In response to these developments, U.S. corporations began a system of subsidiaries and affiliates, which in turn raised the question of how a group of companies is to be taxed. The United States went through several tax regimes. Corporations have been required to consolidate their income statements for tax purposes (1917–21); forbidden to do so except for railroads and a few other companies (1934–41); allowed the option but required to pay at a higher tax rate (1932–33, 1942–63); and allowed the option without penalty (1922–31, 1964 to the present).

Incorporation Game Comes to Europe: The Swiss Canton of Zug

U.S. states innovated in the first pillar of tax havens, attracting nonresident companies by offering amenable regulatory environments. Since the 1920s, some Swiss cantons—led initially by the impoverished canton of Zug, located not far from Zurich—have copied this practice.

There are good reasons why the Swiss were first to copy the Americans. Switzerland is a confederation of autonomous cantons. When modern Switzerland was established in 1848, direct taxation was placed in the hands of the cantons, whereas indirect taxation was in the hands of the confederation. Each canton developed its own system of direct taxation, using different methods of evaluation and different rules. The result was "an orgy of fiscal evasion and dissimulation" (quoted in Guex 1998, 105).

The canton of Zug gained a reputation for being particularly lenient, though for reasons now shrouded in fog. It is not entirely clear whether the Zug authorities innovated or were leaned upon to innovate. In the early 1920s, two of the largest industrial enterprises in Zug demanded considerable tax rebates from the cantonal authorities, threatening to leave the canton otherwise. Their demands were met, explained the Director of Cantonal Finance at the time, because "the result would most certainly have been a loss of substance of five million francs in taxes for the state, but in showing understanding . . . the losses will amount to 1.5 million" (quoted in Guex 1998, 70; authors' translation).

Guex stresses that the development of tax privileges in Switzerland had much to do with competition among the various cantons, and less with the outside world. He gives the example of the relationship between two neighboring cantons, Zug and its richer neighbor Zurich. The Zugoise authorities, often on the advice of lawyers and businesspersons from Zurich, modeled their tax laws specifically to compete with Zurich, both shortly after 1918 and again in the 1930s. The government of the canton of Zug, considering amendments to its tax legislation, contracted a tax expert from Zurich. The expert suggested low taxation to compete with other cantons but he warned "we must take care that the advantages will not be immediately evident" (Guex 1998, 113).

In 1944, Zug again reduced corporate profits tax from 25% to 17.8%—not apparently significant, yet the action made Zug the lightest taxing authority in Switzerland. The devil, as they say, is in the details: far more significant were the various loopholes and rules that established Zug as a veritable tax haven. For example, preferential income rates, much lower than the 17.8%, applied to "business control centers" if 80% of sales were derived from customers outside Switzerland. Other such rules applied to every conceivable type of company, trust, or financial institution. Although impoverished and with a population of only 100,000 in the early twentieth century, Zug is currently home to 18,000 companies including Shell and BASF as well as a famous fugitive from U.S. taxation Mark Rich.

British Courts Create the First Tax Haven

If the U.S. states came up with the technique of bidding for corporations by liberalizing incorporation laws, we must credit the British courts with the technique of "virtual" residencies, allowing companies to incorporate in Britain without paying tax—a development that at least one commentator believes is the foundation of the entire tax haven phenomenon (Picciotto 1992). The series of legal innovations that ended up creating such a facility were not intended, strictly speaking, to establish the UK as a tax haven. Rather, they evolved slowly, through a series of cases in which British courts sought to clarify the concept of "residence" in the context of British taxes. The courts were, and still are, important actors in the tax haven game.

British tax was applied on income from sources in the United Kingdom (Couzin 2002, 1–2), and so liability for taxation hinged on the related question of the characteristics of persons that are deemed residents in the UK. The British courts developed their ideas in light of the law regarding real personalities and applied it gradually to firms—effectively defining firms as artificial personalities in the process. Questions about the method of taxation of British companies arose during the nineteenth century with regard to companies operating in the Empire and beyond. The Inland Revenue, the authority entrusted with the collection of taxes, brought several cases to the courts to clarify these issues. One major decision dates back to 1876, when judges were confronted with the case of two companies, the *Calcutta Jute Mills* and *Cesena Sulphur Mines*, both registered in England but whose production activities were located respectively in India and Italy. In these cases, the judges applied the concept of residence as they saw it:

> The great principle of the law of England in relation to taxation is, that taxation shall only be imposed upon persons or things actually within this country. (quoted in Couzin 2002, 6)[1]

The judges argued that since control and management of the two companies were not in fact carried out from England, the two companies were not resident in Britain for tax purposes and should not be taxed in Britain. The place of registration (or "seat" as it is understood in continental law) was not deemed necessary to prove residence; rather, effective control was the necessary proof.

The principle was reaffirmed in 1901 in a "seminal decision steeped in history" (Couzin 2002, 38). The renowned diamond multinational De Beers registered in the Colony of the Cape of Good Hope in 1888, and located its head office in Kimberley in the Cape. It mined its diamonds in South African, where it also managed its affairs. The company, nonetheless, maintained an office in London chaired by Cecil J. Rhodes. Was De Beers UK resident for taxation purposes? The judges stated that real control of the company's strategy was executed from London, and hence De Beers should be taxed in England. The decision was useful for the British Exchequer: at the time, London was the largest international financial center from which many companies were funding activities throughout the world.

In 1904 the British company Egyptian Delta Land and Investment Co. Ltd. was established to purchase and lease land in Egypt, and moved its board of directors to Cairo. The issue of the company's place of residence for taxation went to court in 1929. This time around judges decided that the company was not liable for British taxation. This was a seminal case. "The decision in Egyptian Delta Land created," writes Sol Picciotto, "a loophole which in a sense made Britain a tax haven: foreigners could set up companies in the UK, which would not be considered UK resident

---

1. *Calcutta Jute Mills, Limited v. Nicholson* (Surveyor of Taxes) and *Cesena Sulphur Company, Limited v. Nicholson* (Surveyor of Taxes), (1876) I TC 83, 88 (HL) at p. 101.

Box 4.1 A brief history of income tax

Taxation, state, and war share a long common history. So do schemes for tax avoidance and evasion, as demonstrated so vividly by the reaction to the infamous window tax, introduced in Britain in 1696 and abolished as late as 1851. It was a variable tax imposed on the number of windows above ten in a building. Following an established pattern, the first income tax system was introduced in Britain in 1799 as a means to pay for the war against Napoleonic France. Considered a temporary solution at the time, the Act of 1799 applied a rate of 10% on the total income of British taxpayers from all sources above £60, with reductions on income up to £200. However, Addington's 1803 Act created the first permanent system of income tax—although the Act deliberately avoided the term "income tax."

In the United States, the first system of income tax was introduced in 1812 to pay for the War of Independence, only to be repealed by Congress in 1817. In 1862, income tax was introduced again to fund the Civil War, only to be repealed a few years later by the courts as unconstitutional. It was, therefore, only in 1913 that the Sixteenth Amendment to the Constitution made the income tax a permanent fixture in the U.S. tax system. Similarly, personal income tax and sales tax were introduced in Canada in 1917, again as temporary measure due to extraordinary expenditures related to World War I—a measure never to be repealed.

In France, four taxes in place from 1792 to 1914 were dubbed "the four oldies." They were based not on declared revenue but on an estimation of wealth and the capacity to be taxed (number of doors and windows of one's main house, land tax based on an estimation of average rents, etc.) (Piketty 2001, 234). The first income tax was voted by the French parliament on July 15, 1914, thanks to pressures imposed by the financing of the war.

Income tax remained relatively low at least until World War I. In Britain in 1914 the standard rate of income tax was 6%, and in France the maximum rate applicable to the wealthiest was 2%. It climbed to 20% in 1917–18, and the standard British rate had risen to 30% by 1918.

Other categories of taxes were introduced during the same period, and broadly for similar reasons. Death taxes, for instance, are very old; the ancient Egyptians were the first to establish such taxes, and later the concept was adopted by the Greeks and Romans. In 1796, Britain introduced Legacy Tax on sums over £20 excluding those to wives, children, parents, and grandparents—again the context was war with France. In 1797, the U.S. Congress followed suit and imposed a legacy tax too, to help fund construction of a U.S. navy. The legacy tax was transformed in 1862 into an inheritance tax, to raise revenue to pay for the Civil War. These taxes went through several changes during the twentieth century, but the first havens specialized in the avoidance of inheritance tax.

Capital gains tax was introduced in the United States in 1913 and in Britain in 1965, as part of the introduction of the British company tax.

under British law because they were controlled from overseas, but might be shielded from some taxation at source because they were incorporated abroad" (1992, 8).[2] As the decision applied to the entire British Empire, it was soon exploited by Bermuda, the Bahamas, and later the Cayman Islands and Hong Kong. The decision also meant that foreign companies could register in the UK, but if they organized their activities abroad, they would not be subject to UK taxes.

The *Egyptian Delta* case is the foundation of the practice of virtual residency practiced by a great many tax havens—it gives the offshore world its "virtual" flavor.

The Rise of the European Havens

The Rise of a Swiss International Financial Center

Swiss bankers have long established a reputation for pragmatism. Voltaire is reputed to have quipped, "if you see a Swiss banker jumping from a window, jump behind him, there should be some money to be won!" Swiss anonymous accounts existed in the late nineteenth century, and Swiss bankers, as well as the subsidiaries of French and German banks, were well aware of the benefits of the rather loose financial regimes maintained by the cantons. Fehrenbach (1966) claims that the principle of bank secrecy was the norm in Switzerland by 1912. As Europe underwent profound changes, Switzerland attracted considerable French, German, Italian, and Austrian capital and became the European "haven for capital."

Yet the early development of Switzerland as an intentional tax haven is not entirely clear. There is talk of the emergence of offshore trusts in Switzerland in the 1920s, used primarily by wealthy Italians to protect their assets. The canton of Zug developed as an incorporation haven, on the Delaware model, at around the same time. In fact, it was not until 1934 and 1944 when, respectively, Switzerland introduced its bank secrecy laws and Zug introduced taxation laws that in effect set it up as a tax haven.

It was rising taxation in Europe during the war years of the 1870s that, according to Roman Kuenzler, triggered the first wave of capital flight to neighboring Geneva, Basel, and Zurich. Two major French banks opened branches in Geneva, the Banque de Paris et des Pays-Bas in 1872 and

---

2. This possibility was ended by the Finance Act of 1988, which provided that companies incorporated in the UK are resident for tax purposes in the UK. However, the control criteria remained relevant for tax treaties. This change brought the UK into line with European states (Picciotto 1992, 8).

Crédit Lyonnais in 1879. In 1872, a group of smaller independent banks founded the Basler (later Schweizerischer) Bankverein which, in addition to the Basler Handelsbank founded in 1862, made Basel the biggest financial center in Switzerland. Most of the capital transferred to Switzerland was destined for reinvestment abroad, and so Swiss bankers were forced to become familiar with international financial markets, controlled at the time by the British Empire. They opened branches in London, Berlin, Milan, and Paris, extending their expertise in the receipt, administration, and multiplication of money from foreign investors.

Various cantons took advantage of the situation. As we have seen, the canton of Zug began emulating U.S. states by offering cheap and liberal incorporation facilities in the early 1920s. The city of Basel was more interested in international capital, allowing virtual holding companies and trusts to set up. This strategy proved successful, as industrialists such as Leopoldo Pirelli settled in the city.

Fehrenbach (1966) believes that Switzerland never intentionally meant to serve as a tax haven. Rather, Swiss bankers, followed by cantonal authorities and the courts, were pragmatic, agile, and discreet enough to overlook legal niceties and allow for informal arrangements effectively made Switzerland what Richard Gordon calls "a haven for capital." This view is true up to a point, as Fehrenbach misrepresents the intentions behind the banking law of 1934. Nevertheless, Swiss pragmatism undoubtedly played an important role.

A Small Detour through Liechtenstein . . .

The tiny territory of Liechtenstein, subject of much debate in early 2008 when the German secret service bought a list of international tax evaders from a former bank employee, has played a long-term if not distinguished role in the establishment of tax havens. Liechtenstein has the dubious distinction of having enacted some of the most stringent secrecy laws. The precise motives behind the development of Liechtenstein's Company Law remain in dispute.

Liechtenstein, a small principality located between Switzerland and Austria, was until World War I closely associated with the latter, and shared in its post-1918 economic disaster. All trade came to a standstill and the Austrian currency was practically worthless. To remedy the situation, Liechtenstein renounced its customs union with Austria in 1919 and associated with Switzerland instead. In 1924 it adopted the Swiss franc as its currency and at the same time enacted its own Civil Code. Glos believes that the Company Law of 1926 "was part of a national strategy of economic revival after abandoning the disastrous reliance on Austria" (1984, 929). Others suggest that it was a German lawyer from Berlin, Heinrich Kuntze, anxious to protect his fortune, who placed his funds in Liechtenstein in the early 1920s and was instrumental in shaping Liechtenstein's thinking about its future.

In practice, Liechtenstein simply synthesized and codified Swiss and Austrian practices, creating a new corporate form, the Anstalt. The new Company Law imposed no requirements or restrictions concerning the nationality of shareholders in Liechtenstein companies. Furthermore, corporations could reach agreements with the Liechtenstein tax authorities concerning the payment of capital and income tax, and these agreements were valid for a period of thirty years. Under these agreements, the corporation had to pay an annual tax of 0.1% of its capital with an annual minimum of FRS400 for the entire duration of the agreement (Marias 1957, 412).

The Anstalt is a unique blend of different rules. It developed in Austria and Germany over centuries as a concept of public and not private law. It is an institution permanently dedicated to a public purpose, usually charitable, medical, or educational (Glos 1984, 930). Conventional Anstalts are therefore home for the elderly, asylums, hospitals, colleges, and universities.[3] The Austrian law of July 19, 1919 on economic enterprises had extended the concept and permitted the formation of an "economic Anstalt" (Glos 1984, 931). The Liechtenstein Company Law of 1926 simply adopted Austria's Economic Anstalt articles 534–551 and blended them with the Anglo-Saxon concept of the trust (unknown in civil law countries). The UK Trust Act of 1925 enshrined the secrecy of trusts, requiring neither that they be registered unless taxable nor that they maintain public records, thereby creating the perfect instrument for offshore secrecy. Liechtenstein's adoption of trust rules converted the innocent Anstalt into one of the most abusive forms of trust.

The Liechtenstein Anstalt is an entity with a legal personality, which strictly speaking is not a corporation or a private type of trust. The key innovation of the Anstalt "has been causing problems to jurists and taxation authorities in Europe" (Glos 1984, 953). The Anstalt is a "reverse corporation" designed "to obtain all the advantages of incorporation for an individual physical person. It is thus a one-man corporation endowed with legal personality for the apparent purpose of concealing the identity of its owner in the carrying out of business which he would not be likely to conduct openly under his own name" (Glos 1984, 954). Glos cannot

---

3. The concept is closely connected with that of a *Stiftung,* which is best characterized as a foundation or an endowment.

think of uses for the Anstalt other than the concealment of property and income subject to taxation.

Today Liechtenstein may be considered the dark side of Swiss banking. As Ramati notes "the large amount of money formally held by Liechtenstein entities are not transferred directly to Liechtenstein proper. Vast sums are held in accounts of Liechtenstein entities in banks outside Liechtenstein, mostly in Switzerland" (1991, 27). Swiss lawyers are allowed to set up entities in Liechtenstein, and in effect, it is used by Swiss banks and financial institutional to by-pass Swiss laws, most of which were introduced in response to international pressure.

As a civil law country, Switzerland does not recognize the facility of the trust. Was it to fall behind Liechtenstein with the innovation of the Anstalt? Not really. Swiss banks were already pragmatic enough to open accounts in the name of foreign trusts even though such legal entities were not recognized by the Swiss courts. When issues concerning trusts eventually came before the courts, Swiss jurists proved equally pragmatic and simply converted these trusts for purposes of the proceedings into the nearest form of civil law arrangements. So why did Liechtenstein introduce the Anglo-Saxon concept of the trust if it could simply have adopted the pragmatic practices of Swiss banking? In our opinion, Liechtenstein saw itself as a competitor to Switzerland and so felt the need to advertise the facility—and did pretty well.

In the beginning of the twentieth century Switzerland was not yet a legislative tax haven, but it had already established its reputation for pragmatism. We may speculate that foreign trusts and foundations initially used Swiss banking less for taxation reasons and more for fear of political reprisals in their volatile home countries. Many noble families and much "old money" were looking to protect their assets from the revolutionary forces that were sweeping through Europe—and in Swiss bankers and cantons they found perfect partners to assist them to protect themselves.

Kuenzler (2007) suggests that a Zurich-Zug-Liechtenstein triangle emerged as the first true post-1918 tax haven. A few offshore holding companies and trusts existed in Switzerland before the war, but the number of holdings increased relentlessly after 1920. The canton of Zurich was not keen on offering tax privileges to these holding companies, but the city's financial elite used the more amenable and much poorer rural cantons of Glarus and Zug, which redrafted their laws on the advice of lawyers and bankers from the Bahnhofstrasse. Those same lawyers and bankers advised Liechtenstein. Through these facilities, Zurich became the center for the Swiss *societé anonyme* and mailbox companies, eclipsing Basel by the end of the 1920s. This was only the beginning of a strategy that emerged clearly in 1934 with a new banking law.

And Luxembourg Too . . .

Luxembourg strenuously rejects the label of tax haven. Its protestation, however, have failed to impress a panel of experts at ShelterOffshore.com who in 2007 nominated it as best tax haven of the year (together with the Isle of Man). The panel noted: "This is incredibly positive news for the jurisdiction and its government who have been actively working to improve the overall appeal of the location for international business and offshore finance in general." Indeed, since the introduction of its Maritime Register in 1990, Luxembourg has emerged not only as an important tax haven but also as a significant actor in the flag of convenience game.

In fact, Luxembourg is one of the older tax havens. Its bank secrecy laws were strengthened in 1981 to match Switzerland's. Luxembourg was also among the first to establish special tax treatment for nonresidents through its 1929 holding company, although it did not emerge as a major tax haven until the 1970s. In 1970, the share of banking and insurance companies in the nation's total value added accounted for roughly 5%; it peaked at 13% in 1975 and fell back to 10% in 1980 (Hübsch 2004). Today Luxembourg is the wealthiest country in the world in GDP per capita terms, and that success can be attributed almost exclusively to its flourishing financial sector.

Luxembourg was among the first countries to introduce the concept of the holding company in 1929. Under the July 31, 1929 law, such companies are exempt from income taxes, Fortune Tax (or wealth tax), tax on the transfer of shares, and withholding tax. In addition, Luxembourg established several derivatives of the classical 1929 holding company that offer even better tax regime (Warner 2004, 556). Under pressure from the EU, the 1929 holding company law has been abolished. But as a company specializing in Luxembourg offshore explains to prospective clients, not all is lost: "Luxembourg has shown its commitment to remain one of the world's foremost tax planning jurisdictions by the introduction in the near future of a new vehicle for personal investment. The new company, the SPF, will allow private investors indirect investment in financial assets and the tax-free hoarding of income. The SPF will be exempt from taxation on income and wealth in Luxembourg."

The Swiss Banking Law of 1934

Swiss bankers already possessed significant advantages vis-à-vis their neighbors in that banking secrecy was guaranteed in Switzerland by civil law. The Banking Act of 1934, in article 47, strengthened the principle by placing bank secrecy under the protection of criminal law. The article is extraordinary and merits quoting at length:

Whosoever as agent, official, employee of a bank, or as accountant or accountant's assistant, or as a member of the Banking Commission, or as a clerk or employee of its secretariat, violates the duty of absolute silence in respect to a professional secret, or whosoever induces or attempts to induce others to do so, will be punished with a fine of up to 20,000 francs, or with imprisonment of up to six months or both. If such an act is due to negligence, the penalty shall be a fine not exceeding 10,000 francs. (quoted in Fehrenbach 1966, 64)

If that were not enough, article 273 of the Swiss Penal Code provides additional protections to holders of Swiss bank accounts. It states:

Whosoever explores trade secrets in order to make them accessible to foreign governments or foreign enterprises or foreign organizations or their agents, and whoever makes such trade secrets accessible to foreign governments or organizations or private enterprise or to agents thereof, will be punished by imprisonment. (quoted in Fehrenbach 1966, 64)

Swiss law demands "absolute silence in respect to a professional secret," that is, absolute silence in respect to any accounts held in Swiss banks—"absolute" here means protection from any government, including the Swiss. The law labels inquiry or research into the "trade secrets" of banks and other organizations a criminal offence. Not surprising, very few academics and journalists have been prepared to risk jail for their research. The law ensured that once past the borders, capital entered an inviolable legal sanctuary guaranteed by the criminal code and backed by the might of the Swiss state.

Why did the Swiss authorities feel the need to strengthen banking secrecy to such an extent? Together with U.S. laws and British virtual residencies, Swiss bank secrecy forms the third pillar of the offshore world, to be copied by other jurisdictions. It is worth our delving briefly into the work of scholars who have studied the history of these laws.

Swiss bankers favor the myth that the 1934 law was created to protect the assets of Jews and other minorities persecuted by Nazi Germany. The historians Sebastien Guex (1999) and Peter Hug (2000) have demonstrated persuasively that the laws had little to do with the Nazis and a lot do with internal debates in Switzerland about banking supervision. The actor seldom mentioned in these debates was France. The background to the laws of 1934 was not Hitler's rise to power the previous year but the financial crisis of 1929, which hit Swiss financial centers particularly hard. In the second half of 1931 Switzerland entered the worst banking crisis in its history. Three of the eight of the so-called big banks went bankrupt, another survived only with massive aid from the federal state, and the remaining four had to be substantially reorganized. The confederation decided in January 1933 on a new banking law aimed at strengthening the regulation and supervision of financial institutions.

Swiss bankers, like their colleagues around the world who faced similar new laws, feared that new regulations and supervision would allow public officials unprecedented access to individual accounts. They were particularly concerned that information might be used for tax purposes both at home and abroad. In exchange for agreeing to general oversight of the financial system, they demanded that access to individual accounts and transactions remain restricted, not available to federal officials, and that bank secrecy laws be strengthened. Article 47 of the Banking Act of 1934 was in fact a part of the first-draft bill of February 1933.

The role that French politics played in the enactment of this Banking Law is little known. In June 1932 the center-left government of Edouard Herriot came to power in France. Herriot's government sought a drastic reduction in the budget deficit, and singled out tax evasion through Switzerland as the culprit responsible for a gaping hole in French finance.

Research in the French National Assembly's archives conducted by one of the authors of this book (Chavagneux 2001) and the historical analysis of Sebastien Guex (1998) allow us to reconstruct the events that followed. At 4:10 p.m. on October 26, 1932, Commissioner Barthelet of the Paris police raids the local branch of the Commercial Bank of Basel, located in a beautiful apartment in the fashionable district of the Champs-Elysées. He discovers, to his surprise, a French senator in the apartment, 245,000 cash in Swiss francs, and crucially, ten notebooks containing the names of 2,000 French citizens. These notebooks reveal that French citizens were using the bank to avoid paying 20% income tax on their foreign investments. Rumors spread like wildfire about the names on the list. The Interior Minister, Camille Chautemps, however, refuses to reveal the names, while Louis Germain-Martin, the Minister of Finance, claims the list is not in his possession.

In this atmosphere the Socialist MP Fabien Albertin takes the podium in the Assembly. With consummate skill, the former lawyer of the Paris Court of Appeals goes through the names of the most famous fraudsters in these notebooks. They include three senators, a dozen generals, judges, two bishops, and directors of major newspapers and big industrialists such as the Peugeot brothers and the owner of the furniture manufacturer Lévitan.

These respectable French citizens had placed about 2 billion francs (about €1.2 billion in today's money) with the Banque commerciale de Bâle. The total tax loss to the French state was estimated as amounting to four billion francs per year. Soon lawsuits were filed against three large Swiss banks, and their assets were frozen. On November 16, 1932 the French authorities summoned two members of the board of directors of the Commercial Bank of Basel and requested an investigation into French accounts at the Basel headquarters. The directors refused the request and were promptly imprisoned for two months On November 21, France officially requested a mutual assistance treaty with Switzerland, which the Swiss government immediately rejected.

The damage, however, was done. Many foreign customers withdrew their money from Swiss accounts. Swiss newspapers began to worry about the effects of these massive withdrawals on its beleaguered banking industry. The Commercial Bank of Basel had to repay large sums, and the Discount Bank of Geneva failed to survive the onslaught. The Swiss banking community realized that another scandal could ruin it completely. It was in this context that voices demanded stricter bank secrecy laws. Many years later a similar onslaught by the United States prompted a similar hardening of financial laws in the Cayman Islands.

Peter Hug (2000) shows that in 1966 Swiss bankers invented a legend about the protection of Jewish assets in response to the grilling they had faced in the U.S. Congress. The myth has been perpetuated ever since by apologists of Swiss banking secrecy. The irony, of course, is that Swiss bankers used precisely the same bank secrecy laws to justify their unwillingness to return Jewish money to Holocaust survivors. It took more than sixty years, and all the might of the United States, to obtain permission in 1988 to open the archives and investigate the amount of Jewish money in Swiss coffers—a small concession that cuts into the legendary secrecy of Swiss banking.

Article 47 proved a great success. Foreign deposits in Swiss banks increased by 28% during the three years that followed (Hug 2000). Several countries considered the new law nothing less than an act of aggression. The United States exerted strong pressure on the Swiss authorities but to no avail. In Franco's Spain, the use of such accounts was prohibited under Spanish criminal law (Fehrenbach 1966). The problem was compounded as other jurisdictions, including Beirut, the Bahamas, Liechtenstein, Uruguay, Panama, and Curacao began to emulate Swiss law. Over time, some European countries have made "improvements" on the Swiss laws. Switzerland still requires that at least two bank employees know the identity of their customers, but Luxembourg now requires that only one official know the customer. Austria has taken that particular "race to the bottom" to its logical conclusion—in Austria, accounts became completely anonymous. (Austria has since revoked its controversial banking laws due to intense pressure from the European Union.) Many jurisdictions allow for banking accounts to be arranged through the Internet, maintaining the practice of anonymity.

Conclusion

The early history of tax havens demonstrates the remarkably close links in the development of the modern economy in the late nineteenth century, including the rise of the modern corporate structure, modern taxation, and tax havens. Ironically, but not untypically, the earliest examples of quasi tax havens in the modern era emerged in the small U.S. states of New Jersey and Delaware, followed by Vermont, Rhode Island, and then Nevada. This may come as no surprise, for by the late nineteenth century the United States was the most advanced economy in the world. As the newest phase of capitalist development reached European shores, so did the phenomenon of tax havens. The European state that most nearly resembles the U.S. federal model of governance, Switzerland, emerged as the earliest key player in the offshore world. A Zurich-Zug-Liechtenstein triangle took shape in the 1920s as the first genuine tax haven to draw the great bulk of its funds from nonresidents. Meanwhile, British courts were entrusted with the task of modernizing British tax rules and residency laws in light of the rise of the modern multinational company. They ended up creating, probably unintentionally, the concept of company residence without taxation, paving the way for the International Business Company model, which is now at the heart of the offshore world.

The emergence of tax havens appears to modern eyes as a perhaps regrettable but unavoidable response to rising taxation. The history of tax havens demonstrates, however, that neither governments nor individuals understood fully the potential for pecuniary gains in the tax haven strategy. In fact, no one state or jurisdiction developed the strategy fully; each appears to have responded to very specific circumstances and only much later, perhaps not before the 1950s, would a fully articulated strategy emerge, based on a wholesale rewriting of tax and regulatory laws with the sole aim of attracting nonresident capital.

Chapter 5

The British Empire Strikes Back

Switzerland was the archetypal tax haven, but the British Empire more than matched it, proving a fertile ground for the development of tax havens. Today, the United Kingdom retains responsibility for fourteen Overseas Territories, eleven of which are permanently populated. Of those, seven are tax havens: Bermuda, Caymans Islands, British Virgin Islands, Gibraltar, Turks and Caicos, Anguilla, and Montserrat. The United Kingdom also maintains sovereignty over the Crown Dependencies of Jersey, Guernsey, and the Isle of Man, all among the world's leading tax havens. Moreover, a former British colony, Hong Kong, shared British law and has developed into a major financial center.

Several reasons can be identified as to why the British Empire has been so important in the development of tax havens. First, the British Empire was the largest empire the world has ever seen, nearly twice the size of the Soviet empire. England was also the home of the first and second industrial revolutions. Until World War II, a considerable portion of the world economy was handled within the British Empire. Second, a key factor in the development of any haven, as we show in chapter eight, is the socio-economic structure of the society. Tax havens invariably develop in countries dominated by commercial and financial elites—which was the case for the British Empire and many of its outposts. Third, English common law proved extremely useful in generating loopholes that were used to develop tax havens. Fourth, in search of quick and easy "savings" to maintain its unwieldy empire, the declining British state was keen to embrace tax haven status for its small colonial outposts, because it kept the local elites happy and lowered payments from London. Finally, the Euro-market and the City of London were critical to the Empire's survival as an offshore center.

The combination of these factors proved a heady cocktail. In time, it generated a unique political economy centered on the City of London, the UK-dependent jurisdictions, some former colonies, and Switzerland and Luxembourg.

Box 5.1 *Partington v. Attorney General*, 1869—Only words matter

---

Common law is exceedingly complex, based on a combination of legislation, statutes, and interpretation. Between 1970 and 2008, British tax legislation alone has grown from 1,297 to 4,580 pages of primary legislation and from 171 to 1,444 pages of secondary legislation—a compound rate of growth of 6% per annum since 1970, over 8% since 1988, and over 12% since 1992. These figures are in stark contrast to the 450 pages French tax codes (plus 400 pages of annexes), and Germany's 450 pages of tax legislation (Avery Jones 1988, 255–56). The longer and more complex the rules, the more opportunities are created for avoidance and evasion.

In retrospect, an important development, which speaks to the very heart of British attitudes to taxation, was "the habit of the courts constructing tax legislation as a matter of words" (Avery Jones 1996, 70). One early statement about how to construe tax legislation is that of Lord Cairns in *Partington v. Attorney General* in 1869.

> As I understand the principle of all fiscal legislation, it is this: if the person sought to be taxed comes within the letter of the law, he must be taxed, however great the hardship may appear to the judicial mind to be. On the other hand, if the Crown, seeking to recover the tax, cannot bring the subject within the letter of the law, the subject is free, however apparently within the spirit of the law the case might otherwise appear to be (quoted in Avery Jones 1996, 70).

The principle that has guided British courts ever since is an emphasis on the words of the legislation, not on their meaning or purpose. The principle was restated in the House of Lords in 1980: "A subject is only to be taxed upon clear words, not upon 'intendment' or upon the equity of an Act. Any taxing Act of Parliament is to be construed in accordance with this principle"(Lord Wilberforce in *Ramsey v. IRC* 54 TC 101 at 184E, quoted in Avery Jones 1996, 70).

Since entry to the EU, British courts have begun to shift their position and are moving increasingly toward the concept of "purpose," in which the courts seek to interpret the Parliament's approach—a development that may have great significance for the future of tax havens.

A British Empire-Centered Economy

It is not easy to pinpoint the beginnings of this British Empire-centered political economy. The evolution of British residency laws, culminating in the *Egyptian Delta v Mr. Todd* 1929 (discussed in the previous chapter), proved extremely important. Since the *Egyptian Delta* case, any colonial outpost could serve in principle as a tax haven. But how many companies or officials were aware of this possibility? And were such developments used intentionally, to attract foreign businesses?

Wherever British colonists settled, they brought with them the common law. However, "subsequent statutes passed by the Parliament at Westminster do not apply to the new colony unless distinctly made applicable by their provisions or by natural inference" (Dill and Minty 1932, 216). The result was lags and delays in the introduction of British law throughout the Empire, resulting in loopholes useful for tax avoidance. By the 1930s British law books had plenty of cases to discuss: some merchant company in the Sudan appears to have taken advantage of a delay in the introduction of a statute to avoid paying tax on some of its activities; Bermuda refused to introduce the British Company Law "to keep out speculators forming realty companies to buy land" (Dill and Minty 1932, 217) and found itself, ironically, being used for tax avoidance purposes as a result. Tax avoidance schemes were rife, but these colonial outposts were not, at least not intentionally, what we would describe today as tax havens.

Bermuda Emerges as a Tax Haven

Bermuda's protectionist impulses unwittingly helped to make the colony one of the earliest Caribbean tax havens. In 1932, Bermuda's Attorney General T. M. Dill was still of the opinion that Bermuda had been prescient in refusing to introduce British company law to the territory, but he was apparently out of touch with what was happening on the islands. In 1936, a Bermuda lawyer, Reginald Conyers, and an attorney, Henry Tucker, found a way around the protectionist legislation to enable the U.S. makers of LifeSavers candy, to shelter their non-U.S. earnings from the U.S. Internal Revenue Service (IRS), creating what many believe was the first exempt company in the world. The company was called Elbon, the family's name spelled backward. "But it was the second exempted company that triggered the island's gold rush: the International Match Realisation Co.," writes Roger Crombie (2008).

Only in October 1947, when Shell established the first international company office in Bermuda, would the modern history of Bermuda offshore begin. In 1958, Bermuda enacted the Exempted Partnerships Act, which permitted nonresidents to operate out of partnerships formed in the colony. A handful of the world's super-wealthy individuals had their affairs managed from Bermuda, including the British playwright Noel Coward and a number of Greek ship owners. Most of the work was handled by the law firm of Conyers, Dill & Pearman. By the mid-1950s, American International had almost 300 employees on the island, mostly on the life insurance side of the business. In 1954, the law firm of Appleby, Spurling & Kempe set up the island's first two mutual funds.

A letter in the London *Times* in 1956 about local shipping laws provided another and instant success: within a year, half the world's fleet was "based" in Bermuda. Next came the captive insurance business. The story, as told by Crombie (2008), is that a former property insurance engineer from Ohio, Frederic Mylett Reiss, invented the business. "The steel mills that Reiss insured also owned coal mines. The coal was then turned into coke solely for their owners' use in making steel. The mines were called 'captives,' and that, according to Reiss's nephew, is the origin of the term 'captive' in the insurance context" (Crombie 2008). Late in 1962 Reiss formed his first captive insurance company in Bermuda. Reiss's business turned into the International Risk Management Group, the captive management and consulting company that he subsequently founded in Bermuda. Bermuda soon became the world's risk capital.

Over time Bermuda has become home to 2,000 investment funds with assets in excess of $210 billion in 2008. The number of captive insurance companies registered on the island has passed the 3,000 mark. Bermuda is still the leading center for captive insurance, albeit it is coming under pressure from Vanuatu and Vermont.

Bermuda remains one of the few "pure" tax havens. It has no income, profits, or capital gains taxes, nor any withholding taxes on dividends or succession duties.

The Bahamas

The Bahamas also began to emerge as a tax haven during the 1930s. The 1937 Morgenthau report to the U.S. president (see Morgenthau 2006) states that Americans have formed sixty-four personal holding companies in the Bahamas between 1935 and 1937, as well as a number of insurance companies. Bahamas was considered the principal tax haven for Americans at the time (together with Panama and Newfoundland [Morgenthau 2006]).

The early pattern in the Bahamas resembles what we see in many early developers—local, outward-oriented, merchant and financial elite established a legislative regime attractive to foreign capital. In the Bahamas, a group dubbed the Bay Street boys, consisting of merchants and attorneys who met regularly in a club on Bay and Charlotte Streets in Nassau, controlled the islands' development—both licit and illicit—until 1967, when the first black prime minister was elected.

Bahamas remained something of a backwater until the early 1960s, when Meyer Lansky, considered the Chicago Mafia's banker, hatched a plan with members of the local elite to replace Cuba as the Caribbean gambling capital (Naylor 1987, 2002). They used the Port Authority to form a company called Grand Bahamas Development Corporation (DEVCO), placing Lansky's associates on board. Swiss-style bank secrecy laws followed in 1965.

By the early 1970s, Bahamas was one of the largest "pure" tax havens. Its financial sector was second only to tourism—at that time the Bahamas attracted 40% of all Caribbean-bound tourists. It was, as Donald Fleming, the Managing Director of the Bank of Nova Scotia Trust Company (Bahamas) and a sometime Minister of Justice, Attorney General, and Minister of Finance of Canada, described it, a "tax paradise." The country, he assured his readers, imposes no income tax, corporation tax, capital gains tax, withholding tax, estate tax, death duties, or succession duties. The Bahamas gained tremendously from the emergence of the Euromarket; by the early 1970s, it accommodated the second largest Eurodollar market in the world after London. It has since been eclipsed by the Caymans.

Mafia links to the Bahamas attracted the attention of the U.S. President's Commission on Organized Crime and of the U.S. Senate's Permanent Subcommittee on Investigations. Both reported on the extensive use of Bahamian offshore banks and businesses by U.S. criminals (US Senate 1983; Presidents' Commission 1984). In 1965, the IRS Intelligence Division established Operation Tradewinds to investigate U.S. criminal activities in the Bahamas. This operation continued into the 1970s, its main success being the penetration of Castle Bank, a small bank with branches in the Bahamas and the Caymans. The Bahamas "brand" was tainted as a result, and other Caribbean havens have since taken over its preeminent position.

The Channel Islands and Gibraltar

Some experts consider Jersey and not Bermuda as inventor of the modern exempt company (Crombie 2008). Several offshore companies located in Gibraltar are also vying for that dubious honor. We can dismiss Gibraltar's claims outright. Although Gibraltar took steps to set itself up as a tax haven in the 1960s, it began to develop only in the mid 1980s, when Spain opened its border with the colony.

Jersey is a different matter altogether. The first Jersey income tax law was enacted in 1928. A Jersey company was subject to tax on its profits if it was managed and controlled on the island. In principle, therefore, companies could be registered on the island but if not controlled there, they could avoid paying tax. It appears that a small number of companies were already taking advantage of this loophole in the late 1920s. But this practice was not uncommon in the British Empire, as the *Egyptian Delta* case of 1929 suggests.

The Channel Islands were known as tax havens since the 1920s. The British government, writes Assaf Likhovski, "exerted pressure on the Islands to tackle the issue of avoidance, urging them to legislate in this matter" (2007, 206). The islanders proved "very stubborn. They argued that the islands were not the only tax haven in the British Empire. They added that they were being unfairly discriminated against and that government intervention would gravely impair their constitutional rights and immunities" (2007, 206). Not much appears to have changed in one hundred years as the same arguments are used today by the Channel Island governments.

The origins of Jersey's exempt company law are often traced to German occupation in 1940. The occupying forces enacted the Corporation Tax Law. One of its provisions was a flat tax rate of £50 on companies registered on the island but controlled from other locations within the British Empire, and a tax equivalent to the income tax if the company was controlled outside the Empire. The 1940 tax law was replaced in 1956 by a new law that imposed a tax of £50 on companies controlled in the British Commonwealth and £100 if controlled outside the Commonwealth. In 1970, the differentiation regarding place of control was removed and a flat rate of £200 was fixed. Ironically, therefore, the Nazi Corporation Tax company is the antecedent of the current Jersey exempt company and serves, perhaps, as the origin of the exempt company worldwide.

To enjoy the Corporation Tax arrangement, control had to be outside the island—that is, all directors meetings had to be outside Jersey. This gave rise to a peculiar practice, the so-called Sark Lark, in which directors purportedly met on the minute Island of Sark. The 1988 Finance Law introduced the exempt company, and the Corporation Tax Law was repealed. This allowed companies owned by nonresidents to hold board meetings in Jersey without incurring income tax liability unless income arose in Jersey. This put paid to the need for Sark Lark meetings.

Like Bermuda, the Bahamas, and many other jurisdictions, Jersey and Guernsey offshore began to develop in earnest only in the 1960s. According to Hampton and Christensen (1999), it was a case of a small economy first being "discovered," then increasingly exploited, by international financial capital rather than a planned, state-led strategy aimed at becoming a finance center.

Entrepôt Centers as Quasi-Tax Havens

Before we turn our attention to the third and crucial stage in the development of UK-centered tax havens, let us recall a third group of states occasionally referred to as tax havens. These disparate jurisdictions include Beirut, Uruguay, Panama, as well as Cuba and Tangier—although there is very little information on the last two, which were known as financial centers during the 1940s and 1950s and were considered tax havens. They represent an "old" offshore that more or less ceased to exist by the 1960s. To this list, we should add the Dutch Antilles. The Dutch authorities developed these islands during World War II as tax havens in order, they claimed at the time, to protect their citizens' financial assets during the German occupation of the homeland.

Beirut, 1943

The region of Mount Lebanon, dominated by merchants and financier interests, served from the late nineteenth century as an intermediary or entrepôt between the Middle East and Europe. After gaining independence in 1943, the elite "set up institutions to facilitate a competitive position in the international market, offering growing opportunities in entrepôt trade, finance and offshore operations" (Gates 1998, 3). The creation of a permissive environment attracted foreign—mainly Arab—capital to Lebanese banks. Beirut's offshore ended, for all intent and purposes, with the outbreak of the civil war in 1966. Lebanon has been trying to regain its position as an offshore center in the past few years.

Uruguay, 1948

Uruguay was developed as a major entrepôt center for the Southern Cone by British interests in the nineteenth century. It was dominated by merchant and financial interests, and development of an offshore center seemed a logical next step. The offshore Uruguay companies (SAFIS) were set up in accordance with Act No. 11.073 of June 24, 1948. The main purpose of SAFIS is to serve as investment vehicles for investments located outside Uruguay. SAFIS pay an annual tax at a rate of 0.3% on their capital and reserves.

According to the act, SAFIS must have their main activity outside Uruguay and must earn foreign-source income exceeding 50% of total income. They are allowed bearer shares and corporate directors, providing anonymity to shareholders and removing the need for an external audit.

Panama

Panama's evolution as a shipping registration center (flag of convenience) dates back to the early 1920s. The development of Panama offshore, however, which boasts a large offshore financial sector and 350,000 companies, took place in the 1970s. Panama adopted the familiar tax haven model, based on the three pillars we have already described: the exempt company, bank secrecy laws, and competitive incorporation laws. In 1970 it introduced a series of rulings that liberalized its banking laws, adopting Swiss-style banking secrecy, abolishing currency controls, and setting up exempt companies (Warf 2002).

The Emergence of the Euromarket

A great deal of confusion surrounds the origins and the nature of the Eurodollar market, otherwise known as the Euromarket or the "offshore financial market." The historian David Kynaston (2001) recalls a joke common in British papers' newsrooms in the early 1960s: asking novice photographers to call on the Bank of England to take a photograph of a Eurodollar. The joke of course was that Eurodollars have no physical existence, nor is the Eurodollar market a physical place.

Some distinguished economists believe that the Euromarket is simply a wholesale financial market, or an interbank market, that began trading in U.S. dollars in the 1950s (McClam 1974; Oppenheimer 1985; Schenk 1998). In time, the Euromarket has come to denote any market trading in non-resident "hard" currencies, such as British Sterling, the Japanese yen, the Swiss franc, the German mark, and the euro.

A different theory suggests that the Euromarket is a very specific market that emerged in late 1957 in London (Burn 1999, 2005). Faced with mounting speculation against the pound after the Suez crisis, the British government imposed restrictions on the use of the pound sterling in trade credits between nonresidents. Commercial City banks, which have evolved for more than a century as specialists in international lending, particularly to Commonwealth countries and the so-called British informal empire in Latin America, saw their core business disappear overnight. They responded by using U.S. dollars in their international dealings, presumably arguing that such transactions had no bearing on the UK balance of payment. At this point the precise steps that gave rise to the Euromarket become uncertain. But it appears that the decision of the Bank of England not to intervene in such transactions was interpreted as implying that the Bank views certain types of financial transactions between nonresident parties undertaken in a foreign currency as if they do not take place in the UK. Because the transactions took place in London, they could not be regulated by any other regulatory authority and so occurred nowhere—or rather, in a new and unregulated space called the Euromarket, or the off-shore financial market (Burn 2005).

How can this turn of events be politically possible? How could international financial institutions deceive the vigilance of central banks, at the height of the Bretton Woods system dedicated to the strict supervision of capital markets, and create an offshore market without any regulation by national monetary authorities? It is inconceivable that the market could have flourished without the blessing of the Bank of England. Gary Burn has demonstrated convincingly that the Bank could have intervened and opposed this new unregulated market. The Bank of England, however, never objected, nor are we aware of its issuing any statement in support of the new market. The Italian historian Gianni Toniolo (2005) shows, however, that in fact the Bank consistently sought to calm fears that other central banks expressed in the BIS. The Euromarket or offshore financial market emerged, according to this view, because of a convention acceptable to the Bank of England, which deemed certain transaction to be taking place elsewhere (Altman 1969; Burn 2005; Higonnet 1985; Kane 1983; Robbie 1975/6). This is why some experts describe the Euromarket as a booking device; it exists in the accounts of banks and financial institutions but is not actually offshore (Hanzawa 1991).[1] The attitude of the Bank of England has led some observers to claim that the British state established the Euromarket (Helleiner 1994).

Unsurprising, many banks were initially unsure about the significance of the new market. The market remained small and practically unknown until U.S. banks discovered it in the early 1960s. It became clear that it was useful not only in overcoming the specific restrictions of the Bank of England but also in overcoming the strict capital regulations imposed under the Bretton Woods regime. The market also received an important boost

---

1. The same applies as we will see to the U.S. and Japanese equivalent, the IBFs and JOM. A report by the Federal Reserve Bank of New York explains: "Despite the use of terms such as 'international banking facilities,' 'international banking zones,' 'international banking branches,' and the 'Yankee dollar market,' which convey a meaning of special offices in separate locations, activities of IBFs can be conducted by institutions from existing quarters. However, IBFs' transactions must be maintained on separate books or ledgers of the institution" (FRBNY 2007). The BIS defines an IBF as "A banking unit in the United States conducting cross-border business unrestricted by many of the rules and regulations applied in ordinary banking with residents. Similar institutions exist in Japan. IBFs and similar institutions are considered residents of the country in which they are located" (BIS 2000, 67).

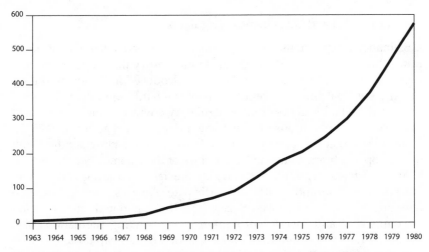

Fig. 5.1 The booming Euromarket, 1963–1980 (stock of assets, in billion dollars, net of double counting due to transactions between banks). Source: BIS, 2008.

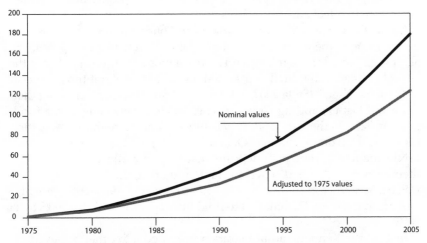

Fig. 5.2 Growth of banking deposits in Jersey since financial market liberalization. Source: Jersey finance data analyzed by John Christensen, Tax Justice Network, 2008.

with the introduction of the Interest Equalization Tax by the Kennedy administration in 1963. As the Euromarket flourished, it transpired that it could also be used to avoid reserve requirements—or any other regulations for that matter. The absence of regulation proved to be particularly important to U.S. banks, which rapidly developed a branch network in London in order to circumvent stringent U.S. banking and financial regulations.

The Euromarket and U.S. Financial Regulations

U.S. financial regulations are the product of two tendencies. One is an attitude that dates back to the late eighteenth century that opposes concentration of financial power. The other was introduced in the 1930s, the so-called New Deal financial regulations of the banking system. Together they produced a highly restrictive regulatory environment. A prominent example was prohibitions on inter-state banking (McFadden Act, 1927), which meant that U.S. money-centered banks could not buy another bank or even open a branch outside the confines of their home state. New York banks, for instance, could only watch the fast-expanding Californian market after 1945 and could not participate. Another example of such regulations was the 1933 Glass-Steagall Act that mandated the separation of commercial and investment banking. U.S. banking regulations also dictated lending no more than about 10% of a bank's capital to one borrower. In addition, Regulation Q, introduced in the 1930s, placed an interest rate ceiling on time deposits in U.S. banks.[2] It kept bank interest rates on time deposits very low, a situation that met with little objection from the banks, for they have to pay very little on time deposits, and so created what were in effect anti-usury laws.

Just as the Euromarket was taking off in London in the late 1950s, U.S. banks, some of them among the world's largest, were beginning to strain against existing U.S. regulations. The regulations ensured that "even the largest of them individually possessed no more than about three per cent of US bank assets" (Sylla 2002, 54). They had difficulties in servicing their large and fast-expanding corporate clients. They were caught in a funding squeeze. On the one hand, they could not lend more than 10% of their capital to any one customer. On the other hand, they could not offer MNEs the rate of return on deposits that foreign banks could pay. Once their corporate clients discovered the Euromarket, they began to bypass U.S. banks and earn higher rates of interest; meanwhile clients were also looking to the same Euromarket to fund their operations (Burn 2005; Sylla 2002).

In 1963 the Kennedy administration proposed a tax that achieved exactly the opposite of what it intended. It introduced the Interest Equalization Tax, a 15% tax on interest received from investments in foreign bonds, in order to make investment in such bonds unattractive to U.S. investors. The tax was supposed to stem the flow of capital out of the United States. In

2. Regulation Q prohibits member banks from paying interest on demand deposits. See Electronic Code of Federal Regulations (e-CFR). The National Recovery Administration, which was set up under the New Deal, sought to fix prices in industry in order to eliminate "ruinous" competition, and Regulation Q attempted to do the same thing in the banking sector.

fact, U.S. corporations refused to repatriate capital in order to avoid paying the interest equalization tax, and in the process they fueled the growth of the Euromarket. U.S. banks soon learned that the unregulated environment in London allowed them (or their London branches) to circumvent many other New Deal regulations. They were able to establish large diverse banks in London, capable of competing in every aspect of finance. German and Japanese banks followed suit.

The Euromarket, the City, and the British Empire

The development of the Euromarket in the City of London proved to be the principal force behind an integrated offshore economy that combined London and remnants of the British Empire. The British Empire is supposed to have more or less disappeared by the 1960s. This is incorrect. The formal British Empire may have collapsed, but the British-led offshore world is alive and kicking.

It is impossible to comprehend the spectacular success of the City of London as the world's premier financial center without the Euromarket and the satellite British tax havens. Formalities aside, we should treat the City of London, Jersey, Cayman Islands, BVI, Bermuda and the rest of the territories as one integrated global financial center that serves as the world's largest tax haven and a conduit for money laundering. How, then, has this City-centered archipelago developed?

Bankers discovered the attraction of these jurisdictions, which responded by drafting the laws and regulations the bankers wanted. Eventually, this process led to an explosion in the number of tax havens, each of which carved out its own niche in the international financial system.

The Islands Discovered

Phase I: Discovery

Mark Hampton notes that "in the official narrative of the Jersey OFC, the story goes that the island's government—the States of Jersey—showed great foresight and leadership and actively created the OFC from the early 1960s" (2007, 4). His research demonstrates, however, that "the emerging offshore centre was driven by international financial capital, merchant banks, who set up in the island to service certain wealthy customers" (2007, 4). British banks began to expand their activities in Jersey, Guernsey, and the Isle of Man in the early 1960s. However, as Johns and Le Marchant note, "prior to 1972 modest growth occurred largely on the basis of offshore UK and expatriate UK business" (1993, 54). In fact, the first to develop an intentional strategy as a tax haven was the Isle of Man, which in 1970 started to compete with its neighbors to attract wealthy English investors.

By 1964, three big American banks—Citibank, Chase Manhattan, and the Bank of America—arrived on the scene (Toniolo 2005, 454). We also know that faced with the high infrastructure costs of a London base, some smaller North American banks "realized that the Caribbean OFCs offered a cheaper and equally attractive regulatory environment—free of exchange controls, reserve requirements and interest rate ceilings, and in the same time zone as New York" (Hudson 1998, 541). The early spillover into the Bahamas and the Caymans, reckons Sylla (2002), was—like the London Euromarket—not motivated by tax advantages, but because it was cheaper to set up branches in these locations. In 1980, "the average annual wages for a bookkeeper in the Bahamas are a meager $6,000, and the annual fee for an offshore banking (Category 'B') license in the Cayman Islands is only $6,098. The total cost of operating a branch in these islands is much lower than in the primary centers of Eurocurrency operations" (Bhattacharya 1980, 37).

Phase II: Niche Development of the British Satellites

It did not take long for banks and other financial institutions to appreciate some very useful synergies between tax havens and the Euromarket. In tax havens such as Jersey and Bermuda, banks were able not only to circumvent stringent financial regulations but also to find "tax-efficient" ways of conducting their business. These so-called offshore financial centers have evolved, on paper at least, for a number of related reasons.

First, they serve primarily as "booking centers": financial transactions are conceived and set up in the main financial centers of London, New York, Frankfurt, and so on, but they are "booked" in the Caymans, and hence a large portion of the profits from the transaction can also be "booked" there (Goodfriend 1988, 50). The figures speak for themselves. Although the Corporation of London claims that the City employs approximately 1 million people, the British National Audit Office estimates that the fourth-largest financial center in the world, the Cayman Islands, currently employs 5,400 people.

Second, Caribbean islands had the advantage of being near the United States, whose financial system was still highly regulated in the 1960s and 1970s. In addition, the Caribbean Islands share New York's time zone. They were developed by the North American banking community to serve as a conduit for Euromarket transactions. Three Caribbean centers—the Caymans, the Bahamas, and Panama—benefited in particular from the rapid expansion of the Euromarket. By the late 1970s, the region accounted for one-fifth of gross Eurocurrency operations (Bhattacharya 1980, 37). By the 1980s, U.S. bank branches in the Caribbean comprised more than one-third of the assets of all U.S. foreign bank branches in the American region (Bhattacharya 1980, 37).

Third, once U.S. banks began to operate in London, the interpretation that had originally led to the establishment of the offshore financial market in London kept UK-based British banks and corporations at a disadvantage. The freedom from regulation and supervision applied only to transactions between nonresidents. A series of UK laws, perhaps unintentionally, would soon allow British businesses and banks to circumvent their disadvantageous position by using Channel Island subsidiaries, through which they could take advantage of nonresident status.

The Cayman Islands

In 1966 Cayman enacted a handful of laws, including the Banks and Trust Companies Regulation Law, the Trusts Law, and the Exchange Control Regulations Law, and it also strengthened its 1960 companies law. In 1976, the Confidential Relationships (Preservation) Law (a codification of English common law) was enacted to protect confidential information in the possession of financial professionals from disclosure—this in response to aggressive action by the U.S. authorities to obtain information from offshore banks. All exchange control restrictions were abolished during the late 1970s. The Insurance Law was enacted in 1979 to enhance and regulate the growing captive insurance industry (driven initially by ill-founded concerns about political stability in the Bahamas).

The Caymans are an astonishing success story. According to the Bank for International Settlements statistics, in 2008 the Cayman Islands were the fourth largest financial center in the world. By the end of 2006, the number of IBCs registered there had grown to 81,783, a 27% increase from 2005. Cayman is the world's number one domicile for hedge funds and for structured finance transactions. It is second only to Bermuda for captive insurance companies. Institutional funds are already around $1.4 trillion and continue to climb (Ridley 2007).

This spectacular rise was due in part to political turmoil in the Bahamas. The sector "took root, significantly assisted by political uncertainty in the Bahamas and the development of the Eurodollar market" (Ridley 2007). But is Cayman truly the world's fourth, fifth, or sixth largest financial center, as various statistics suggest? Is it truly a center for the distribution of world credit? Not really. Cayman's offshore sector is concentrated in short-term trade financing, especially financing for commodity exports. Very little longer-term loan syndication is done directly out of the Caribbean area. In 1980, for instance, only one U.S. bank, First

National Bank of Chicago, did any significant loan syndication in the Caribbean basin.

The 1972 Sterling Rescheduling Act and the Channel Islands

Two pieces of legislation proved to be of great importance to the development of the offshore economies of the Channel Islands. The first, the little-known sterling rescheduling act of 1972, was particularly significant. Although the Channel Islands are constitutionally not part of the UK, they were subjected to a Special Statuary Instrument, the 1947 UK Exchange Control Act. The act created a de facto situation in which "although locally a flexible background of law and procedures existed free from undue restrictions with regard to the establishment and operation of business, in practice the exchange control system gave considerable overriding power to the Bank of England through the vetting and monitoring procedures that this involved" (Johns and Le Marchant 1993, 58). Through these special provisions, the islands were regulated and controlled from the UK mainland.

One of the effects of the 1947 act was that Channel Island banks and subsidiaries had great difficulties in accessing the Euromarket. Companies were regarded as resident for exchange control purposes unless specifically designated as nonresident by the Bank of England—in other words, they were barred from accessing the fledging Euromarket. Companies had to apply to the Bank to obtain the status of "nonresident" and provide detailed information on proposed share structure and other financial matters. According to Johns and Le Marchant (1993), permission, if granted, was subject to many conditions, including:

- The share capital had to be designated in a foreign currency other than Swiss francs and held beneficially by nonresidents.
- The company had to comply with Bank of England conditions.
- Share capital and finance required by the company had to be acquired from nonresident sources.

Points 1 and 3 are, as we saw above, standard conditions of operation in the Euromarket. Point 2, however, ensured that the Bank, as opposed to those operating in the City, would regulate Channel Island companies operating in the Euromarket.

In 1972, the sterling rescheduling act liberated the Channel Islands from such restrictions. "The islands were literally at the stroke of a pen accorded an unprecedented privileged status" (Johns and Le Marchant 1993, 55). In response, merchant banks began to develop both Jersey and

Guernsey as booking centers for their Euromarket operations. The years from 1972 to 1975 are considered by Johns and Le Marchant the "take off" period for their offshore centers.

In 1979 exchange controls in Britain were suspended, ending the Bank of England's control over offshore financial centers in the British Isles. British and Island residents could henceforth invest anywhere in the world.

Niche Development in British-Controlled Islands

British tax havens compete with one another: they emulate each other's legislation and develop niche markets. There are two geographical areas of competition. One consists of the Channel Islands and Dublin's International Financial Centre, and the other is in the Caribbean basin. According to Cobb, "each center's competitive advantage was created through the establishment of a distinct regulatory and legislative regime, particular to that center only" (1998, 19). As he notes, corporate restructuring results in cooperation rather than competition between the OFCs as corporate HQs impose functional divisions of labor. Nonetheless, each island pursues a different strategy. Jersey is primarily an offshore private banking center, Guernsey a dominant captive insurance center, the Isle of Man the fastest-growing life insurance sector, and Dublin (IFSC) is a large fund management center. Bermuda is world leader in captive insurance and reinsurance. The Cayman Islands are a major banking center. BVI are world leaders in the formation of IBCs; Gibraltar provides a broad range of services, including banking, insurance, fund management, trusts, and advisory business.

International Banking Facilities, New York and Japan

The U.S. Treasury fought the Euromarket for years. By 1981 it gave up and decided to set up a more restrictive home for Euromarket transaction inside the United States to fight off the rise of London. This resulted in the International Banking Facilities (IBFs). These facilities enabled depository institutions in the United States to offer deposit and loan services to foreign residents and institutions free both of Federal Reserve System reserve requirements and of some state and local taxes on income.

The IBF, according to Moffett and Stonehill "represents an attempt by US government regulators to 'internalize' the Euromarkets into the US banking system. The purpose of the IBF was to minimize the size and growth of the offshore shell branches of US banks, while providing US-based banks and their offshore customers with a lower cost of funds"

(1989, 89). The Japanese government responded in 1986 by creating a similar facility, the Japanese Offshore Market (JOM). The IBFs and JOM were modeled on the Singapore Asian Currency Market (ACU), set up in 1968. Bangkok followed suit in 1993 by setting up the Bangkok International Banking Facility (BIBF).

Malaysia has a somewhat similar arrangement in Labuan, as indeed does Bahrain. According to some estimates, about one-third of international banking in the United States is undertaken in IBFs, and nearly one-half of Japanese transactions are in the JOM. Although the U.S. and the Japanese IBFs are exempt from some taxes on income, they are not tax havens but if anything "regulatory havens": they primarily emulate the Euromarket in their domestic financial system. They are distinguished from their onshore brethrens by relatively loose regulation not lack of taxation.

The Golden Years, 1960s—1990s

By the late 1960s, the "glorious years" of the post-war period were over. Soaring oil and raw material prices, accelerating inflation and declining growth brought about a crisis characterized by a fall in corporate profitability. It is no coincidence that the explosion in flags of convenience, export processing zones, and above all tax havens began at about this time (Palan 2003). European and U.S. multinationals were seeking ways to augment their profitability, and tax havens were only too happy to help.

There were also logistical reasons for the proliferation of tax havens in the 1960s and 1970s, among them the tremendous strides made in communication and transportation. The introduction of the jet airplane was of great importance. Located in the Atlantic 800 miles from New York, the Bahamas might as well have been on the other side of the planet in the 1930s. The Boeing 707, introduced in 1959, brought Caribbean Islands within two hours' flight of the money markets of New York, let alone Miami. The Caribbean havens had the additional advantage of sharing the East Coast's time zone. As U.S. tourists flocked to the sunny islands, they brought money with them, taking advantage of the absence of taxation. Similarly, the proverbial Belgian dentist, enjoying a comfortable lifestyle fueled by uninterrupted postwar growth, began to make regular visits to nearby Luxembourg to deposit some of his earnings. There he discovered his French and German counterparts doing exactly the same, taking advantage of Swiss-style secrecy laws. Luxembourg even offered lower fuel duty, to help the dentist rationalize the trip. Tuesday, for some reason, is still known as Belgian Day in Luxembourg.

The development of cheap communication rendered tax havens widely accessible. Xerox innovated the Teleprinter, the first fax machine in 1966; ARPANET, the first Internet system, was established in 1969; and the Microprocessor followed in 1971.

Decolonization also played its part. The breakdown of the British, French, and Dutch empires had a huge impact on the geo-economic map of the world. Simply put, there were many more states around. Each was sovereign, each claimed a right of self-determination, and each was looking for ways to survive in the harsher economic climate of the 1970s. Consequently, each wave of decolonization brought new entrants to the tax haven game. The Caribbean havens developed in the 1960s, the Pacific atolls in the 1980s, and the transition economies (former communist countries) in the 1990s. As the world economy expanded, small states in the vicinity of the growth regions of Asia and the Middle East began to adopt the haven strategy; Singapore, Hong Kong, and Brunei in the 1960s, Bahrain and Dubai in the 1970s. New tax havens are still being created in Africa, Ghana being a recent if still fledgling addition to the list just as the continent is at last showing signs of growth.

Independence was not critical. British outposts such as Cayman, the British Virgin Islands, the Channel Islands, and Gibraltar understood that the British brand was of great advantage in an increasingly competitive market. They were right, and by the 1990s were among the premium tax havens of the world.

Yet despite these important structural conditions, the greatest immediate cause of the development of tax havens in the 1960s and 1970s may have been another one of those twists of history—the administrative understanding between the Bank of England and British commercial banks that gave rise to the largest offshore financial market, the Euromarket

Singapore and Hong Kong

Singapore and Hong Kong do not conform to the perfect form of a tax haven. Their tax offerings are not of the classic form, and they are not noted centers for virtual incorporation. The two jurisdictions have, however, evolved as genuine OFCs, serving as intermediaries between the Euromarket and the Asian money markets. Singapore established the Asian Currency Unit (ACU) which was, in effect, the first type of international business facility (although it was not called so) in 1968.

The widening Indo-China war in the mid 1960s increased foreign exchange expenditures in the region, but a tightening of credit occurred in 1967 and 1968, contributing to rising interest rates in the Eurodollar market. As a result, dollar balances in the Asia-Pacific region became attractive for many banks. Singapore responded by setting up incentives for branches of international banks to relocate to Singapore. A branch of the Bank of America was the first to establish a special international department to handle transactions for nonresidents in the ACU. As with all other Euromarket operations, the ACU created a separate set of accounts in which to record all transactions with nonresidents. Although the ACU is not subject to exchange controls, the banks are required to submit detailed monthly reports of their transactions to the exchange control authority (Hodjera 1978).

The second stage in the development of Singapore as a tax haven began in 1998 (Chee Soon Juan 2008). In the wake of the Asian financial crisis, the government decided to make Singapore the financial capital of Asia. In 2001, Lee Hsien Loong, then deputy prime minister, finance minister, and chairman of the Monetary Authority of Singapore all rolled into one (and from 2004, prime minister), met with international bankers to discuss how Singapore could tailor its laws to gain primacy. Following these consultations, he introduced amendments to the Banking Act to revise the secrecy provisions, including stringent laws that are far more robust than Switzerland's. The penalty for breaking Singapore's bank secrecy laws were raised: a fine of up to $125,000 or three years in jail, or both. Swiss banks are now moving much of their client business to Singapore to exploit this fact given that banking secrecy in Switzerland has now proved to be permeable.

There are two other reasons why Singapore is considered a tax haven. First, as an English common law country, Singapore still permits nonresidents to form limited companies but manage them from elsewhere. Neither the UK nor Ireland do so, and Singapore has emerged as the leader in this field. Despite a notional tax rate of 22% on income originating in Singapore, foreign corporate income is not taxed at all. Second, due to a complex arrangement of subsidies and deferred payments, Singapore is considered a low-tax country. Sullivan (2004a, 2004b) puts effective tax rates of U.S. subsidiaries in Singapore at 11%, which is at the high end of taxation among intermediate tax havens.

Singapore is currently emerging as the fastest-growing private banking sector in the world. The main problem Singapore currently faces in its quest to become the world's largest private banking center is what it describes as "talent shortage"—a lack of specialist professional staff, even though the financial center employs about 130,000 people. Asset growth in Singapore has been phenomenal, rising from $150 billion in 1998 to $1.173 trillion by the end of 2007. In response to the perceived shortage in skilled personnel, the government has helped sponsor the Wealth Management Institute at Singapore Management University, set up by the

Swiss bank UBS. It is a college specializing in private banking. Indeed, both UBS and Credit Suisse have set up extensive training programs in the city-state (Burton 2008b).

In contrast, Hong Kong's colonial government adopted a permissive attitude toward the financial sector but it did not actively pursue financial liberalization until the 1970s (Jao 2003, 11). Indeed, the colonial government placed a moratorium on the establishment of new banks in the colony in the 1960s, and the Euromarket developed in Singapore only because Hong Kong did not allow U.S. banks to establish it there. In addition, the Hong Kong government refused to abolish the interest withholding tax on foreign currency deposits (Jao 2003, 12). The result was the extraordinary growth of Singapore, which was happy to accommodate U.S. banks by offering tax breaks and other incentives.

The moratorium on the establishment of new banks in Hong Kong was lifted in 1978. In February 1982, the interest withholding tax on foreign currency deposits was abolished. In 1989, all forms of tax on interest were abolished. By 1995/96, with the government becoming more proactive, Hong Kong had become the second largest IFC in the Asia-Pacific region, and either the sixth or the seventh largest IFC in the world. Like Singapore it maintains close links to the City of London and remains firmly within its sphere of influence.

The Netherlands

The end of the 1970s saw new entrants to the tax haven game from intermediate countries. The Netherlands began to gain a reputation as a conduit country for the capital flows of MNEs wishing to avoid tax (Van Dijk et al. 2006). In the mid-1970s, the Dutch government started deliberately designing tax legislation to make the country attractive to MNEs in search of a "tax efficient" location. As a result, the Netherlands emerged as a headquarters haven for companies such as Volkswagen, Ikea, Gucci, Pirelli, Prada, Fujisu-Siemens, and Mittal Steel.

The Dutch also allowed the creation of shell companies. Dijk et al. (2006) report that by 2005 there were 42,072 financial holding companies registered in the Netherlands, 5,830 of them managed by trust companies. Many are little more than shell operations. The largest management company is Fortis Intertrust (Netherlands) B.V., of Rokin 55, Amsterdam, where 2,387 companies are registered. TMF Management of B.V. Locatelikade 1, Amsterdam has 1,633 companies on its books. Of these shell companies, 43% have a parent in a tax haven jurisdiction such as the Netherlands Antilles, Switzerland, Cyprus, the BVI, or the Cayman Islands. The implication is clear: these are conduits designed to exploit favorable Dutch tax legislation and its extensive network of double tax treaties. The goal is to facilitate foreign direct investment from unknown sources into Europe, with limited tax on the eventual repatriation of income to the parent company.

The "Dutch Sandwich"

One of the most bizarre episodes in the tax haven story must be the rise and fall of the NA conduit companies. Known as Dutch Sandwich, these arrangements were used by U.S., Canadian, and other foreign capital to channel investments into the United States, much as Dutch companies are now used as conduits for investment into Europe. The odd thing about the emergence of the Netherlands Antilles during the 1960s and 1970s as a provider of financial conduit companies was that the United States actually encouraged the arrangement, apparently to permit corporations to avoid withholding taxes and to ease their access to foreign borrowing (Papke 2000). This surprising situation arose as a result of the Kennedy administration's 1963 Interest Equalization Tax Act. The act was a mistaken effort to stem the flow of U.S. dollars into the fledgling Euromarket. It achieved the precise opposite of its stated intent, partly because soon after the U.S. government decided that it would be advantageous if U.S. corporations could borrow at the lower rates available in the Euromarket (Papke 2000). Rather than repeal its Interest Equalization Tax, which it had to do eventually, the IRS authorized the use of N.A. companies to avoid U.S. withholding tax.

The N.A. conduit company continued to play a role until June 1987, when the U.S. Treasury announced that it would end the Antilles tax treaty. Unknown to the U.S. Treasury, 30% of the $32 billion in Eurobonds in issue at that time were held by U.S. companies and banks through N.A. conduit companies. Under enormous political pressure the Treasury had to modify its notice of termination, and tax exemption was not phased out until 1995 (Papke 2000).

Ireland Financial Services Centre, Dublin

Following the success of its Shannon export processing zone, established in 1959, Ireland established the Irish Financial Services Centre in Dublin in 1987. With its favorable tax regime for certain financial activities, low corporate tax rate (12.5% in 2008), and no withholding tax, the IFSC still flourishes, according to the Irish economist Jim Stewart (2005), in what he calls global treasury operation, managing international funds and flows of funds within MNEs.

According to Stewart the total stock of foreign investment in Ireland in December 2003 amount to €1,041 billon, a sum approximately eight times the size of Ireland's GDP that year. Of this sum €749 billion (72%) related to activity within the IFSC. By 2000, over 400 major companies were using the IFSC, of which 50% were U.S.-owned. By that time Ireland had emerged as the largest single location of declared pre-tax foreign profits of U.S. companies ($26.8 billion, followed by Bermuda with $25.2 billion). In 2002, U.S.-owned companies located in Ireland paid €700 million in taxes to the Irish Treasury but all this work was done with low active employment in the Irish economy, the IFSC directly employing only 4,500 people in 1997 (ECOFIN 1999, 61). In contrast U.S.-owned subsidiaries in Canada, France, Germany, Italy, and the UK accounted for 44% of foreign sales, 44% of foreign plant and equipment, and 56% of foreign employee compensation of their parent companies—and yet accounted for only 21% of their foreign profits. It is unsurprising that some have suggested a relocation of profits into the Irish economy.

A second peculiarity of the IFSC is that the largest source of foreign direct investment into Ireland was the Netherlands (€10.7 billion), the second largest being the United States (€7.8 billion). Stewart explains this as a consequence of FDI being routed through a complex web of subsidiaries located in different tax havens, each supplying a conduit through which finance moves with the aim of mitigating tax. His research shows that of

---

Box 5.2 Microsoft in Ireland[1]

Technology and pharmaceutical firms are high on the list of companies maintaining subsidiaries in Ireland. U.S. companies in particular set up IFSC subsidiaries as collection centers for their worldwide intellectual rights. In some cases, companies maintain small operations in Ireland, taking advantage of its low corporate taxation. Microsoft, for instance, set up a company called Round Island One in Dublin. Employing maybe 1,000 people, more than enough to establish a physical presence in Ireland, the subsidiary was used by Microsoft to license the sale of all its products outside the United States. As a result, license income was taxed only at the low effective rates charged by Ireland and not at the much higher rates charged in the countries in which many of the end consumers of these products were located. This unusually named subsidiary helped Microsoft's effective worldwide tax rate plunge to 26% in 2005, from 33% the year before. Nearly half of the drop was due to "foreign earnings taxed at lower rates," Microsoft told the Securities and Exchange Commission in its August filing for 2005. When the *Wall Street Journal* reported the arrangement in 2005, Microsoft re-registered its Irish subsidiary as an unlimited company, meaning that it no longer had to place its accounts on public record, and it thereby avoided future scrutiny of its activity.

1. The box is based on Simpson 2005, to which one of the authors of this book, Richard Murphy, contributed.

the 513 companies whose parent was located in the Netherlands, 102 had an ultimate parent in the UK. These included well-known companies such as Marks & Spencer and BOC. Ninety-three of the companies were ultimately owned by U.S. corporations such as Dell, IBM, and Hewlett-Packard, and smaller number were owned in France (14), Germany (9), and Japan (9). The evidence is clear: corporate structuring is motivated by tax, low-tax conduits seriously alter the flows of investment capital, data on FDI are distorted, and there may well be a significant impact upon reported profitability and taxation in many countries.

The Pacific Atolls

From the work of three Australian researchers—Greg Rawlings, Jason Sharman, and Anthony Van Fossen—we now know a good deal about the origins and development of the Pacific tax havens.

The development of the Pacific havens followed what we have described as the British Empire model, but with a twist. The Australian and New Zealand governments sought to intervene in the development of these tax havens and created their own unique model of a managed offshore environment.

The first Pacific tax haven was established in 1966, in Norfolk Island, a self-governing external territory of Australia. The Australian federal government sought consistently to block the development of the Norfolk haven, largely successfully for international purposes but not for Australian citizens (Van Fossen 2002).

As Jason Sharman noted that once

> Norfolk Island set the precedent in 1966, Vanuatu (1970–71), Nauru (1972), the Cook Islands (1981), Tonga (1984), Samoa (1988), the Marshall Islands (1990), and Nauru (1994) have increasingly taken the standard route of copying legislation from the current leaders in the field and then engaging in fierce competition for business that has often generated only the thinnest of margins. (Sharman 2007)

All these havens introduced familiar legislation modeled on the successful havens, including provision for zero or near zero taxation for exempt companies and nonresidential companies, Swiss-style bank secrecy laws, trust companies laws, offshore insurance laws, flags of convenience for shipping fleets and aircraft leasing, and since the early twenty-first century establishing advantageous laws aimed at facilitating e-commerce and online gambling.

In the case of the British and Australian dependencies, the offshore sector was developed in a deliberate policy to reduce the cost of maintaining the islands. The British government's Department for International

Development (DFID), apparently unaware of the broader picture, is proud of its record of advising the Caribbean and Pacific on "improving" their offshore sector. A study by Greg Rawlings (2004) of the origins of the Vanuatu tax haven demonstrates this point well (for additional information see Sharman and Mistry 2008, chs. 10–12).

The first British legal firm opened an office in the New Hebrides (later renamed Vanuatu) in 1967. Taking advantage of the Egyptian Delta principle, this company was soon followed by others. The Secretary for Financial Affairs in the New Hebrides, Mr. Mitchell, visited Bermuda and the Cayman Islands to learn about the offshore sector. "As a result of these wide-ranging talks and discussions, the British Administration took a policy decision that since the private sector was determined to use Vila as an international investment centre, there was no alternative but to enact legislation to control the situation and seek to gain much-needed revenue to keep down the spiraling grant-in-aid" (Rawlings 2004, 9). In 1970 and 1971, the British administration introduced the Banks and Banking Regulations, Companies Regulations, and Trust Companies Regulations. By 1976 Vanuatu was a thriving offshore center (Sharman and Mistry 2008).

Sharman and Mistry note how difficult it is to assess the financial contribution of the offshore financial center to Vanuatu's economy. Local industry representatives claim that the offshore sector contributes about 12% of GDP. The IMF, in contrast, puts the figures at 3% of GDP and 1–1.5% of government revenue. A more thorough cost-benefit analysis funded by the Pacific Islands Forum Secretariat estimated that in mid-2004, the offshore industry represented 9.7% of GDP and 5.1% of government revenues (Sharman and Mistry 2008, 133). The proportion is highly likely to fall in the future. In 2008 the Australian government ran an aggressive campaign against tax evasion in Vanuatu, leading to the arrest of the senior partner at a firm of chartered accountants on the islands. Consequently, Vanuatu has agreed to reform its financial services sector, although progress to date is not clear.

What does seem clear is that the British policy of using tax haven activity to cut the cost of post-colonial administration has backfired. Although hundred of billion of dollars flow through the Pacific havens every year, of which a good portion is believed to be laundered money (Van Fossen 2002, 2003), the combined direct income for these jurisdictions amounts to relatively little. The Pacific havens remain among the poorest nations in the world.

The Middle East and Africa

In October 1975, Bahrain initiated a policy of licensing offshore banking units (OBUs; Gerakis & Roncesvalles 1983). The OBU was designed to compete with Singapore's ACU, and both centers evolved as what Park (1982) described as "funding" and "collective centers"—regional facilities to either tap or fund Euromarket operations. Gerakis and Roncesvalles report that the initial response to Bahrain was extremely positive. Within four months, thirty-two application had been approved and by 1979, Bahrain authorities judged that a temporary saturation point has been reached (1983, 271). Bahrain had emerged as an important regional financial center. The OECD considers Bahrain a tax haven, although the nation has announced its intention to cooperate with the OECD.

Bahrain has now been eclipsed by Dubai. An oil-rich emirate, Dubai levies no taxes and has no mutual legal assistance treaties or indeed any information exchange agreements with the United States or other countries. Dubai is unlikely to buckle under the OECD campaign against tax havens, and it has refused to participate in the EU savings tax directive as a voluntary member. As a result, and because of the substantial capital that is backing investment there, Dubai is seen as a sustainable long-term tax haven, and with Singapore one of the few where growth seems likely to continue.

The Indian Ocean

The 1980s and 1990s witnessed a great proliferation of tax havens in other regions of the world. Mauritius set itself up as a tax haven in 1990 (Sharman and Mistry 2008, 41). It has always had one focus for its activities, and that is India. Under the terms of its double taxation agreement with India, which predated its creation as a tax haven, capital gains made by Mauritius companies in India are free of tax in the subcontinent. The impact has been significant. The majority of foreign direct investment into India is now routed, as we have seen, through Mauritius. One consequence is that a significant part of the Indian stock exchange is owned through Mauritius-based enterprises, though few observers think that this is the genuine location for control of the companies in question. A serious discussion has taken place within the Indian press on whether the country should in effect buy itself out of the double tax treaty with Mauritius by granting aid as an alternative—the costs to the Indian state likely being much lower. Such policy suggestions are likely to be repeated in other countries as time passes.

Post-Soviet Offshore

Russia began to experiment with manufacturing PTRs in the late 1980s, as did Ukraine. Since the mid-1990s, several regions of the Russian Federation, including Kalmykia, Ingushetia, Altai, Buryatia, Evenkia, Mordovia, and Chuvashiya, and the cities of Uglich, Kursk, and Smolensk, have all obtained tax preferences as territories with "special" federal regulations (Haiduk 2007).

Haiduk reports that the region of Kalmykia, for instance, initially offered a reduction of regional taxes from 19% to 2%, and then replaced its portion of the income tax with a fixed fee of $6,800 denominated in U.S. dollars. The region also permitted the creation of a variant of the shell company. Many businesses were located in "administrative buildings." For example, 249 Lenina Street in Elista hosted as many as 145 companies, including branches of Lukoil, Apatit Trading (one of the major companies of YuKOS), and Sibneft. Specialized "secretary companies" were introduced to deal with regional and local authorities, and they served to maintained secrecy. These domestic offshore territories were, according to Haiduk, used as transshipment points for capital being sent to tax havens abroad. According to one conservative estimate, at least $2 billion per year have been transferred abroad via these "free economic zones" since the mid-1990s.

Conclusion

The British state and the British Empire emerged as the second and soon the dominant hub of the offshore economy. With the advent of the Euromarket in the late 1950s, a City of London-centered economy emerged, closely linked to a satellite system of British dependencies. This British Empire economy combined tax avoidance and evasion with regulatory avoidance in a synthesis now known as OFCs. The powerful attraction of this London-centered offshore economy forced both the United States and Japan to develop their own limited version of OFCs, adopting a model originally designed in Singapore.

Tax havens now span the entire world, serving all the major financial and commercial centers. Modern tax havens are still largely organized in three groups. First and still by far the largest is made up of the UK-based or British Empire-based tax havens. Centered on the City of London and fed by the Euromarket, it consists of the Crown Dependencies, Overseas Territories, Pacific atolls, Singapore, and Hong Kong. The second consists of European havens, specializing in headquarter centers, financial affiliates, and private banking. The third consists of a disparate group of either emulators, such as Panama, Uruguay, and Dubai, or new havens from the transition economies and Africa.

Part III

Tax Havens in World Politics

Chapter 6

Tax Havens and the Developed World

Tax havens may have their origins in the United States, but the last one hundred years have witnessed their evolution into a developmental state strategy. Tax havens are now an essential component of financial and economic globalization, but their impact has been uneven. We distinguish the impact they have had on the developed world, which we discuss in this chapter, from their impact on developing countries, which is the subject of the next chapter.

Tax Havens and Tax Competition

Tax havens offer low or zero rates of taxation, primarily to nonresident businesses and individuals. One obvious impact of this strategy over the years has been to exacerbate tax competition among states.

International Tax Competition and Tax Havens

Since the 1970s, structural changes in the world economy have transformed tax competition. Capital account liberalization combined with technological change and financial innovation greatly increased the volume of mobile international capital. A growing number of states, as well as regional organizations and even municipalities, have responded by developing strategies in order to attract businesses to their domains. These efforts have included targeted industrial policies, the provision of cheap R&D funds, infrastructural support, and a large variety of sweeteners and state subsidies (Palan 1998).

As a result, governments found themselves under growing pressure to lower taxes on capital and businesses. Susan Strange captured the new trend when she wrote: "states are now engaged increasingly in a different competitive game: they are competing for world market shares as the surest means to greater wealth and greater economic security" (1988, 564). Since the early 1990s, the statutory tax rate for corporate taxation has declined almost everywhere in the world. In the European Union as a whole, for example, average nominal corporate taxation declined by an average of ten points, from 35% to 25%, between 1995 and 2007.

Tax competition occurs not only among states but also within states, particularly in federated polities such as the United States (Bestley and Case 1995; Case 1993; LeRoy 2006) and Switzerland (Feld and Reulier 2005). Evidence also suggests pervasive tax competition among counties and municipalities in Europe and the United States (Brueckner and Saavedra 2001; Heyndels and Vuchelen 1998). Swank (2006) argues that nominal tax rates declined in the United States because tax rates were lowered in sixteen other countries in his sample. Similarly, Feld and Reulier (2005) argue that intra-cantonal competition led by Zug was the main reason for declining corporate and personal tax rates in Switzerland.

The extent to which tax havens have pushed down individual and corporate taxation in developed countries is difficult to quantify. They do play a symbolic role, crystallizing opinion on the relationship among taxation, state, sovereignty, and contending conceptions of liberty, so the tax haven debate is also a broader ethical and political debate. Those who broadly favor international tax competition tend to view tax havens as adding a desirable competitive edge. This is the position most commonly associated with U.S.-based right-wing think tanks such as the Heritage Foundation and the Center for Freedom and Prosperity. Those critical of international tax competition tend to view tax havens as harmful and parasitic for the world economy. This is the position of the OECD and some of its key backers, such as France and Germany, and development-related NGOs such as the Tax Justice Network. As we discuss below, these contrasting positions are now at the heart of the debate over multilateral efforts to combat tax havens.

In Praise of Tax Havens

The positive perspective on international tax competition derives from two bodies of ideas: an interpretation of mainstream economic theory, which claims that tax havens are harmless, combined with normative considerations attached to neoclassically derived political science, purporting to show that tax competition increases efficiency.

Not surprising, perhaps, we find that mainstream economists, schooled in the "dismal science," generally come out in favor of tax havens. Their hypothesis is that international tax competition limits the naturally expansionist tendencies of bureaucratic governments. In typical fashion, Hong and Smart (2007) title their much-cited article "In Praise of Tax Havens," and Rose and Spiegel (2005)—apparently responding to Palan and Abbott (1996) and Slemrod and Wilson (2006)—argue that tax havens are symbiotic rather than parasitic. This positive perspective hypothesizes, correctly in our view, that the staggering FDI statistics reported in chapter 2 are a sham, and that tax havens are no more than conduits for capital flow.

There are variants to the argument. Hong and Smart (2007) maintain that because companies shift fiscal activities to tax havens, such as financing, insurance, and intangibles, they are less likely to shift "real" investment offshore. Paradoxically, they conclude that "tax planning tends to make the location of real investment less responsive to tax rate differentials, even as taxable income becomes more elastic" (2007, 3). The overall effect on taxation revenues is, therefore, less drastic than observers have assumed. In similar vein, Desai, Foley, and Hines (2004a, 2005) argue that use of tax havens as conduits results in higher growth rates for company activities in non-tax havens. As we will see in chapter 9, similar ideas had already appeared in the 1970s debate on tax havens. The theory comes down to the familiar argument that tax havens attract virtual rather than real investment, and so the tax revenues attached to real investment, such as income tax, may not be affected by havens to the extent that many believe.

Hejazi's (2007) analysis of the use of conduit jurisdictions by Canadian companies claims to show great benefits. The favorite conduit jurisdiction is Barbados—a country approved by the OECD for its transparency and cooperation—although Hejazi notes that Canadians may use other less savory havens. He concludes that "outward FDI that flows through conduits such as Barbados results in higher Canadian trade [exports] than FDI that flows through high tax jurisdictions, and hence higher amount of capital formation and employment" (2007, 29). Hejazi and other economists of this ilk fail to understand that what they have actually discovered is empirical evidence for transfer pricing abuses and not evidence that conduits create jobs.

Rose and Spiegel's (2007) analysis is centered on the effects of OFCs and is relevant to the next section, where we discuss the impact of OFCs on financial stability. Using the familiar neoclassical models, they admit "that successful offshore financial centers encourage bad behavior in source countries, since they facilitate tax evasion and money laundering" (2007, 1332). However, they continue, "offshore financial centers created to facilitate undesirable activities can still have unintended positive consequences. In particular, the presence of OFCs enhances the competitiveness of the local banking sector" (2007, 22–23). In other words, they advance the standard argument that competition generates efficiency and innovation. They presume that a competitive financial market is a good thing in and by itself—a large assumption, as we have learned from the 2007–8 subprime crisis. Rose and Spiegel provide no empirical evidence to demonstrate that OFCs in tax havens have become more efficient.

The more entrenched thesis marshaled nowadays in favor of international tax competition is not based on these arguments but instead on political science theories that extended neoclassical economics into the sphere of politics. It is also pernicious, for it is explicitly anti-democratic. It suggests that market discipline should override democratic governments, an idea no more than implicit in the theories we have already noted.

Neoclassical economics is used to describe the behavior of individuals and firms as "economic agents." Modern economists and political scientists have extended the neoclassical model to other spheres of life, postulating different sort of markets. In what proved to be a seminal article applying the neoclassical rationale to public policy, Charles Tiebout (1956) argued that individual choices of location are not dissimilar to consumer behavior in the market. Tiebout was writing about an evolving competition among incorporated municipalities in the Los Angeles metropolitan area in the 1950s. He saw evidence that competition was developing among different municipalities for wealthy inhabitants. Due to the high mobility of the U.S. workers, he argued, individuals surveyed the range of policies, including taxation, provided by different suburbs and opted for those that offered the best value. Municipalities that correctly balanced taxation and public services tended to attract wealthier residents and as a result were able to expand rapidly. Others witnessed decline and a rising proportion of low-paid workers and the unemployed. Tiebout suggested that competition among municipalities produced efficiency improvements in the delivery of municipal services in the Los Angeles basin.

Tiebout's theory is often advanced in favor of international tax competition by modern-day politicians, particularly by George W. Bush's administration. In a nutshell, the argument holds that international tax competition forces otherwise idle governments to think long and hard about the balance between taxation and public services, and hence to respond to consumer need. Based on this view, tax havens push governments to enhance their "efficiency."

Tax Havens as Parasites

The opposing view maintains that international tax competition resembles only superficially the neoclassical model of market competition. According to this view, the application of neoclassical methods to tax competition conflates micro-economic theory of the firm with political economic theory of the state—a fallacious notion, say opponents, because tax havens affect income distribution rather than efficiency or optimality. International tax competition is a double zero sum game: the tax receipts earned by some territories are tax receipts lost by others; but also, the diminished fiscal burden for some translates into an increased burden on others. Consequently, the neoclassical rhetoric of competition advances the parochial interests of particular groups and sections in society. It is not simply an analytical tool through which to understand the impact of tax havens on the world economy.

Take the tax havens themselves. The idea that tax havens have pioneered or have contributed to a reduction in tax rates is misleading. The tax rates for ordinary people who live in Switzerland or Luxembourg are not particularly low when compared to the taxes imposed on the middle classes elsewhere. Some tax havens, such as Jersey, have robust laws to make sure that their residents cannot take advantage of the services of other tax havens. Jersey's anti-avoidance provision, designed to tackle what the island sees as abuse from neighboring Guernsey is a model of its type.[1]

If tax havens were meant to reduce tax rates for all, then they must be considered failures. The overall rate of taxation has risen in the past three decades, even in the United States and the UK. In the past decade, tax to GDP ratio went up in a significant majority of the OECD countries, by an average of 1.3% (OECD 2007, 43). Tax havens are used by only a small portion of the population, the wealthy and multinational businesses. International tax competition does not contribute to a saving in taxation at all, but simply contributes to a distributional shift. Clearly, if the burden of taxation has not declined, and wealthy individuals and corporations are reducing their tax bills because of their use of tax havens, then someone else has had to bear the costs. The big losers from the tax haven games are the salaried middle classes.

A decline in nominal and real corporate tax in OECD countries contrasts with a rise not only in income tax rates but in other forms of taxation as well, such as consumer taxes (VAT and the like) and social security

---

1. See Income Tax (Jersey) Law 1961 as amended, http://www.gov.je/NR/rdonlyres/ B7ED7163-EA89-44B6-A376-8C6FB90621D3/0/IncomeTaxLaw1961_RevisedEdition_ 1February2008.doc (accessed May 5, 2008).

contributions (Norregaard and Kahn 2007), both of which have disproportionate effects on the middle classes and the poor. The ratio of consumption spending to income is, inevitably, higher for the poorest members of the community. Social security contributions, for instance, apply to income derived from labor and hence affect the rich only marginally. In addition, most social security systems have earning caps above which further contributions are not made.[2]

In addition, and despite the claims of its advocates, tax competition exerts little meaningful pressure on governments to be more efficient. Governments are not profit-maximizers and do not collude with one another to raise tax levels in the way that businesses do to raise price levels. The purported "innovations" generated by tax competition have led to no discernible improvement in the provision of public services at lower costs. On the political side, democratic governments are accountable to their electorates, who are keenly aware of tax levels. The aim of an artificial competition between states to reduce taxation is a direct attempt to undermine the ability of electorates to choose between otherwise viable tax alternatives.

Is There a "Race to the Bottom"?

A related debate concerns whether tax havens are contributing to a global "race to the bottom." Simply stated, the race to the bottom thesis predicts a gradual erosion of regulatory and tax regimes under the pressures of international economic competition and capital mobility.

It is important to first address the question of whether we can isolate the pressure on taxation and regulation that is generated by tax havens from other pressures such as financial and economic globalization. The race to the bottom, if there is such a thing, may be stimulated by other factors or by a combination of factors, and separating these factors is very difficult. We are not aware of any systematic empirical or theoretical work that has tried to separate the different causes. Nonetheless, some arguments suggest that the race to the bottom is not as compelling an argument as it appears at first sight.

There has been a decline in statutory tax rates among OECD countries but interestingly not a decline in corporate tax receipts as a percentage of GDP. One explanation for this oddity is that declines in statutory rates "have generally been accompanied by a broadening of the tax base through a scaling back of generous deductions and exemptions" (Nor-

---

2. For example, in the UK in the tax year 2008/9 the upper earnings limit for employees is reached at £40,040, above which the contribution rate falls from 11% to 1%. At most 12% of UK income earners have income above this amount.

regaard and Khan 2007, 8). Governments are adept at presenting themselves as actively engaged in international tax competition while at the same time safeguarding their tax receipts. This should come as no surprise: governments need to maintain political stability at home as well as the infrastructure and the health and education systems to compete internationally. A race to the bottom is simply not a realistic option. However, most recent research suggests that the sustaining of tax revenues from corporations is the result of what is called "corporatization"—takeover by a corporate sector over previously non-corporate sector income (Clausing and Clausing 2007; Piotrowska and Vanborren 2008; Sorensen 2006). The implications are clear: real corporate taxes have declined. Nonetheless, revenues from corporate taxation are holding as a larger volume of taxable profits is taxed at lower rates.

There is, however, an important related competitive game, stimulated by intermediate tax havens such as Ireland, the Netherlands, and Belgium. The most obvious sign arose in the UK in the spring of 2008, as companies located in that country and quoted on the London Stock Exchange (LSE) began re-registering their companies in Jersey, but making them tax resident in Ireland while maintaining their head offices in the UK and keeping their LSE quotation. This highly publicized move was described by business lobby organizations as motivated by intolerably high corporate taxation in the UK. However, it is notable that the first two companies to make the move—Shire plc and United Business Media plc—have a high proportion of their earnings arising outside the UK (more than 90% in the first case), and neither pays much tax in the UK. Shire paid just £1 million between 2000 and 2004, and United Business Media paid £5 million total in worldwide taxes in 2006. What seems to be in dispute here is the role of the UK as a tax haven, traditionally lax in taxing the overseas earnings of companies quoted on the LSE. A threatened change in UK tax rules, proposed at the behest of business itself, created some losers, especially among those using the UK as a haven in its own right. In this case Jersey and Ireland are exploiting the situation for their own benefit, but there is no apparent change in the economic substance of the transactions taking place.

In fact, tax havens make the race to the bottom argument as they face pressure to re-regulate their economies: if they do so, the money will flow to less regulated territories. According to InvestmentInternational.com, a website dedicated to providing "useful insights into offshore financial services," "If Guernsey is forced to compromise on either tax equality or information exchange, it would see any potential tax evaders flee the island."[3]

3. "Channel Islands Banking," http://www.investmentinternational.com/_channel_islands_banking.asp (accessed July 5, 2008).

The argument is self-serving and at least in part dubious. In reality taxation and regulation in the major havens such as Caymans, Jersey, and Bermuda are light and are unlikely to be affected by minor increases in taxation. Furthermore, all the evidence suggests that tax havens are developing niche strategies and offering tailor-made legislation to appeal to different segments of the market. Guernsey, for instance, was the first territory to offer protected cell companies—an easy way of creating a pool of reinsurance funds, each with a separate liability, yet within a common corporate entity, thereby saving on administrative costs. Guernsey may have secured first-mover advantage by introducing these entities in 1997, but it was quickly followed by Delaware, Bermuda, the British Virgin Islands, the Cayman Islands, Anguilla, Ireland, Jersey, the Isle of Man, Malta, the Seychelles, and Gibraltar. It is clear that competition degrades the product rather than the tax base. Eleven years after introducing protected cell companies Guernsey is renewing its legislation to reflect the relaxation in protection and controls commonplace in other domains. As director at KPMG Isle of Man notes, "the offshore environment has been changing over the years. It adapts new solutions when legislative regimes come into play. An example of this is Protected Cell companies. They have been used for funds but now they are being used for Capital Gains Tax planning" (Huber 2008). A model created for regulatory purposes is now being used for tax planning, exemplifying how the two issues interact.

Competition and niche strategies should not be confused with a race to the bottom. The "consumers" of tax havens—firms and wealthy individuals—are sensitive to tax and regulatory differentials when choosing where to invest, but only up to a point. Logistics, habits, and most important, political stability and reputation play at least an equal role. Doubtless, firms actively and often aggressively engage in tax planning, re-arranging financial flows in a "tax efficient" manner (Desai et al. 2002; Gruber and Mutti 1991; Sorensen 2006; Sullivan 2004b). However, there is less evidence to show that firms and wealthy individuals are specifically targeting those countries that offer minimal taxation and regulation.

Sharman and Rawlings (2006) report that some of the most extreme unregulated and untaxed havens, the Pacific atolls, are also some of the least successful tax havens. They have succeeded in attracting money laundering flows but rarely serve as booking centers for large financial and industrial institutions. Respectable MNEs, banks, and hedge funds are not too keen to attract attention to themselves by associating with disreputable havens. There is a premium for those tax havens with a reputation for solidity and at least the appearance of a regulatory environment. Tax havens are like a good music system: the more expensive the system, the more likely it limits the distortion of the original sound.

Tax havens are competing to create as little distortion as they can, in the sense that they offer secrecy and anonymity. They compete in the business of appearing not to exist.

Although the shrewder tax havens play carefully orchestrated games, reducing regulation and taxation to the bare minimum, those who really play a role in globalization cannot play the zero regulation game. We suggest therefore that the race to capture rent from large financial and capital flows is centered not on a race to the bottom. It is a race for minimal rather than no regulation and taxation.

Tax Havens and Financial Stability

One of the least discussed aspects of the tax havens phenomena is the issue of financial stability, which is likely to be changed by the 2007/8 financial meltdown. Analysis of the links between tax havens and the current financial turmoil is still in its infancy, and so we draw primarily on research done since the East Asian financial crisis of the late 1990s.

From the exchange rate crisis that ended the Bretton Woods system in the early 1970s to the Asian financial crisis of the late 1990s, most explanations for financial instability and crisis centered on currency values, budget deficits, external imbalances, and the health of the banking sector in the affected economies. This was true for developed as well as developing countries. As a result, little analytical work was devoted to the role of institutional factors—tax havens among others—in financial instability. Only at the end of the 1990s, when financial instability engulfed diverse economies around the world and generated systemic risk, did analysts begin to raise uneasy questions about how opaque and murky the financial system has become, and what types of risks are being disguised and propagated by using intricate financial structures and complex investment practices (Nesvetailova 2007).

It was not until the late 1990s—with the East Asian financial crisis, the Russian financial crisis, and the near collapse of the Long-Term Capital Management (LTCM) hedge fund—that several experts started to raise concerns about the role and function of tax havens in financial crises. LTCM was registered in an offshore center. Even the Italian central bank was tempted by the high yields it offered and invested in its highly secretive funds. Equally, the Russian central bank, confronting debt default and fearing that its assets might be seized, hid $150 billion of its reserves in a fund incorporated in Jersey. In these two cases offshore locations were implicated, but only indirectly.

In the East Asian crisis, the quality of data on bank lending from centers such as Aruba, the Bahamas, Hong Kong, and Singapore was singled out as a serious prudential problem (CRS Report 1998). Some experts blamed large capital inflows into the East Asian economies, most taking the form of bank and private sector borrowing through OFCs and turning quickly into even larger outflows, exaggerating both trends and leading to financial volatility (Radelet and Sachs 1998). Others specifically blamed the activities of new financial institutions such as offshore hedge funds, allegedly trading in ways different from their onshore funds (Kim and Wei 2001).

In April 1999, following the East Asian crisis and the collapse of LTCM, and in an effort to strengthen the international financial architecture, a small secretariat was set up at the Bank for International Settlements under the heading of the Financial Stability Forum (FSF). One of the FSFs first actions was to establish an ad hoc Working Group on Offshore Financial Centers. The Working Group addressed the thorny issue of the impact of tax havens on the financial stability of the world economy.

As one would expect, different views exist on the contribution of tax havens/OFCs to the financial system. A minority position, often held by economists, maintains that tax havens/OFCs strengthen the financial system. We have already mentioned Rose and Spiegel's theory that OFCs force onshore centers to improve their performance and efficiency, producing what these two authors believe is optimality. Fehrenbach (1966) put forward a more original argument, maintaining that capital flows to the secretive Swiss banking system adds to stability. He argued that tax evaders, money launderers, racketeers, bribe takers, and more generally people who do not wish to attract attention tend to be long-term savers, demanding relatively low rates of return on their investments. Hence the Swiss banking system could also take a long-term view on investment. Another theory suggests that booking centers and regional centers such as Singapore help channel funds to and from the main financial centers to developing countries and therefore serve an important role in development (Park 1982). Research suggests, as we have already noted, that the flow of money tends to be primarily in the opposite direction, from developing to developed countries (Baker 2005).

The more widely held opinion, however, is that tax havens/OFCs add little to the health and strength of the international financial system. There are divisions among those who take this view. Some believe that tax havens exacerbate existing tensions and problems in the financial system (for instance FSF 2000b). Others argue that tax havens add a distinct layer of instability to the financial system (e.g., Summers 2008). This difference in opinion has, however, more to do with risk assessment than with solid empirical evidence.

An embattled FSF (in a struggle with the IMF, which seeks to take charge of the issue) took a politically wise decision arguing that at least "to date, [OFCs] do not appear to have been a major causal factor in the creation of systemic financial problems" (FSF 2000, 4). Can we suggest that, in diplomatic language, the FSF is suggesting that tax havens have been a contributing factor in the creation of financial instability? The FSF implies that tax havens/OFCs raise two fundamental issues: supervision and systemic risk. First, they add a layer of opacity to an already opaque financial system. It is, however, difficult to ascertain the degree of risk associated with this additional layer. Second, they attract financial entities that are specifically designed to avoid regulation or detection. In the words of the FSF, "the lack of due diligence with which financial institutions can be formed in many OFCs can facilitate inappropriate structures, or inappropriate ownership, that can impede effective supervision." (FSF 2000, 2) But what does that mean in concrete terms?

The Use and Abuse of SPVs

Financial crisis in East Asia as well as scandals associated with the dot com bubble, Enron, World Com, Parmalat, and to some degree Northern Rock and the 2007–8 crisis have been blamed, at least in part, on the opacity of current accounting practices and the use of tax haven affiliates for either fraudulent or opaque purposes. The argument is that opacity benefits the one who is, as one Enron director reputedly quipped, "the smartest man in the room." The small investor, if not the dumbest in the room, is the one least equipped to handle complex and rapidly changing information. But these crises revealed a more critical dimension: scandals and frauds not only cheat investors, they leave many workers without pensions and jobs, and affect an entire economy that ultimately bears the risk without enjoying the risk premium that created it.

The offshore entities that seem to have caused most of the problems are special purpose vehicles or special purpose entities (SPVs or SPEs). SPVs and SPEs raise severe prudential problems. Tax havens have made it exceedingly easy to set up offshore SPVs, but they do not have the resources and expertise to perform due diligence on what are very sophisticated financial vehicles. For example, the Cayman banking system holds assets of over 500 times its GDP. Jersey holds resources of over 80 times its GDP. It seems obvious to ask whether such small jurisdictions can allocate sufficient resources to monitor and regulate such colossal sums of money. Cayman tends to cooperate well with the U.S. government when specific evidence-backed requests are made, but it rarely if ever initiates its own investigations (GAO 2008).

Enron
SPVs hit the headlines following the collapse of Enron. A congressional committee investigating Enron affairs discovered that Enron's fraud was organized through 3,000 SPVs "with over 800 registered in well known

offshore jurisdictions, including about 120 in the Turks and Caicos, and about 600 using the same post office box in the Cayman Islands" (U.S. Senate 2002, 23). Offshore locations were implicated heavily in Enron's collapse. The committee, chaired by William Powers Jr., reported that Enron created complex financial arrangements, partnerships, and SPVs to shift debt around and pay money illicitly to its directors. The report states that "many of the most significant transactions [of Enron] apparently were designed to accomplish favorable financial statement results, not to achieve *bona fide* economic objectives or to transfer risk" (Powers et al. 2002, 4).

Despite the newspaper headlines, neither the Powers report nor the congressional hearings demonstrated that offshore structures were palpably more poisonous than the onshore ones. It appears that Enron's offshore SPVs were set up primarily for tax avoidance purposes, although they did hide some debt, whereas onshore SPVs were used primarily to hide debt. Both, it appears, contributed to the fraud (GAO 2008, 38).

In the same manner, the opaque conduits—another name for SPVs—used by banks during the buildup to the subprime crisis and since labeled "a shadow banking system," operated onshore as much as offshore by using different methods of regulatory and supervisory avoidance.

Northern Rock and Granite

Another interesting case resulting from the subprime crisis and associated with an offshore SPV came to light with the collapse of Northern Rock. Northern Rock was a UK mutual building society that was converted into a public limited company in 1997. Building societies raise money they lend in a conventional fashion, by attracting it from depositors. Conversely, banks have the option of accessing larger sums somewhat more easily from the money markets. With demutualization, Northern Rock became a bank and began an aggressive expansion. Its 2006 audited accounts showed that it raised just 22% of its funds from retail depositors and at least 46% from bonds.

Those bonds were issued not by Northern Rock itself but by what became known as its "shadow company." This was Granite Master Issuer plc and its associates, an entity owned by a charitable trust established by Northern Rock. After the failure of the company, it became clear that this charitable trust had never paid anything to charity and that the purportedly benefiting charity was not even aware of Granite's existence. Granite's sole purpose was, as a part of Northern Rock's financial architecture, to guarantee that Northern Rock was legally independent of Granite and that the latter appeared to be solely responsible for the debt it issued.

This was, of course, a masquerade, and one helped by the fact that the trustees of Granite were, at least in part, based in St. Helier in Jersey.

When journalists tried to locate these Granite people, they found no such employees in Jersey. In fact, an investigation of Granite's accounts showed it had no employees at all, despite having nearly £50 billion of debt. The entire structure was managed by Northern Rock, and therefore (and unusually) was treated as being "on balance sheet" by that entity and so included in its consolidated accounts.

The dilemma this situation created for Northern Rock was apparent. Granite was used to securitize parcels of mortgages on the money market through bond issues. When the money market lost its appetite for that debt in August 2007, Northern Rock's business model failed: it could no longer refinance the debt and as a result had to support Granite in meeting its obligations to its bondholders, even though Granite was notionally independent.

Confusion arose as to whether Northern Rock was onshore or offshore. In practice, its location included elements of both. When Northern Rock was nationalized, the House of Commons saw late night debates on whether this meant that Granite was also nationalized. The issue was not resolved. No one seemed to know whether a company wholly managed by a state-owned enterprise but notionally owned by a charitable trust was under state control. Notwithstanding, the government had little choice but to extend its guarantees to Granite bondholders.

It appears that the majority of British banks used such charities. HBOS, another troubled UK bank, maintained a Jersey-registered debt-finance fund with £19 billion in debts. HBOS was forced by the British government to take Grampian, its in-house, Jersey-registered, debt-financed fund, back on its books (Hoskins 2007). U.S. corporate and banking sources claim that such a practice is unheard of in the United States, yet the GAO investigation into the Cayman made specific reference to U.S. owners masquerading as charitable trusts (GAO 2008, 19). U.S. Treasury data show that as of the end of 2006, U.S. investors held about $119 billion in asset-backed securities issued by the Cayman Islands, more than any other foreign country (GAO 2008, 13). This type of structured finance vehicles is at the heart of the 2007–8 crisis. They can be organized onshore in some countries, such as the United States, or offshore in others, such as the UK. Why so many SPVs were set up in tax havens is not entirely clear—the reasons for going offshore tend to vary (GAO 2008). Nor is it clear what proportion of the structured finance market was set up offshore. Unfortunately, we have no good research yet on the subject. The GAO (2008) inquiry into the Caymans is probably the best available right now—although the study reports on the great difficulties it had in obtaining data and, more significant, in verifying the data. GAO does report, for instance, that of the 18,857 entities registered at one address in Cayman, Ugland House, owned by the law firm Maples and Calder, 5% were wholly owned by U.S. entities and 40–50% had their billing address in the United States (2008, 7). But what exactly this U.S. relatedness means was not clear to GAO researchers. The report continues: "structured finance entities are not typically carried on a company's balance sheet, and ownership can be through a party other than the person directing the establishment or the entity, such as a charitable trust, or spread across many noteholders or investors in deals involving securitization" (2008, 19). The GAO report believes there are many reasons why U.S. entities use Cayman conduit companies, including the islands' insolvency laws, which provide specific protections for creditors and investors and, of course, tax advantages (2008, 8). We can only presume that regulatory permissiveness, costs, and sometimes tax, must have played a role.

The widespread use of offshore SPVs or conduit companies is creating serious confusion about ownership and liabilities. SPVs such as Granite and Grampian indicate the problems that the use of SPVs, often "orphaned" from their parent through the artificial use of charitable trusts, can create. This structure is commonplace among British banks and has been widely used with regard to the securitization of sub-prime mortgages. In fact, Northern Rock was a relatively clean case compared to many in the UK, and yet its failure exposed uncertainty on how to deal with the situation on the part of almost every regulator. Ambiguity survives even after Northern Rock was nationalized by the UK government. The GAO report confirms that opacity of ownership is endemic throughout the system because of tax havens. We know that 26% of the U.S. asset-back securities (ABS) market is foreign-held—but not much more than that (Beltran et. al. 2008).

The use of complex entities such as SPVs, Structured Investment Vehicles (SIVs), protected cell companies, and the like appear to have contributed significantly to problems in the financial markets. The accounts of banks and other financial institutions cannot be trusted, as they can easily and legally maintain scores of entities offshore, holding debt instruments of all sorts. The links between such entities and the "mother" institution can be discovered only retrospectively, once a bank has folded, and even that may take years. In many cases even the institutions themselves do not know which offshore entities belong to them, and examples certainly exist of SPVs being claimed by two separate banking groups. During the good times financial actors have been surprisingly trustful of each other, and during the bad times they demand the others "own" up to their debts, not knowing whether to trust the figures eventually produced. Governments, in turn, are forced to offer blanket guarantees to cover unknown amounts of debt, much of it registered offshore, to try to unblock a frozen market. The staggering reports of financial activities in OFCs notwithstanding, none of the "pure" tax havens has offered a cent in support—they were, after all, not serious actors in the game, they were merely conduits for a fee. In effect, the governments of the major countries ended up subsidizing not only the disgraced financial actors but also the tax havens.

Hedge Funds

Hedge funds, and in particular offshore hedge funds, are suspected as another transmission belt for financial instability. The Prime Minister of Malaysia, Mahathir Mohamad, famously described them as the "highwaymen of the global economy." Hedge funds have been implicated in a number of speculative currency attacks, from Black Wednesday in the UK in 1992, to 1999 when hedge funds reportedly launched attacks on various currencies, including the Philippine peso, the Thai baht, and the Indonesian rupiah. Following the collapse of LTCM in 1998, the U.S. Congress held no fewer than six separate hearings on the industry. Some hedge funds were also implicated in the subprime crisis; two Cayman-registered hedge funds were strongly linked to the collapse of Bear Sterns.

There is no formal definition of a hedge fund. The term is used "to describe a great variety of institutional investors employing a diverse set of investment strategies" (Becker and Doherty-Minicozzi 2000, 3). Hedge funds' most controversial aspect is that they are generally either unregistered or registered through offshore private investment partnerships that use leverage to carry their investment. They are intentionally structured to minimize both regulatory supervision and tax in most cases. They are nonetheless, still subject to some regulation, especially if located in populous states. That is one reason why one-third of the U.S. hedge fund industry is believed to either reside in or have subsidiaries in tax havens. The Cayman authorities maintain that 85% of the world's registered hedge funds are located in tax havens. Whichever figure is correct, tax havens offer three great attractions, making them irresistible to the industry: secrecy, non-disclosure of trading performance, and low taxation.

The often-mentioned starting point of the hedge fund industry was in 1949, when Alfred Jones opened an equity fund, but the industry has grown significantly since the 1960s. What hedge funds have in common is that they make their money by exploiting pricing anomalies in markets. Trading in risk or using arbitrage techniques, hedge funds maintain their own "secret" set of strategies, theories, and aims. Many hedge fund managers claim to have discovered complex and sophisticated mechanisms that help them beat the market's average return. In this atmosphere of secrecy, it is unsurprising that they favor tax havens such as Bermuda, Switzerland, and the Cayman Islands. Many however, though notionally located in these places, are managed from London and New York.

There is another reason why many hedge funds like to keep a firm foot offshore. Following the collapse of Long-Term Capital Management, U.S. Congress hearings concluded that if any country sought to regulate the hedge fund industry, it would simply push the industry offshore. Yet again offshore explicitly served as the great deterrent against necessary regulation (Becker and Doherty-Minicozzi 2000). Despite the prohibitive costs of the LTCM fiasco, the light-touch principle of regulation remained in place even though the U.S. Treasury's examination of LTCM raised familiar concerns about offshore funds (Becker and Doherty-Minicozzi 2000, 28).

Another issue with the hedge fund industry is its sheer size. Size combined with light-touch regulation and the implicit incentive to operate on the "edge" may aggravate financial instability. The industry has attracted considerable attention, and money has poured in, primarily from institutional investors who believed that the sector was able to offer higher returns. The very high leverage used by most of these institutions resulted in combined resources that packed considerable market punch.

In terms of systemic stability, the problem is that "investing" in a hedge fund is largely a matter of trust and faith. This does not seem to have deterred banks, pension funds, and other financial institutions from committing funds to these entities. Estimates of the sums involved vary. Most think that a little less than $2 trillion is committed to hedge funds (IFSL 2007a). The sheer size of this resource in an opaque financial market, with little or no regulation, concerns many observers.

Very few studies of offshore hedge funds have been conducted, and those few are concerned primarily with performance. Some analysts argue that because offshore funds are less moderated by tax consequences, and are subject to less supervision and regulation, they trade more intensely and so increase volatility. Kim and Wei (2001) have investigated this allegation but found that fundamentally offshore funds are no different from their domestic counterparts. Kim and Wei may have been operating on a false premise, namely, that some of the hedge fund industry is offshore and some of it is onshore. GAO research into the Cayman Islands presents what we believe is a more accurate picture. Hedge funds normally set up a "master fund" entity for holding assets and making investments, through which the fund achieves economies of scale. When U.S. investors invest in offshore funds in the Caymans, they typically prefer doing so through a "feeder" entity that is formed in the United States, usually in states such as Delaware (GAO 2008, 21). As a result what may appear as separate hedge funds located in different jurisdictions are in fact related funds. An official of the British Financial Service Authority (FAS) was quoted to the effect that there are no hedge fund registered in the UK (Clark 2008). Yet London is considered a major hub of the hedge fund industry! Obviously all these British hedge funds are registered off-shore. The classic booking role of offshore is maintained in the hedge fund industry.

There is no empirical evidence at present to suggest that offshore investment vehicles pose any greater threat to financial stability than their onshore counterparts. The problem rather is that practically any type of entity that the finance whiz kids dream up can be set up if not onshore then within hours offshore. If not in Cayman, then in Jersey, if not in Jersey, then some place else. If strictly speaking the UK does not have a hedge fund industry, in Ireland the government boasts that it takes two hours to register a hedge fund. A 400-page application can be submitted at 3 o'clock in the afternoon, and it will be approved by 9 o'clock next morning. Assuming that Irish officials go home at 5 p.m., they have exactly 2 hours to approve a new hedge fund.

In truth, regulators know little about the offshore hedge fund industry. Considerable rumors point at the role of hedge funds in precipitating the crisis, but we have no solid research to back them. Until now, the U.S. Fed has chosen to rely on the good will of the industry and on "market discipline." Others (the SEC, the British FSA, the German Bafin, the European central bank) raise concerns about systemic risk, fearing a domino effect in which the failure of a big hedge fund could bring the collapse of the big banks that made loans to them, and they push for more regulation.

Debt Mountains

Perhaps the greatest worry in the current global financial system is the growth of debt, particularly unhedged debt. "Unhedged debt" is the credit risk created when money is lent without any collateral or security or—as it often the case—against poor forms of collateral, obscured through sophisticated financial instruments. The complexity of today's financial system obscures the issue.

Each financial crisis since the late 1990s has shared a basic characteristic: that debt mountains had been secured against "assets" such as shares or loans (as in the case of the Japanese bubble and the subprime crisis), which of course are worth only what the market believes they can be traded for. When confidence evaporates, the value of these assets vanishes. Worse, as the subprime meltdown of 2007–8 revealed, a combination of complex innovation, securitization, and the hedging of risk created considerable opacity in this unhedged debt. The issue is further compounded by valuations at market worth on corporate balance sheets under accepted Accounting Principles and International Accounting Standards and under IFRS rules in Europe. These valuations gave the impression of considerable earnings growth during the market upside but created a negative feedback loop, which has helped compound losses since market confidence in the underlying assets evaporated. This is a developing problem within the private equity sector, built on the basis of rising share prices which, it was assumed, would continue to underpin very high levels of leverage.

The FSF has noted this trend, saying that because of opacity, no one picked up on the buildup of unhedged debts in offshore affiliates before a wave of crises, including in Latin America (1994–95), East Asia (1997–98), and the Anglo-Saxon economies (2007–8). In Thailand during the early and mid-1990s, the build-up in use of Bangkok International Banking Facilities (BIBFs) to finance foreign currency lending domestically ("out-in lending"), which was largely unhedged, increased the banking system's vulnerability to foreign exchange and maturity risks. Inability to detect the rise in the proportion of risky credit was compounded by the use of tax havens, which further increased the opacity in the system. Another problem is that nonbank financial intermediaries (such as hedge funds) are not subject to disclosure of their commitments in tax havens.

In addition, the FSF raises growth in over-the-counter activity linked with OFCs, which escapes scrutiny and regulation: "The growth in assets and liabilities in centers such as Caymans, together with suspected growth in the off-balance sheet activities of OFC-based institutions (about which inadequate data exist), increases the risk of contagion."(JFSC, para 36) BIS data show that more than 80% of the entire derivate market is conducted over-the-counter, suggesting that colossal amounts of capital escape almost all scrutiny and supervision.

Critics argue, therefore, that the opacity offered by tax havens allows very large risks to develop undetected—risks insufficiently known to, or not fully understood by, the monetary authorities and the financial institutions until they unravel. The principal worry is the unknown dimensions of the operations of highly leveraged institutions such as hedge funds, which are not required to divulge information on their investors or their commitments.

Conclusion

Research on the aggregate impact of tax havens on the industrialized world is relatively recent. Until the late 1990s, tax havens were treated as a relatively minor issue of tax avoidance and evasion. BIS data from the early 1980s, combined with an important IMF study in 1994 (Cassard 1994), raised awareness of their significance to the world economy. Still, the debate is in its infancy. The two leading policy concerns associated with tax havens are taxation and financial regulation. Yet the overall effect of tax havens on the industrialized countries is difficult to measure. The debate, unfortunately, tends to be highly ideological. Pro-market ideologists tend to favor tax havens, viewing them as useful counterbalances to the expansionist tendencies of "rent-seeking" bureaucracies and states, as well as offering useful competition to onshore financial centers. Left-wing activists and social democrats view tax havens as vehicles of oppression, a key component in a gigantic parallel "shadow economy" that spans the entire world and operates for and by the rich and the powerful. This shadow economy relies on the mainstream onshore economies to provide the necessarily legal, political, and logistical infrastructure that sustains a flourishing world economy, whereby the costs of financing such a sophisticated economy falls largely on the shoulders of the salaried middle and lower classes.

Such debates notwithstanding, tax havens are a significant contributory factor to one well-known fact of globalization: the rising gap between rich and poor.

Chapter 7

Issues in Development

Tax havens have played a significant role in shaping the economies of developed countries. They may play an even greater role in shaping the lives of those who live in developing countries.

Most developing countries do not possess sophisticated tax systems. Typically, they are characterized by large and undertaxed informal economies, and in some of the extreme cases economies that are not taxed at all. Research has shown that an effective tax system is a critical factor in development. Not only does a functioning tax system raise the necessary revenues for development; it also builds the institutional capacity necessary for long-term development, and it encourages consensus and political conversation between private and public actors (Bräutigam, Fjeldstad, and Moore 2008). There are many obstacles to overcome in building an effective tax system, and tax havens must count as among the most significant hurdles.

Trevor Manuel, the South African minister of finance, has described how "off-shore tax havens, transfer pricing, multiple income streams and complex supply chains" have become a burden on developing countries (OECD 2008a). Tax evasion and avoidance, however, are more of a future than a current worry. Individual and corporate tax rates are much lower in developing countries, and enforcement is at best patchy. The biggest issue is not the use of sophisticated tax avoidance schemes or even tax evasion, but rather capital flight from developing to developed countries.

Capital Flight, Money Laundering, and Corruption

Raymond Baker, a leading expert on international capital flight, distinguishes legal capital movements from illegal capital flight. Well-documented and properly reported flows of wealth on which proper taxes have been paid are a legitimate part of everyday commercial transactions. Funds fleeing Asia during the Asian crisis of 1997–98, for instance, broadly conformed to this model (Baker 2005, see also Beja 2006). Illegal flight is an altogether different matter.

The illegal flight of capital is simply the movement across international borders of money "that is illegally earned, illegally transferred, or illegally utilized if it breaks the laws in its origin, movement, or use" (Baker 2005, 23). Illicit capital flight results from deliberate misreporting, though it often occurs through channels similar to those used for the legitimate transfer of funds. This, combined with the secrecy and opacity offered by tax havens, creates great difficulties for authorities as they try to identify the circuits of capital flight. At best we have very rough estimates of the worldwide volume of capital flight.

Substantial amounts of illicit money undoubtedly flow out of developing countries. The most up-to-date estimates of cross-border illicit money flows are $1 to $1.6 trillion annually. Baker believes that half of this money flows out of developing and transitional economies and into the major international banking centers of the developed world. A related study conducted by Dev and Cartwright-Smith (2008) put the figures for illicit financial flows from developing countries slightly higher by 2006, at between $800 billion and $1 trillion. Their study also concluded that between 2002 and 2006, illicit financial flows from developing countries grew by 18.8% on average per year.

Table 7.1 Cross-border flows of global dirty money (in billions US$, annual)

	Low	High
Criminal	$331	$549
Corrupt	30	50
Commercial, of which:	700	1,000
Mispricing	200	250
Abusive transfer pricing	300	500
Fake transactions	200	250
Total	1,061	1,599

Source: Baker 2005.

If correct, this figure is about 5% of all international banking transfers from developing countries. What is worse, and unlike illicit flows of money between developed countries, which tend to be multilateral (e.g., Swiss firms transfer illicit money to the United States, and U.S. firms transfer money to Switzerland), these flows tend to be one-directional, from the developing to the developed, from the poor to the rich. According to Baker, some 80–90% of all illicit money transfers from the developing world are permanent outward transfers. Whatever does return to developing countries is likely to be categorized as FDI. In the majority of cases, the money that does return to developing countries takes a "round trip"—a process to which we return below.

What is of greater concern is that illicit capital flight considerably exceeds current overseas aid to developing countries—about $100 billion a year from all sources, according to official OECD figures. At best, therefore, overseas aid replaces 20% of illicit capital flight. In fact, the sums involved in illicit money transfers are much larger than all other deleterious effects on development, including the transfers identified by traditional dependency theory.

Baker (2005) distinguishes three forms of illicit money transfers across borders:

1. The use of fraudulent transfer pricing techniques. Baker estimates that 60–65% of all global illicit money transfers take this form. It amounts to an annual flow of between $600 and $1 trillion, half of which flows from developing countries.
2. The transfer of the proceeds of criminal activities such as drug trading, racketeering, counterfeiting, contraband, and terrorist funds. The criminal component is, according to Baker, about 30–35% of all illicit money or $300 to $550 billion annually.
3. The proceeds of bribery and theft by government officials. The cross-border component of bribery and theft by government officials is the smallest of the three categories and accounts for only about 3% of the global total.

As is often the case with tax havens, the least important factor in terms of aggregate flows—corruption—has gained the greatest media attention. The most significant, transfer pricing, has attracted the least attention.

It is difficult to say what proportion of illicit money transfers, globally or from developing countries, is routed through tax havens, but it is likely to be high. It is estimated that MNEs' intra-group sales (i.e., transactions across international borders but between companies with common ownership) account for more than 60% of world trade (OECD 2002), and as we have already seen, about one-third of the world's FDI passes through tax havens. It is unlikely that these two numbers are unrelated. Indeed, they cannot be unrelated, for the existence of very large numbers of tax haven subsidiaries of multinational corporations is contributing to both statistics. The secrecy provided by tax havens offers a powerful temptation to undertake transfer mispricing, and there can be no doubt that much, if not most, of the mispricing flows through such jurisdictions. Not surprising, Baker, along with other experts in capital flight and money laundering, considers tax havens as the central component or the basic infrastructure of a global shadow economy.

Transfer Pricing

The process of setting the prices at which sales take place among related companies in an MNE is called "transfer pricing." In principle, transfer pricing is completely legal. Mispricing of transfers may be illegal, however, depending on the countries involved.

Let us recall the argument in chapter 2 on transfer pricing. Since World War II, intra-company trade has worked on an arm's length basis. The aim was to ensure a just allocation of the profits earned to the country in which they were generated.

Companies can decide whether they want this outcome, although we must stress that it is not always as straightforward as it may appear. There may be great difficulties in determining the "third party" price for some products transferred across international borders, for example the price of a part of a finished component that will never be sold on the open market. Estimates have to be made of an arm's length price for such products. Such estimates can be undertaken in good faith or, as is quite often the case, with the intent of disguising the reallocation of profit. Likewise, companies can decide to operate arm's length pricing only in locations where a challenge to their policy is likely, such as the major economies where these matters are now subject to routine inquiry by tax authorities. In developing countries a challenge is rare and the incentives to operate such schemes in good faith are even rarer. In December 2004, one of the Big Four international accountant firms, Deloittes, reported that it had never seen a successful transfer pricing challenge out of Africa (TJN 2005). Most African countries do not have the legislation, the expertise, or the commercial confidence to raise such challenges against the MNEs that operate in their territories.

If a company decides to reallocate profits between jurisdictions, several methods may be used:

1. Under-invoicing the value of exports from the country from which cash is to be expatriated. Goods are sold on at full value after they

have been exported, the excess earned from the sale being the value of the flight capital. This is reputedly the principal method used by Russian capital flight in the 1990s. Russian goods, such as oil, gas, minerals, and other raw materials were priced deliberately low, whereas imported goods were priced deliberately high. Tikhomirov (1997) calculates that about $2.5 billion fled Russia between 1990 and 1995 using this method. Predictably, front companies in tax havens were heavily implicated, but so were domestic or onshore companies. Tikhomirov (1997) believes that the vast majority of this capital flight occurred in trade between Russia's eastern region companies and U.S. West Coast companies.

2. Over-invoicing the value of imports into the country from which cash is to be expatriated, the excess part of which constitutes capital flight.
3. Misreporting the quality or grade of imported products to assist the over- or under-statement of value, for the reasons noted above.
4. Misreporting quantities to assist the over- or under-statement of value for the reasons noted above.
5. Creating fictitious transactions for which payment is made. This tactic includes paying for imported goods or services that do not materialize.

The Extractive Industries—Development Blight

One of the most problematic sectors in developing countries is extractive industries. They have emerged as specialists in the use of tax haven subsidiaries and in ensuring low costs in developing countries, using bribes and other such arrangements to facilitate the trade (Shaxson 2007). Cases involving major companies reveal that these companies use a combination of methods to pay little or often no tax at all.

To begin with, the MNE may seek a favorable position for itself by negotiating special tax arrangements under the terms of its mining or oil concession. Companies typically negotiate a tax holiday so that tax is not paid during the first several years of the project's life. Ten years of tax holiday has become commonplace (Global Witness 2006).

In addition, companies negotiate special tax allowances for investment—for example, a 100% write-off of capital costs—to create early-year trading losses, and as a result tax is not paid for a considerable time (Christian Aid 2008, 11). They often secure grants, allowances, or subsidies and negotiate exemptions from domestic tax laws, such as withholdings from dividend payments, so that profits may be extracted tax-free (Global Witness 2006). In many cases, special tax rules ensure that few questions are asked about the expenses charged against profits within the local operation of the MNE, thereby reducing taxable profits.

At the same time, MNEs agree to special transfer pricing arrangements, for example to permit the export of ore or oil at prices below market rates. Often the price is fixed based on production costs plus a fixed mark-up, whatever the price of the raw material may be in the open market. Sometimes the tax code contains no references to transfer pricing arrangements.

MNEs also seek permission for the vast majority of capital invested in the local operation to be in the form of loans, so that "thin capitalization" can take place and profits can be extracted from the host country by way of interest payments (Riesco et al. 2005). Prior negotiation may ensure no limits on the interest rate that may be charged, ensuring that domestic profits are kept minimal, and ensure no limits on royalty and license fees.

The problem with such arrangements is that the concessions granted in the host country negate the benefits of double tax treaties with major financial centers where these MNEs have their headquarters. It is normal that, for the treaty to apply, local taxation law should apply without any concession having been granted in either state party to the agreement. As a result companies create entities to ensure that the profits that flow from a host country are routed to a low-tax state with reasonably good double tax treaties (Cyprus, a full member of the EU, has emerged as a favorite) and thereafter flow through what are called "participation agreements" in jurisdictions like the Netherlands (van Dijk, Weyzig, and Murphy 2006). The benefits of low or no taxation are preserved as profits flow either into the parent company or, more likely, into a group financing operation in the country running the participation agreement (usually specialist mid-size tax havens such as the Netherlands, Switzerland, and Ireland). Group financing operations are effectively intra-group banks; they ensure that low-taxed profits do not reach countries with higher tax rates but are instead loaned to them—usually at a hefty rate.

This is only the beginning. The supply of services and capital equipment from within the group offers additional opportunities for illicit transfers. Prices charged can be manipulated to ensure that profits flow to low-taxed countries. This has the dual advantage of reducing the taxable income of the host country operation and inflating its cost of production of ore or oil, which will probably also reduce the royalties due to it. Typically, capital equipment is sold or leased to the host country operation from another company within the MNE, and that company is likely to be registered in a tax haven or a low-tax area or a country that allows a double tax deduction to be made on leased equipment costs by claiming the expense in two locations—a process known as "double dipping." The process is made possible because some states allow the claim for the cost of leased capital equipment to the lessees and others to the lessor: leasing between states with these differing rules can give rise to relief in both states.

Management services and seconded staff will be supplied from off-shore locations to reduce the tax paid locally on employment costs, thus reducing the benefit to the host country and enabling such services to be sold to the host country at inflated prices, with the resulting benefit being transferred to a low-tax state. In addition, payroll taxes due for such staff may be reduced by paying them from a tax haven (Stockman 2008).

Furthermore, charges will be made for the use of MNE-owned patents, copyrights, and management know-how, the ownership of which will be located in offshore tax havens. The value of this knowledge will be hard to prove and so is particularly difficult to challenge under transfer pricing rules. At the time of writing, the use of tax haven subsidiaries for this activity is precipitating a major crisis in the management of UK corporation tax (Hinks 2008).

Finally, cash needed to fund the operation will be provided by group finance companies in locations such as the Netherlands, Ireland, and Switzerland where low rates of tax are charged on the receipt of such income. This tactic supports the great FDI statistics attached to tax havens, but it has a serious cost to developing countries (Van Dijk, Weyzig, and Murphy 2006).

Box 7.1 Copper mining in Chile[1]

In 2002, Exxon Corp. announced it had agreed to sell Disputada de Las Condes, a medium-size copper mine it operated in the Andes, to Anglo-American plc, a London-based and London-quoted company, for $1.8 billion. Exxon had bought the mine for $70 million in the mid-1970s and had run it, ostensibly at a loss, for twenty-three years. It did not pay any taxes on the mine but did accumulate some $500 million of debt, which it passed on to Anglo-American as tax credits as part of the sale agreement. Exxon also announced that the transaction with Anglo-American was to be signed in a foreign country, apparently to avoid paying some $300 million in capital gains tax to the Chilean state.

Commentators asked how a consistently loss-making mine had appreciated so much in value. Conversely, as Manuel Riesco asked, how had Exxon avoided Chilean tax for so long by declaring accounting losses for a company that must, he presumed, have been profitable to justify the sale price? The president of Exxon Corporation himself recognized the profitable nature of this operation in a speech to his shareholders, where he estimated real profits from Disputada amounted to around 20–21% of sales.

Exxon succeeded by use of some of the techniques we have already described. The principal technique used to expatriate funds from Chile was through the payment of interest on loans from Exxon financial affiliates in offshore havens. Exxon substantially over-indebted Disputada to the point that it was technically insolvent due to the debt owed to Exxon Financials, its own Bermuda-based financial branch; huge interest payments had been expatriated from Disputada to Exxon Financials, and the resulting income in Bermuda would have been subject to little or no tax.

This practice was common in the Chilean private mining industry; one company reached an unsustainable debt: equity ratio of 16.9. Riesco claims that all private mining companies, with the sole exception of BHP Billiton's Escondida have used this mechanism to reduce tax payments.

Given special dispensation under Chilean law, foreign companies were lightly taxed. Yet many were not satisfied with low taxation and used transfer mispricing to facilitate money transfers. Typically, mining companies did not account for the gold, molybdenum, and other precious and high-value metals included in the copper concentrates they exported, thereby understating its value. The result was a further loss of revenue for Chile.

1. The box draws heavily on the work of Riesco et al. 2005.

Criminality, Black-Market Currency Deals, and Petty Smuggling

One favorite technique used for capital flight is wire transfers, in which a bank or a non-banking financial institution transfers money out of a country illicitly. Other mechanisms include the smuggling of cash and other high-value mobile assets such as diamonds, gems, gold, and silver. In one typical case, "from 1993 to 1997, Guinea reported 2.6 million carats of official diamond exports at an average of $96 per carat to Belgium. Belgium, however, through the Diamond High Council, reported imports from Guinea of 4.8 million carats at an average of $167 each" (Campbell 2002). Luxury yachts are regularly sold and moved across oceans to shift capital from one country to another—it is widely believed that this mechanism was used to aid capital flight out of South Africa during the apartheid years. Other high-value commodities such as art, antiques, and rare coins also serve as means to take wealth out of poor countries.

Drugs, and to a lesser extent arms, are the main sources of criminal money transfer, and tax havens undoubtedly play a large role in these businesses.

The Corruption Business
Capital flight is often associated with corruption, theft, and embezzlement. Topping the list of corrupt leaders are Sani Abacha of Nigeria, Mobutu Sese Seko of Zaire, Ferdinand Marcos of the Philippines, and

Pavlo Lazarenko of Ukraine. Of course, it is not only heads of state who are implicated in corruption; corruption leads to capital flight at all levels of government. Many cases involve intermediaries who arrange government contracts or licenses in return for payment, always into foreign bank accounts.

Switzerland was traditionally a favored destination for embezzled money, although the Swiss claim, with some justification we believe, that London has overtaken them as a destination for this form of flight capital. Unfortunately, there are no reliable statistics as to the level of Swiss deposits from citizens of developing counties. What we do know is that at least 16% of the wealth owned by the world's wealthy originates in Africa and Latin America, both continents being subject to very high rates of capital flight, and a further 22.5% comes from the Asia-Pacific region, where such practices are also common. With over 38% of the world's wealthy in these areas—disproportionate to their overall contribution to the world economy—deposits in developed country banks from these sources tend to be disproportionately high (Capgemini 2007).

The Corruption Index Controversy
One big problem in addressing the issue of corruption is that it has been defined too narrowly, largely because definitions have ignored the role of tax havens in facilitating capital flight and tax evasion.[1] Secrecy and corruption are symbiotic; tax havens, by offering secrecy, foster corruption and must be brought to the center of the corruption debate.

The Berlin-based Transparency International brought corruption onto the development agenda in the 1990s, and its Corruption Perceptions Index (CPI) is now characteristic of the way corruption is perceived. It defines corruption as "the misuse of entrusted power for private gain." The World Bank defines corruption more narrowly as "the abuse of public office for private gain." This focus on the public sector is not just arbitrary but has been described by the Tax Justice Network as "wrong, and indeed pernicious."

Like every other type of economic transaction, corruption has a supply side and a demand side. The demand side involves those who would practice corruption, whereas the supply side includes those who offer, provide, and facilitate opportunities for corruption. Currently, the World Bank and Transparency International define corruption as purely a demand-side issue. But if the supply side is ignored, strange things can happen. To give one example: Transparency International's Bribe-Payers' Index (BPI) ranks the tax haven of Switzerland—which, as we have seen,

---

1. This section has been developed with the active cooperation of the Tax Justice Network, http://www.taxjustice.net/cms/front_content.php?idcat=2.

is one of the world's leading destinations for embezzled money—as the world's "cleanest" country. In fact, over half of the countries ranked in the CPI's "least corrupt" quintile are offshore tax havens. Yet all the evidence shows that these places are depositories for much of the proceeds of corruption.

The problem arises from the use of discrete units of analysis. Current perceptions ignore the systemic problem that one country's secrecy and tax haven policies harm other countries. Take this into account, and our understanding of the nature and geography of corruption changes. Indeed, a broader understanding of the geography of corruption must include offshore bankers, lawyers, and accountants who facilitate a central part of the corruption problem.

Tax evasion has the same effects as more traditionally defined forms of corruption, and they share the same political and social dynamics. Both involve elites avoiding and evading their responsibilities to the societies that sustain them. This "Revolt of the Elites" has two main components: first, elites remove themselves from carrying the costs involved in maintaining healthy societies; second, they remain actively involved in democratic (or other) processes of government, notably through lobbying. Tax evasion and corruption both worsen poverty, and both corrode faith in the integrity of the political and economic structures of governance. Both involve the abuse of the public interest by narrow sectional interests. Both have the use of tax havens at their core.

"Round Tripping"

Not all the capital that flees developing countries stays out. Some of it comes back disguised as foreign direct investment. This process is called "round tripping." Preferential treatment accorded to many foreign investors provides an incentive to engage in this process. In the case of China, for instance, foreign investors typically enjoy lower tax rates, favorable land use rights, convenient administrative supports, and even favorable financial services. They also enjoy superior protection of their property rights.

Because of these incentives, it has been estimated that as much as a quarter of the more than $100 billion that China loses every year to capital flight (Dev and Cartright-Smith 2008) comes back as round-tripping FDI. It is believed that the Chinese market accounts for the largest number of new companies registered in the British Virgin Islands (Sharman 2007), and Hong Kong and the British Virgin Islands are the largest foreign investors in China. The same holds true for Brazil, Russia, India, and China. According to some unconfirmed reports, a considerable portion of the "emerging markets" investments into Latin America in the 1990s was "round tripping" as well.

Tax Havens as a Development Strategy

Being a tax haven has proved in a few cases to be a successful developmental strategy. Luxembourg, for instance, is currently the wealthiest nation in the world in GDP per capita. Ireland and Switzerland are not far behind, and Singapore is rising fast through the ranks. Some smaller island locations, such as Jersey, Bermuda, and Cayman, appear to do even better, although problems in measuring GDP in such locations may distort results.

Yet some tax havens are among the poorest nations in the world. The least successful tax havens are Pacific islands. Other relative failures are many of the independent Caribbean islands (those that severed their colonial links), as well as the new transition economies.

The question arises why only some tax havens have proved so successful. Suss et al. observe that there "has been very little measurement of the contribution of OFCs to the general economy" of a tax haven (2002, 13). Notwithstanding, we identify three types of states for which a tax haven strategy has proved extremely successful.

1. Mid-size European onshore/offshore jurisdictions: Luxembourg, Switzerland, Ireland, Cyprus, Belgium, and the Netherlands;
2. Dependent jurisdictions: Caymans, Bermuda, the Channel Islands, Gibraltar, Dutch Antilles;
3. Asian entrepôt centers: Singapore, Hong Kong, Abu Dhabi, Panama, Uruguay.

Why Tax Havens Are Successful: Agglomeration Economies

Economic geographers talk of the importance of regional economies as the mainstay of economic growth. The research, admittedly centered on a very few successful cases in places such as northeastern Italy, Baden-Württemberg, Silicon Valley, Route 128 in Boston, and the City of London, suggests that positive agglomeration effects are created though proximity.

Adrian Tschoegl (1989) employs the same theory to argue that successful tax havens are those that have created an agglomeration effect. Initially the offshore sector of many tax havens was dispersed as countries attracted foreign capital indiscriminately. However, as revenues grew, those governments that were able to reduce tax further, or alternatively provide modern infrastructure, began to attract serious business into their territory. As additional banks and financial institutions enter the local market, competition intensifies, raising the reputation of the center for

efficiency and competitiveness. In time agglomeration economies generate pockets of expertise, and a tax haven develops a reputation in certain
specialized markets.

This theory may explain the success of some centers and the tendency
toward niche development. Switzerland, for instance—and Geneva in
particular—has developed as world leader in private banking, a sector in
which it still controls perhaps 40% of the market. The same is also true for
Luxembourg, although the country relies heavily on a foreign professional population. The theory works spectacularly well for the City of
London. Other successful examples are Guernsey with reinsurance, Cayman with hedge funds, and Jersey with securitization.

Doyle and Johnson (1999) argue that such agglomeration effects include
the local population as well. They report that in the Bahamas and Cayman,
foreign institutions initially hired local staff only in lower-level positions,
often relying on expatriates for professional work. Over time, however, foreign institutions have realized the benefits of training local staff to take
over professional responsibilities.

Agglomeration theory makes sense, but lacking good systemic comparative research, we are left with assertions and presumptions and not
facts. Doyle and Johnson do not provide statistics on the trickle-down effect of the offshore sector, and there are good reasons to doubt them. The
Cayman government claims that nearly 50% of people living on the island
are expatriate workers, primarily from the UK, Ireland, Canada, Australia, South Africa, and New Zealand. The same holds true for Jersey and
Guernsey. In addition, it is notable that Cayman, in its published budget
for 2004–5, had as an objective that "All residents have at least subsistence
levels of income" (Cayman Island Government 2004)—little evidence of
trickle-down working in what is, in per capita terms, one of the richest
countries in the world.

The Spillover Effect

Several of the most successful tax havens became popular tourist destinations at around the time they were developing their offshore sector. Was
there a link? According to Palan and Abbott (1996), there are synergies
between tourism, construction, and offshore. Like tourism, the offshore
sector relies on infrastructure support, such as telecommunication, transportation, hotels, and catering. The two sectors also raise the profile of
small jurisdictions, thus helping each other. In this way, the development
of an offshore sector may have important spillover effects on the wider
economy. This theory makes sense, but again there is little research on the
subject. In some places, like Jersey, the evidence points in the contrary

direction: the financial services sector has harmed tourism by pricing many facilities out of the tourists' reach.

A more debatable variant of spillover theory maintains that sophisticated offshore banking sectors lead to the development of a highly efficient domestic capital market that facilitates investment and growth. Little evidence exists for such a spillover effect. Indeed, a study by David Taylor (2006) on the formation of the East Caribbean stock exchange shows that the offshore sector played no role in modernizing the domestic Caribbean financial sector.

No Choice Theory: Lack of a Hinterland

Another argument draws on the observation that the majority of tax havens are among the world's smallest states, in terms of both population and territory. The theory is founded on the premise that whereas large, heavily populated states have a great many instruments of competition at their disposal, the smallest states cannot realistically compete for large-scale production or manufacturing facilities, nor can they compete in high-value sectors. Besides locational advantages, such as splendid sandy beaches and beautiful mountains that attract tourists, their only "competitive advantage" is their smallness and their sovereign right to write the law. Due to their small size—many tax havens have a population no larger than that of a mid-size town—they have no need for a costly army, and indeed they have no choice but to rely on international law and norms for their security. They also have relatively low infrastructure costs, as many of them have few roads and no universities or big hospitals to maintain. Dependencies under the protection of the UK government receive subsidies for basic infrastructure costs even when their nominal income per head is higher than that of the UK.[2] The cost of maintaining the state and government is, therefore, relatively small.

Baldacchino (2006) points out that many well-known tax havens gained their independence between 1960 and 1970 and quickly realized how difficult it was to survive. Britain, however, was unwilling to subsidize its former dependencies. The British government charged the Department for International Trade (DFID) to find a viable solution for the British dependencies. DFID in turn commissioned an in-depth report, the so-called

---

2. See, for example, the House of Commons Committee of Public Accounts Seventeenth Report of Session 2007–08, Foreign and Commonwealth Office: Managing Risk in the Overseas Territories, which notes that the UK subsidizes civil aviation in the British Virgin Islands by £600,000 a year even though the BVI has considerably higher income per head than the UK, http://www.publications.parliament.uk/pa/cm200708/cmselect/cmpubacc/176/176.pdf (accessed May 5, 2008).

Edwards report published in 1998, which recommended among other things continued support for the offshore sector.

The Edwards report pointed at the absence of a substantial hinterland as the major problem faced by these jurisdictions and hence at a lack of alternatives for development (Edwards 1998). The report argues that the offshore sector is largely "virtual," involving few significant domestic transactions, and does not require considerable human resources. Even the Cayman offshore sector, which makes the Islands the fourth- or fifth-largest financial center, employs only 5,000 people (NAO 2007). Compare the number with London, which directly employed 338,000 people in 2005 (Corporation of London 2005). Other havens employ fewer people, and in some cases the job is subcontracted or itself goes offshore, to foreign companies located in the industrialized world. The great advantage of the offshore sector is that it does not rely on the local economy. It is largely a rent-gathering exercise or commercialized sovereignty. Lacking hinterland, of course, small jurisdictions are less vulnerable to the deleterious impact of tax havens. They do not have a large welfare state to maintain, they do not have to maintain large-scale infrastructure, and so on. In the words of Godfrey Baldacchino, "Banks and insurance companies on (low/no-tax) islands as enclaves of larger states allows for a reaping of the benefits of the industry while containing the associated costs" (2006, 52).

Lack of a hinterland also shapes the social and political structure of these countries. Small, densely populated territories starved of land—such as the city-states of Singapore, Hong Kong, and Luxembourg, or even Bermuda and Malta—inevitably orient their economies to entrepôt businesses, including offshore finance. The absence of a hinterland inhibits the formation of a land-owning peasantry or plantocracy seeking protection from cheaper imports and contributing to higher costs of food items to consumers (Baldacchino 2006). As a result, many such states are dominated by an internationally oriented merchant class that has moved with ease from the import-export business to the provision of financial services (Marshall 1996). Also due to their size, many of these jurisdictions are dominated by oligarchic power in the hands of wealthy families, for which the construction of economic and legal opacity poses no problem.

Agglomeration Theory: A Critique

An offshore sector may have negative long-term impact on development. The problem, witnessed particularly among the most successful finance centers, is that offshore tends to crowd out existing industries such as agriculture and small-scale manufacturing. At the same time, agglomeration economies and commercialized sovereignty produce what Kakazu

(1994) describes as rentier economies—an economy that is oriented toward capturing mobile capital. The problem is that when an entire economy (and society) is oriented toward the most mobile element of what is already highly mobile capital, it is in a vulnerable position. The offshore sector creates an even stronger link with metropolitan powers and renders tax havens subject to their economic cycles.

This trend has contributed to the great vulnerability of these island economies. They may suffer, as they are now beginning to realize as the offshore sector comes under pressure from the EU and the OECD, from a Gold Rush or "boomtown" syndrome. Their enormous wealth relies too heavily on one sector and if the sector should fail for any reason (e.g., another center proves more popular, pressure from the developed world), then the absence of an alternative will begin to hurt. For example, the introduction of the EU Code of Conduct gave Jersey and Guernsey a very difficult dilemma. They were forced either to raise taxation on nonresident businesses or to reduce taxation for all businesses. Both islands chose the latter course, offering what appeared on the surface to be zero percent income tax rates to companies trading within their domain. Yet although they are known as tax havens, the two islands relied heavily on the 20% corporate tax on local businesses and were, as a result, in danger of running a substantial budget deficit. They sought to recover taxes by creating a complex but ultimately futile system of voluntary contributions from local businesses.

In fact, serving as satellites to financial centers such as London and New York, many tax havens are extremely vulnerable to changes in these centers. Changes in British or U.S. law and practices may have a fast and brutal impact on a satellite. It would, for example, only need the United States to enact the Stop Tax Haven Abuse Act, tabled in February 2007 by Senators Levin, Coleman, and Obama (Levin 2007), to ensure a substantial shift in U.S. opinion on tax havens. In May 2008, the European Union pledged to reform the EU Savings Tax directive, which may also have significant impact on some of the havens.

The agglomeration effect also leads to a tremendous rise in property prices and a growing gap between rich and poor. Hampton and Christensen (1999) point out the terrible impact on local people of Jersey's spiraling property prices, which outstrip even some of the wealthiest boroughs of London. The indigenous population is being priced out of decent housing on their own island, and they live in poverty. Similarly, a 2007 editorial in the *Cayman News* notes that "in general, the cost of living is around 15–20% higher than in London." The same editorial notes the growing local gap between rich and poor. "The phenomenon is observed world wide," the editorial goes on, "but in Cayman and other tax havens, the problem is exacerbated because of lack of taxation, progressive or not, to balance out the effects of spiraling house prices."

The agglomeration effect works at best for mid-size economies, countries that can attract and develop indigenous professional services and that are not entirely dependent on the offshore sector. For the smallest countries and jurisdictions, agglomeration is a double-edged sword. There are signs of rising social conflict in many tax havens as the gap between rich and poor increases. This problem has been noted in Jersey, Cayman, BVI, and the Turks & Caicos. Although rarely discussed, it may undermine the stability of tax havens (Murphy 2008a).

Capture of the State

Hampton and Christensen argue that the smallness and insularity of many tax havens precipitate what they describe as the "capture of the local state" by international financial capital, such as international banks and large accountancy firms (Hampton and Christensen 1999). Christensen reports that during his tenure as adviser for the Jersey government, foreign bankers and financiers would draft and sometimes dictate financial laws.[3] Swiss political scientists are similarly critical of the role of the financial sector as an antidemocratic force in Swiss politics (Guex 1998). Persistent reports, as we have seen, note the role of U.S. organized crime in the development of Bermuda's and other Caribbean offshore centers in the 1960s (Naylor 1987).

Although they claim their sovereign rights, these states have an independence that is more apparent than real, for their developmental and social goals are subject to the whim of foreign capital. As a rule, tax havens do not lack transparency only in financial matters—opacity pervades the entire state. The majority are controlled by a small, often invisible, oligarchy.

"When the Big Shark Is Corrupt, the Benefits Are Spread Around"

Little noted but very real is the risk that because tax havens are deeply implicated in financial crime, such behavior "spills over" into other areas. Maingot observes how indiscipline is spreading wide and deep through these societies. He describes the Bahamas as "a society experiencing deep social ills" (Maingot 1988, 173). Cayman is at last openly discussing social ills such as alcohol, drug abuse, child abuse, and sexual molestation.

---

3. Private communication with John Christensen.

These ills result from poverty in the midst of plenty, and from the corruption of a regime that ignores corrupt practices. Some have even suggested that a child sex abuse scandal reported in Jersey in 2008, concerning events that happened many years earlier, was not reported at the time the incidents occurred because of the secretive nature of a tax haven society. This claim cannot be proved, but it is clear that tax haven status may have detrimental effects on any location that adopts it.

Conclusion

Tax havens have had a significant, if largely ignored, deleterious impact on development in the third world. The latest study by Raymond Baker and colleagues (Dev and Cartwright-Smith 2008) suggests that illicit financial outflows from developing countries, many of which they think are facilitated by tax havens, amount to between $850 billion and $1 trillion annually. This is a sum between eight and ten times bigger than current global aid flows. The sum is also considerably bigger than those attributed to and by the theories of underdevelopment that were popular in the 1970s and 1980s.

A considerable portion of third world debt (and by some estimates over half of Latin America's loans in the early 1980s) was placed in Swiss banks and other key OFCs. Although these facts were in most cases known to lenders at the time, including the IMF, they then insisted that third world countries take on the burden of debt payments. Meanwhile, the large Swiss banks who are the main recipients of third world "hot money," made a strategic decision in 1957 to invest only a small portion of their assets in third world countries.

Ironically, the tax haven strategy has proved to be a successful developmental policy for some of the smallest and poorest island economies in the world. At least notionally, some now enjoy among the highest GDP per head of population in the world. Yet even successful havens such as the Caymans, Bermuda, and Jersey have placed themselves in an extremely vulnerable position. Their economies remain far too reliant on the offshore sector and a relatively large community of expatriates, and the unequal distribution of rewards within their communities is now being illustrated in increasing social tensions. From both angles the tax haven's contribution to development must be questioned.

Part IV

The Battle for Hearts and Minds

Chapter 8

Signs of Discontent

The emergence of tax havens has not gone unnoticed. Policies aimed at combating tax abuse coincided with the emergence of tax havens after World War I. The battle against tax abuses, capital flight, and money laundering was conducted simultaneously on three fronts: national law courts, national legislators, and bilateral and multilateral treaties. Yet until late 1990s, "governmental interest in offshore was largely restricted to the concerns of revenue departments of larger nations" (Hampton and Christensen 2002, 1658). It was a period of politics without conviction, intermittent action, and little obvious success. Yet in retrospect, the key battles that shape today's politics were defined in those early days.

Transfer Pricing Regulations

Historically, the first issue of international concern that touched on tax havens involved double taxation and the practice of transfer pricing. Transfer pricing is both normal and legal. It happens whenever two entities under common control trade with each other across an international boundary. As a result, however, they can set prices that allocate profits in a way not determined by the market. Tax liabilities are thus reallocated between jurisdictions to suit the objectives of whoever controls the trading entities involved. It can constitute tax evasion if it breaches the regulations enacted to control this activity.

International policy coordination on this form of tax evasion dates to the early years of the League of Nations (Godefroy and Lascoumes 2004), during the International Finance Conference held in Brussels in 1920. This conference asked the League to deal with the problem of double taxation, a topic that, as Radaelli and Kraemer (2005) observed, was of great interest to diplomats who could be taxed both in their country of origin and at their workplace. A conference in Genoa in April 1922 extended the League's mandate to the issues of capital flight and tax evasion.

A committee of technical experts was set up to advise the League and its recommendations centered on effective exchange of information between tax authorities. There followed a game, repeated on numerous occasions across the century, in which national positions can easily be guessed. The French, in particular, pushed hard for strong measures against tax evasion. Switzerland led the opposition, soon to be joined by the Netherlands and Germany as well as representatives of the International Chamber of Commerce (the lobby group of international business). The proposals of the committee of experts were whittled down to two draft conventions on "administrative assistance in matters of taxation" and "judicial assistance in the collection of taxes" (Rixen 2008)).

The financial crisis of 1929 and the depression that followed led to unilateral legislation in leading countries, which proved to be of greater significance. By the late 1930s, as the UK government became aware of the uses being made of the 1929 Egyptian Delta case, it introduced new laws to regulate the manipulation of residence status for tax purposes (the Finance Acts of 1936 and 1938). The U.S. Congress, meanwhile, had raised concerns as early as 1921 about the use by U.S. corporations of foreign subsidiaries for the purpose of tax avoidance. Although no substantial legislation was introduced during the 1920s, the media and Congress saw considerable debate about individuals who transferred assets to tax havens.

President Roosevelt embarked on a moral crusade against tax cheats as part of the New Deal. In 1937 a report tabled by his finance minister, Henry Morgenthau, provided indication, perhaps for the first time, of tax avoidance perpetrated by U.S. citizens through tax havens such as the Bahamas, Panama, and Newfoundland (which at that time functioned like a tax haven for U.S. citizens). Some of the best-known U.S. industrialists—Alfred Sloan, the Mellons, and the Du Ponts—were implicated in the investigation. The Morgenthau report singled out the role played by professionals: "One of the most disheartening facts disclosed by our investigation is that lawyers of high standing at the bar are advising their clients to utilize devious tax avoidance devices, and they are actively using them themselves" (Morgenthau 1937, 10, cited in Morgenthau 2006). In response, the United States enacted legislation against "foreign personal holding companies," which taxpayers were using to shelter income from U.S. tax authorities (Picciotto 1992, 97–109). Then came the war, and nothing much was done.

A 1943 international conference in Mexico City returned to the subject of tax evasion. Another, in London in 1946, established a committee on international taxation. But it was not until 1960, when the Committee on Fiscal Affairs of the OECD followed up on the League's efforts, that modern policies against tax evasion began to evolve. In one of the periodic bouts of retrospection and concern about the decline of U.S. competitiveness, U.S. MNEs were accused of shifting U.S. taxable incomes to offshore subsidiaries and manipulating intra-firm sales for tax purposes. Congress directed the Department of the Treasury in 1962 to issue new guidelines on transfer pricing. An amendment to the Internal Revenue Code was published in 1968, and the OECD followed that model in 1979.

The OECD Guidelines and Transfer Pricing Today

The OECD required the use of the controversial arm's-length principle for the pricing of goods and services transferred between entities under common ownership. This principle states that goods or services should be priced as they would be priced in an open market, with participants negotiating as if they were independent parties. The idea seems logical, but the sheer volume of intra-group trade suggests that transfer pricing is the norm in international trade. This limits the number of market comparisons available for establishing an appropriate price. In addition, some goods and services are made available only on an intra-group basis, and in such cases no market comparison is available to help determine an appropriate price. This happens, for example, with components traded in a half-finished state and when intellectual property or management services are traded.

For traded tangible goods, models have been built to overcome the problem, and the resulting techniques have become tried and tested over many years of use to establish what is and what is not acceptable practice. As a result, disputes among countries that have effective transfer pricing regimes in operation have probably diminished over time.

The situation with regard to intellectual property is different, not least because such assets can be easily relocated to tax havens and low-tax jurisdictions, where little activity of real substance occurs. It is these arrangements that were the subject of attack in the UK from HM Revenue & Customs in 2007, which provoked a serious backlash. Some companies threatened to move their head offices to Ireland, itself a tax haven, suggesting that the practice is widespread and any measure to stop it would be costly to companies and effective to a revenue authority that could enforce it (see also box 5.2). Clearly little has changed since Morgenthau tackled the issue—except for the sums involved and the complexity of the issue. As Ernest & Young noted in their Global Transfer Pricing Report for

2007, 40% of all MNEs thought transfer pricing the single biggest tax issue they faced, and service transactions were much more likely to face challenges than those relating to the supply of goods (Ernst & Young 2008). A significant proportion of these issues related to supply through tax havens.

For multinational corporations using those locations, transfer pricing is probably the biggest issue they face, not least from the perspective of reputation. Baker (2005) has identified the significant rate of tax evasion he thinks is facilitated by transfer pricing abuse through tax havens. In 2008 the UK-based charity Christian Aid (2008) suggested that such abuse might cost the lives of 350,000 children a year as a result of revenues lost to the governments of developing countries. Debate on the issue is not likely to end in the foreseeable future.

The debate is being fueled by a proposal from about twenty members of the European Union for the creation of a Common Consolidated Corporate Tax Base (CCCTB). This is, in effect, a proposal to create a unitary basis of taxation within a substantial part of the EU, and the only countries not participating are the UK, Ireland, Malta, Cyprus, Estonia, and Latvia (all, it should be noted, tax havens). The proposed unitary basis is likely to require large, and by implication multinational, companies registered in the EU countries concerned, to apportion profits earned to the tax jurisdictions in which they operate based on a formula that gives significant weight to the location of third-party customers, employees, and tangible assets. Tax havens are bound to lose out in this arrangement, and it poses a challenge to states that depend for tax revenues on the relocation of intangible assets used in intra-group trading. If adopted, the CCCTB would fundamentally change tax competition, by creating a multinational bloc that agrees not to compete on the tax base and to cooperate to defend that base. They will then be able to compete openly on the tax rate. The threat to tax havens in this approach is significant, and it is no surprise that it is Europe's most significant corporate tax havens that are objecting to the proposal.

The Controlled Foreign Company
(Subpart-F Legislation)

A second and related measure is "controlled foreign company" legislation. The U.S. government was discontented about the erosion of its tax base when companies operate through foreign subsidiaries in tax havens. The Kennedy administration's goal was, in president's words, the "elimination of tax deferral privileges in developed countries and 'tax havens'" President Kennedy, 2001).

A proposal submitted to Congress in 1961 met with resistance from the business lobby and the Republican opposition. Critics argued that unless U.S. corporations could divert profits to tax havens and reduce their global tax burden, they would be disadvantaged vis-à-vis foreign competitors. Ultimately, a compromise singled out certain kinds of "tax haven income" of the so-called Controlled Foreign Corporations (CFC) that might be taxed in the home jurisdiction. The rules implemented in 1962 did not include all income from foreign subsidiaries in the tax base. Rather, they singled out passive income attributable to foreign subsidiaries that had at least 50% U.S. shareholders. According to Thomas Rixen (2008), the resulting solution distinguished between "good," active business income that should continue to enjoy deferral (under the assumption there was a real economic rationale for the relocation of active business functions) and "bad," passive income that was shifted merely for tax purposes. The same solution continues to be used. In 2007 the UK sought to modify its rules for the taxation of the foreign income of companies registered in its domain using exactly this distinction (HMRC 2007).

CFC rules have been amended many times in the United States and have been adopted, despite considerable controversy, by many other countries. In 1987 the OECD suggested that all member countries should introduce unilateral anti-avoidance measures and support them with increased multilateral cooperation (Eden and Kudrle 2005). Many countries did just that. It was the UK's decision to modify and enhance these rules in 2007, so as to capture more of the passive income of MNEs headquartering in the country that led to companies threatening to relocate to Ireland (HMRC 2007). Many companies responded to CFC rules by using the technique of corporate inversion (see chapter 2). Many well-known American companies, including Ingersoll-Rand, Stanley Works, Fruit of the Loom, Tyco, and Cooper Industries have used the technique (Desai et al. 2002). Congress responded by enacting new anti-avoidance legislation against such corporate inversion schemes as part of the Jobs and Growth Tax Reconciliation Act of 2003. The rules include most of the income of inverted corporations in the domestic U.S. tax base. This issue remains unresolved. CFC rules may not be sustainable in the long term, but if they are not, then serious alternatives are needed.

"Treaty Shopping"

By the early 1980s, governments began to realize that their double tax agreements were being increasingly subject to treaty shopping by citizens of third countries. Those planning an international transaction sought more than just an ideal location for their economic activity; they also sought a preferred route in and out of the transaction so that the returns would enjoy minimal taxation. A U.S. firm wanting to invest in China might route its investment through a subsidiary incorporated in an intermediate territory such as BVI (for more on this see Vleck 2008). The technique raised the significance of locations such as Switzerland and the Netherlands, which had extensive networks of double tax treaties but which also operated favorable regimes for the taxation of dividends, royalties, and other investment income. One example of a favorable tax rule is what are called "participation exemptions," in which income already taxed before its arrival in those states suffers little or no further tax when routed through their domains, and no withholding taxes.

The first country to engage in efforts to counter this phenomenon was the United States. Many tax havens did not conclude double tax agreements themselves, being refused the right to do so because of local secrecy provisions that prevented information exchange. However, they could, either as a result of agreements dating from the early post-colonial era or by a combination of entities in different locations, achieve the same effect. For example, the U.S. treaties with the Netherlands and the UK extended to former overseas territories of both countries unless they chose to be exempted (as Cayman, for example, did in the late 1960s).

The Carter administration appointed a top tax official, Richard Gordon, to investigate tax avoidance and fraud by U.S. multinationals. The Gordon report, published in 1981, was the first serious examination of tax havens. The report proposed, in particular, unilateral termination of treaty abuses. Opponents of the proposal, led by Chase Manhattan Bank, succeeded in derailing the report. In the same year the United States abandoned its opposition to the offshore financial market (the Euromarket) and set up its own version of offshore, the IBFs. The United States sought, nonetheless, to conclude agreements on effective information exchange, among which the 1983 Caribbean Basin Initiative was the most significant. It also recommended renegotiating the U.S. tax treaty with the Netherlands and the Dutch Antilles.

Attacks on Trusts in Europe

The other issue of great concern as the 1980s progressed was the use of offshore trusts. The UK, in particular, was increasingly aware of the use of such arrangements by those not domiciled but resident in the country to avoid tax. In fact, many who were supposedly taxable in full in the UK were using these arrangements to avoid capital taxes in particular. For a brief period the UK threatened to change both its residence and its domicile rules of taxation, but the scale of opposition to the move meant instead that from 1989 on, the range of trust benefits for those fully resident in the country was reduced. These measures were replicated in other states. It is noteworthy that these were seen as issues created not by the havens themselves but rather as flaws in the UK's domestic tax legislation. There was as yet no appreciation that this was a systemic issue.

The Changing Attitude of Tax Administrations

Another response to the rise of tax havens developed through national courts and national legislations. Tax havens pose two distinct sets of problems to tax authorities: one has to do with avoidance, and the other with evasion. In terms of avoidance, tax havens are often used to defer tax, to avoid tax withholding or, in combination with other regulatory avoidance, to increase returns on capital (Belotsky 1987). There was already some discussion of the role played by the Channel Islands in facilitating tax avoidance on the UK mainland (Likhovsky 2007). However, much of the work to close loopholes, which began in the 1960s, was aimed at identifying and then terminating such arrangements. Conversely, evasion is facilitated primarily by the tight secrecy provisions provided by tax havens and results in an outright and deliberate failure to pay tax.

With regard to both sets of problems, the Gordon report states that "the Congress has never sought to eliminate tax haven operations by U.S. taxpayers. Instead, from time to time, the Congress has identified abuses and legislated to eliminate them" (Gordon Report 1981, 42). The U.S. approach was piecemeal, driven in part by media attention. Beltovsky believes that the most successful unilateral measures were the income tax treaties concluded with other countries. This "is of vast importance in relation to the tax havens problem" (Belotsky 1987, 61). It should be noted that this comment has a particular U.S. context: the United States has far more of these treaties with tax haven states than any other nation simply because of its economic power; some contain unique provisions. For example, the treaty between the United States and Cayman that permits the latter to turn over bank records in cases involved tax fraud and false tax statements. The treaty however does not cover simple tax evasion, because the islands do not have tax laws. Indeed, exchange rarely happens when there is no domestic interest in an issue. The Caymans, with no income taxes, need not hold records on the income of either corporations or natural people and as such cannot exchange it. As the havens move toward zero percent corporation tax. Such practice will become increasingly commonplace. For example, as Jersey moves to this rate for all companies it is abandoning the requirement that any company submit a tax return. At the same time, as it is beginning to enter into tax information exchange agreements, it is ceasing to hold the information other countries might need.

It is not clear whether this is the result of policy or convenient coincidence, either one of which suits those using tax havens (Belotsky 1987).

Border Skirmishes

One of the most interesting developments in the 1970s and in the 1980s was what Hudson (1998) calls border skirmishes, referring to disputes over the coverage of legal sovereignty between nations. The United States took a leadership role in pressuring Caribbean OFCs and Switzerland to relax their bank secrecy laws adopting an expanded interpretation of its own sovereignty.

In 1965 IRS Intelligence Division established Operation Tradewinds to gather information about the illicit activity of U.S. criminals in the Bahamas. The main success of the operation was the penetration of Castle Bank, a small bank with branches in the Bahamas and Cayman. Castle was involved in web of money laundering, linked to Meyer Lansky. Tony Field, the resident manager of Castle Bank in Cayman, was subpoenaed on January 12, 1976 as he waited to board a Cayman-bound flight at Miami airport. He refused to testify in front of a grand jury, citing Cayman law. The Cayman authorities eventually relented and allowed him to testify. The actions of the United States undermined Cayman as a secrecy haven. The latter responded by passing the 1976 Confidential Relationships (Preservation) Law, strengthening its bank secrecy promises.

The next important border skirmish was *United States v Bank of Nova Scotia* (1982), immortalized in the 1987 movie *Wall Street*. The Canadian bank's branch in Miami was asked to give to a grand jury a document held in its Bahamas branch about the banking transactions of a U.S. taxpayer. U.S. agencies subpoenaed the Miami branch of the Bank of Nova Scotia for the documents, and when the offshore branch refused to hand over the documents, citing Bahamian confidentiality laws, the bank was fined $50,000 a day for contempt of court, later increased to $100,000. "In effect, the Miami agency was held to ransom" (Hudson 1998, 550). Eighteen months and $1.8 million later, the bank relented. In this and other cases, the United States demonstrated its willingness to pressure the small Caribbean havens to a greater extent than international law seemed to permit.

This tendency has not ceased. In May 2008 Martin Liechti, a senior executive with the private banking division of the major Swiss bank UBS, was arrested at Miami airport. Liechti, Mario Staggl, an executive with a trust company in Liechtenstein, and others are accused of helping U.S. billionaire Igor Olenicoff evade taxes. According to the indictment, about $200 million (€129 million) was sheltered from tax authorities "in secret bank accounts in Switzerland and Liechtenstein." Prosecutors allege that Staggl's attorney in Gibraltar helped Olenicoff hide the details of his ownership of a 147-foot yacht, and that those indicted forged the special forms that Swiss banks use to report their U.S. customers' capital gains to the U.S. tax authority, the Internal Revenue Service. The case presents UBS with a dilemma. It needs to protect its employee if others are not to lose confidence in the bank. It also needs to protect banking secrecy, but at the same time it wants to retain its license to operate in the United States. It seems likely that the move against bank secrecy is now entering a new stage in which the employees of global banks are pawns in the game.

Criminalization of Money Laundering

Money laundering seems to provoke more public indignation than tax evasion and is considered by some to have "been the most prominent ostensible theme of the anti-OFC campaign" (Van Fossen 2003, 251). The quest to "take the profit out of crime" has targeted bankers, lawyers, accountants, and professional advisers (who created offshore structures for their clients) as much as conventional criminals.

The United States once again took the lead. In the early and mid-1980s the U.S. Senate Permanent Subcommittee on Investigations exposed the criminal use of offshore banks in the Northern Marianas (U.S. Senate 1983). The subcommittee's work did not get much media exposure; nevertheless, it prompted the passage of the Money Laundering Control Act of 1986. This legislation (the first in the world to criminalize money laundering), was followed by an expanded and far more comprehensive International Counter-Money Laundering Act of 2000.

The new initiatives faced considerable opposition, and Democrats appealed to Republicans by framing the problem in terms of drugs and a new Cold War against (Russian) organized crime. James Woolsey, former CIA director, testified in congressional hearings that Russian capital flight and laundering had the potential to corrupt U.S. institutions, destabilize Russia, and increase anti-U.S. sentiments there. Congressional hearings on Russian money laundering "constructed a vision of how the new Russian threat had evolved out of the KGB and the former USSR" (quoted in van Fossen 2003, 249). Money laundering efforts were later linked with the struggle against terrorism finance in the United States.

The UK Treasury versus the UK Inland Revenue

The UK has, as we have noted, played a unique role in the development of tax havens. Some of the more successful havens are UK dependencies, and "successive governments encouraged the overseas territories and dependencies to establish themselves as tax havens" (Hampton and Christensen 1998, 1659). But while the Treasury and Foreign Office worked together to develop UK dependencies as tax havens, the Inland Revenue took a different view. In 1981, the UK Inland Revenue issued a Consultative Document—propositions about official policy regarding tax havens. The document led to conflicting public sentiments. Many changes were suggested, including the concept of a person's residence in the UK and his or her right to use tax haven trusts. The former did not happen, the latter did. Just as significant was another change, in the rule established in the Egyptian Delta case locating a company where its center of control was based—usually where its Board of Directors met. The UK changed its law so that a company incorporated in the UK was usually resident in the UK for tax purposes. As HM Revenue & Customs' manual notes,

> There has never been a statutory definition of what makes a company resident for the general purposes of the Taxes Acts. Yet it has long been recognised that the residence of a company is determined according to where its central management and control is to be found. That is still so even though since 1988 a company incorporated in the United Kingdom is, with some exceptions, regarded as resident in the United Kingdom for the purposes of the Taxes Acts. That rule overrides but does not eliminate the test of central management and control. (HMRC 2008)

It is important to note the exception: even now a UK company can be non-resident if it can convince HM Revenue & Customs that it is wholly taxable in a country with a double tax treaty with the UK. Some tax havens have such treaties and so ambiguities remain, at least in theory.

German Reaction

Next to the United States the country that traditionally pushes hardest against tax havens has been Germany. In the 1980s, Germany introduced a series of laws to counter the widespread flight of German capital, much of it to the neighboring states of Switzerland and Luxembourg. The German government pursued a two-pronged policy. First, it closed certain tax loopholes and then introduced additional regulations to prevent the outflow of MNE funds to specific tax havens. The U.S. Real Estate Investment Trusts (REITS) and Regulated Investment Companies (RICs), which are not taxed in the United States as companies, have been considered a problem in Germany. Germany also renegotiated its double tax treaty with Ireland to prevent some opportunities for abuse that arose from the establishment of the Dublin Financial Services Centre and from other Irish tax incentives. In 1994, Germany decided to cut its corporate tax rates, citing international competition. This is a process that continues, and the complexity of the German tax regime is still quoted as a reason for German tax evasion. The matter came to a head in 2008 as the Liechtenstein affair became a major political issue in Germany and in those neighboring countries that supply the services used to undermine its tax regime. In May 2008 Konrad Hummler, a partner in the Swiss private bank Wegelin & Co., told *Der Spiegel* that "German tax evasion is a legitimate defense by citizens attempting to partially escape the current grasp of the administrators of a disastrous social welfare state and its fiscal policies. Swiss-style saving outside the system is something to which not only the wealthy, but also productive small and mid-size businesses are entitled. These people must be protected" (quoted in Balzli and Hornig 2008). Some might say that the battle lines have been drawn.

Policy in France

France adopted tax avoidance legislation as far back as 1933 (Godefroy and Lascoumes 2004). Yet serious political mobilization against money laundering and tax havens occurred only in late 1990s. The advent of a Socialist government in 1981 stimulated considerable capital flight from France, and stories told of backpackers serving as couriers and carrying sacks of cash from Paris to Luxembourg. A French Assembly report at the time implicated shell companies in Luxembourg, Switzerland, and the Channel Islands as the principal conduits for capital flight.

In 1996, seven European judges made the now famous "appel de Genève," condemning leniency regarding tax havens. Two members of parliament followed the appeal by launching a parliamentary investigation of Liechtenstein, Monaco, Switzerland, Luxembourg, and the UK (Peillon and Montebourg 2000, 2001). In 1998 France became one of the principal backers of the OECD campaign. Indeed, the minister of finance, Dominique Strauss-Kahn—currently managing director of the IMF—went so far as to call publicly for international sanctions against tax havens (Les paradis fiscaux, 1999).

Conclusion

Tax avoidance and evasion was emerging as an important issue of national politics in the 1920s in the majority of industrialized countries. By the 1930s, a dedicated professional literature on evasion and avoidance had emerged (Likhovsky 2007, 207). However, avoidance and evasion were debated largely within a domestic context. With the rare exception of legal cases and even rarer exceptions of public uproar, tax havens did not attract much attention before the 1980s. Even then, criticisms remained largely at the national and regional levels.

From the 1980s on, the new phenomenon of what Hudson calls border skirmishes between the large industrialized countries and individual tax havens began to grow. Led initially by the United States, and then by Germany, these local skirmishes yielded some successes in specific cases. Nonetheless, the 1980s and 1990s were the golden years of the tax havens.

Chapter 9

Institutional Attacks on Tax Havens

By the late 1990s, the left-of-center governments of the United States, France, and Germany led international organizations toward a much more aggressive attack on offshore financial centers. As we have seen, the United States took the lead throughout the twentieth century in developing unilateral measures against tax havens, particularly those located in the Caribbean. The Clinton administration sought to extend the same methods and tactics multilaterally.

The years 1998–2000 saw the beginning of a new phase in international efforts to combat the deleterious effects of tax havens. A coordinated three-pronged attack was pursued by separate international organizations. The OECD developed its campaign against harmful tax competition at the request of the G7, the FSF tackled financial stability, and the FATF money laundering. The Clinton administration, in particular, saw clear links between money laundering and tax evasion and so linked the FATF and OECD campaigns.

The first major joint report on anti-laundering strategies by the U.S. departments of Treasury and Justice was released in 2000. It explicitly linked laundering, tax avoidance, and a weakening of the global financial architecture as related problems to be pursued with offshore centers. There were already close links between the FATF and the OECD—not least because the FATF secretariat is located at OECD headquarters in Paris—and an OECD report published in 2000 drew links between bank secrecy, money laundering, and tax evasion.

To clean up such practices, the OECD chose a technique unusual in international affairs, "blacklisting" countries and territories that were harming their neighbors. This politics of "name and shame" put political pressures on tax havens.

The Committee on Fiscal Affairs of the OECD got the ball rolling in April 2000 with a report on "harmful tax competition." The report condemned practices aimed at attracting foreign capital. Forty-seven tax havens had been identified at the end of 1999 as practicing harmful tax competition, but the list that the OECD made public in June 2000 included only thirty-five jurisdictions. Six territories had been removed from the list before publication after pledging to make immediate reforms: Bermuda, the Cayman Islands, Cyprus, Malta, Mauritius, and San Marino. (The other six territories dropped from the list are unknown.)

The Financial Stability Forum (FSF), established in 1999 to help build a new financial architecture after the crises of the 1990s, established its own list of non-cooperating jurisdictions. Forty-two countries were listed by the FSF in 2000, divided into three groups according to the estimated level of risk.

The same year saw the publication of a third list, by the Financial Action Task Force on Money Laundering (FATF), established in 1989 as a financial arm of the international fight against narcotics trafficking. The FATF identified twenty-nine territories by the end of 1999 and listed fifteen "non-cooperative countries and territories" in June 2000.

FATF: The Politics of Name and Shame

Criminalization of money laundering began in the early 1980s, but multilateral efforts soon followed. In 1988, the United Nations adopted the Convention against Illicit Traffic in Narcotic Drugs and Psychotropic Substances, the so-called Vienna Convention. It was the first international agreement to require the criminalization of narcotics-related money laundering. A year later FATF was established.

The FATF is a group of experts set up under the auspices of the G7 group of nations, charged with making recommendations on legislative and regulatory measures to combat money laundering. In its deliberations, the group distinguished two sets of difficulties with current cooperation against laundering: direct legal or practical impediments to cooperation, and indirect ones (FATF 2000b, 2). Among the latter, the FATF raised the alarm about "obstacles designed to restrict the supervisory and investigative powers" (2000b, 2). Most countries that had gone out of their way to set up such obstacles were, of course, tax havens. The FATF in particular flagged its concern with loopholes in financial regulation, excessive secrecy provisions, lack of an efficient or mandatory reporting system for suspicious transactions, and the backbone of the tax havens' strategy—shell corporations and nominees. It considered these tactics, widely used mechanisms to launder the proceeds of crime, and bribery as key issues (2000b, 5).

The FATF made little progress during the 1990s. Led by the United States, it ran out of patience with its consensual, lead-by-example approach and adopted the name and shame method in 2000 (Wechsler 2001). Sharman calls it a shift from "white listing" and capacity building toward blacklisting. By 1999 the FATF had begun work on a list of Non-Cooperative Countries and Territories (the NCCT list), jurisdictions accused of failing to meet minimum standards. It published the first NCCT list in June 2000. Subsequently, countries said to have "serious systemic problems" in their approach to dealing with money laundering were added. Sanctions were set out for those listed countries and territories that failed to take action. A jurisdiction can be removed from the list only on demonstrating that it has introduced and is implementing a specified package of laws and regulations.

The Forty Recommendations and the Reaction among Tax Havens

Central to the FATF process was a list of forty recommendations, drawn up in 1990 and subsequently revised on several occasions. The recommendations are highly detailed, comprehensive, and clear. FATF recommendations emphasize the role of national legislatures, including those of tax havens, in combating money laundering. The FATF established clear principles of due diligence, clarified the problems with non-financial institutions in tax havens, and suggested measures to rectify the problem. It identified in particular the difficulties in the use of bearer shares and offshore trusts. It noted with concern, as Morgenthau had in 1937, "the use of professionals, such as lawyers, notaries, and accountants, by organized crime and other criminals" and added that "In many countries, these professionals also specialize in the creation and management of companies and other legal entities or arrangements, thus providing other services useful to the money launderer" (2006, 1–2). Although not concerned specifically with tax havens, FATF appears to be the most successful of the three-pronged attacks upon them, perhaps precisely because its focus has been on a different problem.

The problem is that the reaction of tax havens to the FATF has become ritualistic. It has gone through a series of stages typical of their reaction to other campaigns. The initial reaction is negative and accusatory. FATF was accused of "institutional imperialism." George McCarthy, financial secretary of the Cayman Islands and former president of the Caribbean FATF, declared himself "astonished" that the Caymans should be categorized as non-cooperative. The Cayman Islands, he claimed, had long adopted a policy of cooperation with international bodies. For example, in 1996 it had, in response to the forty recommendations, introduced its Proceeds of Criminal Conduct Law, established related anti-money laundering regulations, and set up the Cayman Islands Monetary Authority (CIMA). The FATF, however, was not persuaded and placed the Caymans on its list all the same.

Then, with one or two exceptions, most tax havens declared themselves ready to cooperate with the FATF. The shrewder havens such as Switzerland, Cayman, and Jersey passed FATF recommendations into law as soon as possible. Switzerland penalized insider trading from 1988, money laundering from 1990, stock-market manipulation from 1997, and bribery of foreign officials from 2000 (Chaikin 2005, 100). Under pressure from the FATF, Switzerland amended in 2003 its money laundering laws and now requires Swiss banks to identify customers by name when transferring money abroad (2005, 102). Similarly, Cayman introduced new laws and regulations, including the Securities Investment Business Law in 2001, and provided for the licensing of investment managers and advisers. By 2001, it finally managed to have itself removed from the FATF list. Among the Pacific islands, the Cook Islands, Nauru, and the Marshall Islands also took quick action to get off the blacklist (Van Fossen 2003, 256).

But in our opinion, the reality is not so positive. Rules are either not enforced or unenforceable, a description that holds true for other campaigns as well. Indeed, Hampton and Christensen suggest that "the rush to legislation might be a window dressing exercise" (2002, 1662). They have a point, and a British National Audit report of British overseas territories in 2007 says as much (NAO 2007). Noting apparently intense efforts to create laws and regulations, the report concludes that "the main challenge across all Territories is to respond adequately to growing pressure to reinforce defenses against money laundering and terrorist financing" (NAO 2007, 5). Reporting of suspicious activities is still "suspiciously low" (NAO 2007, 23). Table 9.1, reproduced from the report, is unfortunately self-explanatory. The report also notes that superficial signs of success—Jersey reported 1,162 cases of suspected money laundering, and the Isle of Man 1,652—are misleading. It adds (in small print) "very high levels of reporting can be indicative of defensive reporting of trivial cases" (NAO 2007, 23). This is confirmed in appendix 3 of the Jersey Police Report of 2006 (Jersey Police Report 2006), which states that not a single case of criminal money laundering had been reported in that jurisdiction in 2006, and so none had been investigated. The Cayman Islands, the fourth- or fifth largest financial center in the world, has had just five successful prosecutions of money laundering since 1997, while in Switzerland, "Geneva prosecutors have yet to achieve successful prosecutions in a variety of cases in-

Table 9.1   Level of monitoring and investigation of suspicious financial activity

Territory	No. of suspicious reports 2005	Est. employees	Financial intelligence and investigative capability	No. of successful prosecutions
Bermuda	313 (2006)	4,000	11	0
Cayman Is.	244	5,400	21	2
BVI	101	1,600	5.5	0
Gibraltar	108	1,500	8	0 (1 pending)
Turks	17	700	5	0 (3 pending)
Anguilla	2	150	1	0
Montserrat	1	150	1	0
Jersey	1,162	11,800	22(2003)	
Isle of Man	1,652	7,010	22	

Source: NAO 2007, 23.

volving Russian-related money laundering" (Hampton and Christensen 2002, 1662). The reality on the ground is not encouraging.

The FATF process suffers on two other counts. First, Anthony Van Fossen reports a perception among Pacific offshore centers that they were disproportionately stigmatized because they lacked powerful allies.

> Intensive lobbying by France was said to be responsible for the exclusion of Monaco from the FATF blacklist. The United Kingdom insisted that Bermuda, the British Virgin Islands, Gibraltar, Guernsey, the Isle of Man, and Jersey not be included, but it had to concede the Cayman Islands (which was listed in June 2000 but later removed from the blacklist in June 2001). Canada successfully intervened to have the Caribbean countries that it represents at the International Monetary Fund (Antigua and Barbuda, Belize, and St Lucia) dropped from the blacklist. Mexico, a FATF member country that is sometimes considered to be a major non-OFC laundering center, interceded to help Panama, which was removed from the blacklist in June 2001. (Van Fossen 2003, 247)

He could have added the biggest anomaly of the FATF process, which is the widely held view that the principal conduits for money laundering are the world's largest financial centers, London and New York.

Allegations of political favoritism appear not without substance, particularly when seen in the context of a very thorough report by the U.S. Bureau for International Narcotics and Law Enforcement Affairs. The INCSR Report contains a list of fifty-seven countries and jurisdictions considered "countries of primary concern for money laundering" (2008, 70). The list contains all the major industrialized countries including the United States, the UK, Germany, Japan, and China. Tax havens are a

minority of the countries of primary concern, but among them are some
that were removed from the FATF list because of alleged politicking. The
tax havens considered by the Bureau to be of primary concern are: Antigua and Barbuda, Bahamas, Belize, Cayman Islands, Costa Rica, Cyprus,
Guernsey, Hong Kong, Isle of Man, Jersey, Latvia, Liechtenstein, Luxembourg, Panama, Singapore, and Switzerland. This U.S. list does not correspond closely to the FATF blacklist. It appears that FATF has concentrated
on the small fish.

The politics of blacklisting has damaged the campaign considerably.
Most experts agree that money laundering worldwide is not in retreat,
nor has the role of tax havens declined in facilitating criminality (see in
particular INCSR 2008).

The Nine Recommendations on Terrorist Financing

The FATF found an unexpected ally in Osama bin Laden. In response
to the terrorist attacks of 2001, the United States in particular sought to
clamp down on "terrorist financing" that it suspected was operating
through tax havens. R. T. Naylor (2002) says that the United States has good
reason to be worried about the financing of terrorist activities through tax
havens; the CIA, after all, used tax havens for its clandestine operations for
many years. The FATF jumped on the bandwagon with a release in 2001 of
nine Special Recommendations on terrorist financing, lifted from the
FATF's forty recommendations of 1990 (FATF 2001).

The FATF had categorized money laundering, terrorist financing, and
tax crime as the same (Masciandaro 2004). The mundane reality was that,
as the Bush administration correctly pointed out, anti-laundering measures would not have stopped the terrorist attacks of 9/11 because the
funds used to finance those attacks were not criminal in origins and so
had not been laundered (Rawlings 2005, 296). The few terrorist-financing
prosecutions to date in the United States involved domestic banking institutions (INCSR 2008, 52–58). Notwithstanding, a Council on Foreign
Relations report noted that "For years, Al-Qaeda has been particularly
attracted to operating in . . . under regulated jurisdictions, places with
limited bank supervision, no anti-money laws, ineffective law enforcement institutions, and a culture of no-questions-ask ban secrecy" (2002,
9). Among such jurisdictions the report names regional banking centers
in the Middle East, Dubai, Kuwait, Bahrain, and Lebanon, but also Paki-
stan and the Caribbean offshore, Liechtenstein, and the United States itself (2002, 9).

In line with these contradictory messages, the U.S. Patriot Act removed
any mention of tax havens but reemphasized the measures contained in
the FATF's forty recommendations. It reaffirmed the power of the Trea-

sury Secretary to prohibit transactions with jurisdictions "of primary money laundering concern," most of which, as we have noted, are not conventionally recognized tax havens.

Creation of the "Know Your Client Concept"

Underpinning the entire approach to money laundering and tax evasion has been the requirement that financial service intermediaries "know their clients." As the FATF said in 2006, "it seems clear that prevention of corporate vehicle misuse for money laundering purposes could be improved by knowing or being in a position to determine in a timely fashion who is the ultimate beneficial owner of a company and who are the trustees, settlors, beneficiaries involved with a trust" (FATF 2006, 21). "In theory," the report adds, "it matters less who maintains the required information on corporate vehicles . . . provided that the information on beneficial ownership exists" (2006, 21).

The Financial Stability Forum (FSF)

The Financial Stability Forum was established in the aftermath of the 1997–98 Asian financial crisis to help establish "new international financial architecture." The FSF's brief is not directly related to tax havens, and it distanced itself from the OECD's initiative against harmful tax competition (Sharman 2006). Yet as we saw, the FSF ad hoc Working Group on Offshore Financial Centers ended up concentrating on tax havens.

The FSF is a select group of predominantly large, rich countries that set down universal standards and rate how nonmember jurisdictions measure up. Aside from endorsing broad principles of transparency and good governance, the FSF adopted the "name and shame" method by classifying countries and jurisdictions into three groups: (I) co-operative jurisdictions with a high quality of supervision; (II) those having procedures for supervision and co-operation where actual performance falls below international standards; and (III) those with a low quality of supervision and non-co-operation (FSF 2000, 46). An FSF press release in May 2000 listed the following countries in group III: Anguilla, Antigua and Barbuda, Aruba, Bahamas, Belize, British Virgin Islands, Cayman Islands, Cook Islands, Costa Rica, Cyprus, Lebanon, Liechtenstein, Marshall Islands, Nauru, Netherlands Antilles, Nauru, Panama, Samoa, Seychelles, St. Kitts and Nevis, St. Lucia, St. Vincent and the Grenadines, Turks and Caicos, and Vanuatu. The FSF did not create a clear set of incentives for jurisdictions to get off the list: "It more or less passed the buck to the IMF" (Tranoy 2002, 14).

Predictably, these offshore centers criticized the FSF "for being merely a collection of anecdotal views of a number of metropolitan onshore regulators" (Van Fossen 2003, 255). One serious problem is the FSF's method of data collection. It relies almost exclusively on national supervisors for information and for their judgment of the quality of supervision. The cats are put in charge of the cream, with predictably anodyne results.

The FSF has yet to achieve the impact of the FATF or the OECD. As to tax havens, it recommended that the IMF be made responsible for coordinating assessment of OFCs.

The Campaign against Harmful Tax Competition

The most significant development in the battle against tax havens came in 1998 with the publication of a landmark OECD report titled "Harmful Tax Competition: An Emerging Global Issue" (OECD 1998). The OECD and FATF reports were published at about the same time and the FSF report followed soon after, creating the impression of a concerted global campaign against tax evasion. The three reports generated great media and academic interest. They overshadowed, at the time, a separate if related announcement by the EU Council of a code of conduct on business taxation (ECOFIN 1999). Combined, these developments signaled the beginning of a new stage in the life of tax havens.

The 1998 OECD report makes extensive references to the EU Code of Conduct. The two, however, are rather different, and the differences, which are discussed below, somewhat explain why the OECD has been sidelined while the EU has emerged as a key institution in the battle against tax havens.

The origins of the OECD report can be traced back to the early 1990s, to the coming to power of left-of-center governments in all the major industrialized countries. These governments had a commitment to socialized health and education, redistribution, and the conditions of the poor in their societies. Yet they were not prepared to sacrifice the so-called neoliberal goals of low inflation, low budget deficits, and low taxation. An enforcement of tax rules and the eradication of tax abuses appeared a logical solution that would reconcile these two apparently contradictory goals.

As we saw in the previous chapter, the Clinton administration identified clear links between money laundering, criminality, and tax evasion, and strongly favored multilateral efforts to curb all three forms of abuse (Kudrle 2003). By the early 1990s it was clear that serious and concerted international efforts were required to achieve these goals (Kudrle and Eden 2003; Eden and Kudrle 2005). The turning point came in 1996 (Radaelli 2003; Sharman 2006), when at their 1996 summit in Lyons, the finance ministers of the G-7 called upon the OECD to "develop measures to counter the distorting effects of harmful tax competition on investment and financing decisions . . . and report back in 1998" (OECD 1998, 3).

Before we discuss the report campaigns, we need to deal with other important issues often ignored in such discussions.

The OECD Campaign and the End of Neoliberalism

The OECD frames its report within two sets of theoretical understandings. First, it seeks to link the timing and rationale for the report to changes in the international environment, specifically to globalization. Globalization is considered broadly a positive development but left to its own devices, the report warns, it can generate negative effects, particularly in the area of taxation and fiscal policies. Second, the OECD report accepts and indeed promotes the principle of international tax competition.

The reference to globalization is significant. The report states clearly: "the OECD believes that the progressive liberalization of cross-border trade and investment has been the single most powerful driving force behind economic growth and rising living standards" (1998, 9). But, it warns, "globalization has, however, also had the negative effects of opening new ways by which companies and individuals can minimize and avoid taxes and in which countries can exploit these new opportunities by developing tax policies aimed primarily at diverting financial and other geographically mobile capital" (1998, 14). Economic liberalization set in motion a double-edged competitive dynamic, as "tax schemes aimed at attracting financial and other geographically mobile activities can create harmful tax competition and could lead to the erosion of national tax base"(OECD 1998, 7).

The OECD clearly seeks to present its proposals on harmful tax competition as measures intended to support liberalization and globalization. It calls for adjustments to be made to the international system to "safeguard and promote an open, multilateral trading system" (1998, 9). Combined with an explicit commitment to the principles of international tax competition, the report is unambiguously neoliberal in tone. Yet the report, as well as the campaign that it helped to launch, could be seen—and indeed was seen by its critics—as signaling a fundamental change in the direction of the multilateral regime. In the name of preserving the gains from globalization, multilateral efforts have shifted from narrow neoliberal concerns—deregulation and privatization, low inflation and low taxation—toward reregulation of the markets and "good governance," leading to current concerns with climate change and unfettered capitalism (Chavagneux 2009).

These shifts in policy are typical of left-of-center governments in Europe and the United States. It was no surprise that as a Republican president came to power in 2001, the United States soon abandoned the OECD campaign. The campaign has seemed to falter ever since, leading to considerable soul searching and criticism of the OECD (Sharman 2006). Yet the OECD campaign was not an isolated incident. Under the Bush administration, the United States abandoned multilateralism and reverted, at least for tax havens, to its traditional policy of aggressive unilateralism. Seen narrowly in terms of the issues of money laundering, tax evasion and avoidance, and criminality, the faltering OECD campaign may be interpreted as a political coup perpetrated by well-organized tax havens and their supporters. Seen from the broader perspective of the battle between a go-it-alone Bush administration and the post-neoliberalism of the EU, it is not at all obvious that the campaign against harmful tax competition is faltering. On the contrary, the EU has taken over, becoming the standard-bearer and driving international policy regarding tax havens.

The OECD and Harmful Tax Competition

The OECD's 1998 report was seen at the time as different from both the FATF and FSF reports, for its uniquely strong and unambiguous language describing the deleterious effect of harmful tax competition perpetrated in particular by tax havens. The report alleges that harmful tax competition has the following effects:

1. Affects location of financial and other services,
2. Erodes the tax base of other countries,
3. Distorts trade and investment patterns,
4. Diminishes global welfare,
5. Erodes the fairness of the tax system and undermines taxpayer confidence in the integrity of the tax system.

The report raises two sets of concerns, and the tension between them was not resolved. One concern is of a macroeconomic nature, and the other has to do with democracy and justice. The macroeconomic concerns raised by the OECD report have to do with the distorting effects of tax havens on markets. The assumption is that market distortion of any sort damages the markets' ability to deliver optimum results, or in the language of the report diminishes global welfare. The other concern has to do with a sense of injustice and eroding fairness, which may lead to a lack of confidence in the system of taxation.

Although the report does not distinguish between the two issues, the OECD is clearly far more concerned with the first than the second. Not only is the second set of concerns mentioned less frequently, often as subsidiary issues, but the OECD's proposals are aimed primarily at macroeconomic distortions in the belief that the sense of injustice will dissolve if the distortion problem is fixed. The OECD's principal objection to tax havens is that "location decisions [of MNEs] should be driven by economic considerations and not primarily by tax factors" (1998, 9), meaning that tax havens and harmful tax competition should be viewed as distorting mechanisms. The implication is that despite appearances, low taxation should be equated not with liberalism but with the distorting practices perpetrated by states.

The OECD's proposed solution was intended to prepare what it described as a "level playing field." The concept of the level playing field is ambiguous; it has an ethical ring to it, but the OECD primarily intends it in macroeconomic terms, to ensure markets free of political distortion. FDI and relocation decisions should be driven by economic goals. Here we agree with critics of the OECD. The OECD perhaps should have learned from the long experience of the EU, which never succeeded in converting the theory of market distortion and fiscal competition to tangible policy (Radaelli 2003). Only after the EU made the crucial link to abuse in 1996, did its policies begin to gather pace (Radaelli 2003; Sharman 2006).

The Politics of Blacklisting

The OECD and the EU faced the same intractable problem of definitions that we discussed in chapter 1. They both solved the problem by establishing a distinction between two sets of states, tax havens and those states practicing harmful preferential tax regimes (PTRs) (OECD 1998, 8). Tax havens are defined by the OECD along the lines of the "pure" tax havens, while PTRs are more complex. PTR countries offer a great variety of preferential treatment to foreign investors not available to domestic investors (OECD 1998, 57–79). The distinction between the two categories was motivated, Thomas Rixen (2008) believes, by the idea that the two types of countries should have different incentives to cooperate against harmful practices. However lucrative PTRs may be to vested interests, several tax havens rely on their offshore sector for the bulk of their revenues. From the outset the OECD expected that tax havens would be a much harder nut to crack, and developed its policies accordingly.

There are no objective criteria for distinguishing harmful from harmless tax competition. As we saw earlier, Germany was concerned more by U.S. investment vehicles, Belgium's coordination centers, and the so-called Irish doc companies than by the traditional tax havens. Yet the OECD, as a club of rich nations, found a way to separate good and bad in a way that appears to critics to be rather advantageous to its membership. The OECD recognizes that the wide array of investment incentives and so-called sweeteners might be considered tax competition but excludes them from its definition of harmful practices (1998, 15). The OECD also recognizes the problem of "mismatching," the unintentional loopholes that emerge because of different tax regimes, but seek to differentiate them from "poaching," which it labels harmful (1998, 16).

The OECD recognizes that Switzerland and Luxembourg are tax havens but seems to be unwilling or unable to force them to change their policies. Its progress reports contain useful descriptions of the practices of each country. They are checked off as either "amended to remove potentially harmful features," "not harmful," or "harmful." When it comes to Switzerland and Luxembourg, some boxes are left unchecked, without explanation. Boxes are checked only when a country eventually amends its rule. By keeping silent about certain practices, the 2004 progress report was able to given the impression of very good news.

Tax havens are in a much weaker position vis-à-vis other countries, not least because they are not subtle about their techniques. Lack of taxation or minimal taxation, "ring fencing," "exempt companies," bank secrecy laws, lack of transparency, and lack of effective exchange of information are fairly uncontroversial cases of abuse. Indeed, some tax havens go out of their way to advertise themselves as "tax minimization vehicles," announcing loud and clear their intention of poaching revenue from other countries. Tax havens are described by the OECD rather forcefully as "free riders of general public goods created by the non-haven country" (1998, 15) and "poachers" (1998, 16). The OECD goes so far as to invent a new "industrial sector" to describe them, noting that "many havens have chosen to be heavily dependent on their tax industries" (1998, 10)—"tax industries" being a creative term for "rent."

The OECD set up three criteria to identify harmful regime. They all match up well with the practices of tax havens:

   i. Does the tax regime shift activity from one country to the country providing the preferential tax regime rather than generate new activity?
   ii. Is the presence and level of activities in the host country commensurate with the amount of investment or income?
   iii. Is the preferential tax regime the primary motivation for the location of an activity? (OECD 1998, 34–37).

The OECD is a think tank and in reality could do little more than build up peer pressure by naming and shaming states that practice harmful tax competition (Webb 2004). The key to the OECD process was a promised list of non-cooperative jurisdictions, to be released by the end of 2001. Ominously, the 1998 report recommends that its members adopt serious defensive measures against non-cooperative countries. These measures include terminating tax treaties; disallowing deductions, exemptions, credits, and so on related to transaction with non-cooperative jurisdictions; effectively boycotting such jurisdictions; and terminating nonessential assistance to these jurisdictions. The OECD chose a tight deadline for tax haven cooperation but a more lenient five-year deadline on removal of PTRs.

The Neutering of the Campaigns

The OECD posed a serious challenge to tax havens. The publication of the report was greeted by tax havens in a familiar way, with accusations of bullying, imperialism, and interference with the sovereignty of small states, followed by declaration of intended, or apparent, cooperation. By 2001, the OECD was able to declare a modicum of success and it reported that six countries had already complied with its recommendations. A 2000 report lists thirty-five countries and territories (OECD 2000) that were asked to sign a "Memorandum of Understanding" (MOU) with the OECD by July 31, 2001 with an understanding of changing their regimes.

Van Fossen (2003) notes that the response of tax havens was highly uneven. The British and Dutch dependencies have tended to comply, or make all the right noises suggesting that they have complied, whereas the more independent and perhaps less savvy Pacific islands put up stiffer resistance. A few tax havens with small offshore centers lost the will to fight and surrendered to the OECD demands. Tonga repealed its offshore banking legislation in August 2001, as did the Seychelles, the Netherlands Antilles, and the Isle of Man. Soon, however, the OECD began to falter, for reasons that are still debated today.

The more successful tax havens were not prepared to give up without a fight. The authorities of Barbados led the offensive, establishing in 2001 the International Tax Investment Organization (ITIO), a pressure group in the service of tax havens. Among the Pacific atolls, the Cook Islands, which managed to get itself on all three blacklists, shaped the regional response, which was one of defiance (Van Fossen 2003). The ITIO is judged to have been a great success in derailing the OECD campaign.

In fairness, the battle against the OECD had begun before the publication of the 1998 report. Luxembourg and Switzerland abstained from the 1998 report, complaining that "by voluntarily limiting itself to financial activities, excluding industrial and commercial activities, the Report . . . adopts a partial and unbalanced approach" (OECD 1998, 74). Both pointed out a bias against highly mobile capital, their specialty, as opposed to the traditional sweeteners practiced by virtually all OECD countries. It may come as no surprise that neither saw any necessary link between bank secrecy and harmful tax practices, and both sought to remove references to bank secrecy from the agenda. Switzerland complained that the report "does not give territories that make tax attraction a pillar of their economies an incentive to associate themselves with the regulation of the conditions of competition" (OECD 1998, 78). Switzerland, which like Luxembourg denies that it is a tax haven, signaled its concerns about rising competition from Singapore and the Caymans, simultaneously managing to deny and confirm its status as a tax haven.

The ITIO adopted many of Luxembourg and Switzerland's points. Some believe that business interests were involved behind the scene in derailing the OECD campaign, as they had done in the inter-war years and again in the 1980s. Libertarian groups were certainly heavily involved in the battle against the OECD, believing for one reason or another that tax havens are advancing a libertarian agenda. In a highly detailed and careful examination, Jason Sharman (2006) found little factual evidence for any concerted business lobbying campaign. Other observers blame the confused message and the lack of impartiality from the OECD, combined with a lack of political will on the part of its member countries (Godefroy and Lascoumes 2004; Maillard 2001). To this Sharman adds a further factor: the sophisticated politicking and rhetorical tactics used by tax havens.

The ITIO put forward three counterpoints. First, tax havens were not consulted during the early stages in the design of OECD policies. Thus, an externally imposed set of criteria reflected OECD membership and interests. This was the familiar set of accusations about imperialism and neo-colonialism. Second, the ITIO pointed out that while the OECD threatened economic sanctions against blacklisted non-cooperative countries, it did not threaten OECD members with any sanctions (Van Fossen 2003, 257). In addition, the ITIO pointed out that the two-year timetable for cooperation was very short and suggested that the OECD was not serious about cooperating with tax havens. Furthermore, the OECD showed remarkably little interest in U.S. states such as Montana and Colorado, which passed offshore banking laws in 1997 and 1999, respectively, that appeared to violate OECD demands (Van Fossen 2003, 259).

The ITIO argued that the OECD may have violated the nondiscrimination provisions of international trade law because it differentiated between tax havens and PTRs. Several Pacific and Caribbean centers threatened to take the matter to the World Trade Organization. This gave credence to the argument that the OECD initiative attempted to protect the privileged positions of its own financial centers (e.g., Paris, Frankfurt, New York) against incursions from other centers with comparative tax advantages in a period of growing financial deregulation and mobility. Thus, they argued, the OECD was attempting to change the rules of a free market and proposing to enforce a comprehensive system of protectionism with an array of punitive sanctions (Sharman 2006).

Last but not least, some tax havens claimed, correctly, that they had been advised by institutions like the IMF and the World Bank, as well as their home countries (in the case of British and Dutch dependencies), to specialize in financial services. Now the mood had changed, and they were left high and dry.

These were strong arguments. Yet perhaps the most significant reason for the faltering OECD campaign had little to do with the quality of the arguments and more to do with changes that took place in the United States in 2001.

The Bush Administration

The Clinton administration, as we saw, supported the OECD project and planned to implement the OECD recommendations in national legislation. All payments to any of the thirty-five listed tax havens would have had to be reported to U.S. tax authorities. The government also considered the termination of credits for taxes paid at source in these countries (Kudrle 2003; Rixen 2008). The arrival of George W. Bush in the White House changed the political situation.

In May 2001, the new U.S. finance minister, Paul O'Neil, signaled a radical shift in policy. The OECD project, he announced, was "too broad and . . . not in line with this Administration's tax and economic priorities." The United States, he declared, "does not support efforts to dictate to any country what its own tax rates or tax system should be, and will not participate in any initiative to harmonize world tax systems" (U.S. Department of Treasury 2001).

Some observers believe that the right-wing Heritage Foundation and its Center for Freedom and Prosperity played a key role in changing U.S. policy. Others believe that banks and financial institutions that made significant contributions to Bush's presidential campaign were able to persuade the administration to change policy. Republican representatives, meanwhile, joined forces with the congressional Black Caucus, which had close links with the Caribbean, to urge the United States to withdraw from the OECD initiative.

O'Neil's intervention proved decisive. The OECD project was not completely abandoned, but it was changed almost beyond recognition. To begin with, the criterion of missing substantive economic activity was removed from the definition of an unfair tax practice. The project was now restricted narrowly to the fight against harmful practices in the area of passive portfolio investments (Rixen 2008). Second, due to U.S. prodding, the project was aligned more closely with the FATF and was concerned primarily with issues of transparency and more effective information exchange.

In addition, and in concession to the ITIO point about the uneven treatment of tax havens and PTRs, the OECD conceded that defensive measures against tax havens could not take place before PTRs were removed. As PTRs had been given a five-year timetable for removal, and Switzerland and Luxembourg showed little interest, the decision in effect left the project in suspended animation (Rixen 2008). The savvier tax havens could now declare their adherence to the OECD project but do nothing, waiting for the PTRs to do their job for them. By 2004, only five tax havens had somehow failed to understand the opportunities they were given and remained on the list: Andorra, Liechtenstein, Liberia, Monaco, and the Marshall Islands.

Following U.S. intervention, the OECD was forced to resume its traditional, highly unsuccessful method of dialogue and persuasion (Sharman 2006). By 2004, an OECD progress report announced the excellent news that most PTRs were no longer considered harmful. Webb (2004) shows that little had changed; in reality most states merely rearranged their PTRs to get OECD approval. Luxembourg and Switzerland were not prepared to comply fully with the OECD and were left in the category of "further investigations." In May 2006, the OECD was able to report even better news: most countries were now able to access information on banking and company ownership, at least for criminal matters. Not to be outdone, the FATF reported the best news of all: thanks to the effectiveness of its actions since October 2005, it declared, only two territories were still on its list: Myanmar (formerly Burma) and Nigeria. This view contrasts sharply with the somber assessments we have already discussed of the UK National Audit (NAO 2007) and of the U.S. report on money laundering (INCSR 2008).

The United States and the EU, the two big signatories on the OECD progress reports, appeared somehow less convinced by the accumulation of good news. The United States may have abandoned multilateral efforts, but it redoubled efforts on a series of bilateral treaties signed with Antigua and Barbuda, Aruba, the Bahamas, BVI, the Cayman Islands, Jersey, Guernsey, the Isle of Man, and the Netherlands Antilles. Predictably, these treaties are controversial. In 2003, for instance, under enormous pressure the Bahamas enacted the US Tax Information Exchange Agreement Act. Nevertheless, by now some of the leading tax havens such as Jersey, Bermuda, and BVI have signed TIEAs with most of industrial countries in the world.

2001–2002: End of Phase One: OECD, FATF, FSF

Extensive political and media discussion of tax havens, combined with attempts to stigmatize them on various published blacklists, resulted by the end of 2002 in an impasse. The FATF appeared to be the most successful of the three organizations, and the OECD was losing credibility fast. It became clear that many countries lacked the political will to implement the severe policies recommended by the OECD.

Appearances notwithstanding, the different organizations were aiming at different things (Godefroy and Lascoumes 2004). Some of the OECD's backers were concerned with declining revenues, but in fact the OECD's goal was to lower tax rates worldwide through international tax competition. The OECD had tried to advance far too complicated a political agenda, which involved the removal of market distortions perpetrated by tax havens and PTRs, to reduce tax levels worldwide. The FSF, by contrast, was concerned with the international financial architecture and showed little appetite for reforming tax havens. The FATF appeared to be making headway, but new laws against money laundering are universally judged to be of little practical consequence.

Since about 2001, the International Monetary Fund, an organization desperately searching for a new role, and lately the World Bank have been leading the multilateral discussions with tax havens. These organizations are far better resourced than the FATF or the FSF to deal with the complex and intricate problems involved. The IMF could immediately assign fifty researchers to study tax havens, five times as many as the entire research department of the FATF. But the IMF's involvement indicates a fundamental ambiguity in multilateral efforts against the havens. The IMF, after all, is the organization most closely associated with neoliberal ideology, financial deregulation, and the lowering of tax rates. Will it be willing to pursue vigorous policies against tax havens?

The IMF set up a process for evaluation, and by 2005 it had reviewed forty-one territories. Its studies showed that significant reforms had been undertaken in many tax havens—even though it acknowledged the not-so-minor issues of international cooperation, exchange of information, and regulatory policies were still problematic. Otherwise, all was well! Commenting on these reports, in March 2005 the FSF cheerfully noted that "the 2000 list has served its purpose." It appears to us that no goal has been achieved and that the FSF and IMF are negligent in their work. The current crisis shows very clearly that problems remain.

The IMF was also encroaching on FATF territory. It requested the suspension of the FATF list of non-cooperative jurisdictions to allow it to make its own assessment. FATF officials learned in 2004 that their mandate for dealing with criminality and money laundering was to be renewed, despite pressures from the IMF. Nonetheless, or perhaps because of its turf war with the IMF, the FATF then declared itself a success. However, the good news emanating from the FSF and the FATF defies common sense. There is little evidence that the United States, the EU, and developing countries, some of which are beginning to develop their own countermeasures against tax havens, are persuaded or even interested in hearing this good news.

The consensus among observers is that the first phase of the battle against tax havens produced at best mixed results. It raised awareness of tax haven abuse, yet it paradoxically legitimized tax havens, which for the first time in their long history are being treated as nearly equal partners in international discussions about the future of the financial system and of fiscal policies. The decision to condemn some tax havens, particularly the Pacific atolls, without a word spoken about Monaco or Luxembourg, London or New York, raised doubts about the seriousness of the three organizations' determination to tackle abuse. The City of London, in particular, had been associated with financial scandals since the BCCI affair,[1] yet was never named in the campaigns against tax havens. The politics of blacklisting, as Van Fossen suggests, may have been the politics of scapegoating. The financial system still thrives on mobility, lack of transparency, and regulatory and tax avoidance—or so it appeared until the credit crunch struck with a vengeance in August 2007.

For better or for worse but for the first time tax havens are being treated as legitimate and respectable partners on the world stage. Before the campaign began, tax havens were regarded as anomalies of international finance, peripheral islands of no political significance. They are now referred to as "participating partners" in multilateral forums. They succeeded in shifting the discussion toward new standards designed to ensure what they call the shared "positive role" they can play in the world economy. All the haggling has certainly led to general recognition of their right of existence and the right to pursue their own national interest.

Tax havens have also learned to cooperate. As they mobilized against the OECD, they understood that they are not only competitors but have common interests to defend. They employ the expertise of professionals, the big law and accounting firms, and public relations firms to help them plan and coordinate their responses. They also established what are from their perspective very useful links with conservative U.S. think tanks, most notably the inappropriately named Center for Freedom and Prosperity, which serves as a powerful lobbyist in the halls of Congress. The

---

1. The Bank of Credit and Commerce International (BCCI) was the seventh largest private bank in the world when it collapsed in 1991. Investigators found that the bank perpetrated a huge fraud, which the Bank of England, BCCI's principle regulator, failed to spot.

center has branded the OECD a "global tax cartel" working for the benefit of a handful of high-tax nations.

The objective of the tax havens has been simple but effective: to obtain the highest possible recognition in exchange for the lowest possible level of regulation. The case of the Dutch Antilles is exemplary. The Dutch Antilles parliament voted a "new fiscal framework" and amended its tax treaty with the Netherlands, removing preferential treatment of foreign companies and gradually imposing a new tax rate on profits of 34.5%, which entered into force in 2002. At the same time, legislators introduced an "exception clause" or "transitional arrangements" to keep the old tax rate of 2.4–3.0% for foreign firms until 2019. Subsequently, a new type of company has been created that allows those who register under the new regime to choose a tax rate of zero percent. Yet, "informal discussion with senior OECD officials suggest that the institution is satisfied with the changes in the Netherlands Antilles" (Cavalier 2005, 16).

Still, not all is doom and gloom. To date we have only one independent and systematic study of the effects of the new measures. Rawlings (2005) reports that international initiatives have been having some impact on the offshore sector, the principal one being greater compliance costs for offshore firms and regulators associated with the due diligence and "Know Your Customer" standard. The measures have increased the costs of running an offshore center, but otherwise have had little change in substance.

The European Union Enters the Fray

As the OECD was preparing its report on harmful tax competition, the EU council was agreeing, on December 1, 1997, to a package of measures to tackle harmful tax competition within the Union (ECOFIN 1999). The package included a code of conduct on business taxation, taxation of savings income, and withholding taxes on cross-border interest and royalty payments between companies. As we saw, EU and OECD discussions were linked, yet there were important difference between them, in terms of motivation and ultimately in what they wanted to achieve.

The European Code of Conduct

The series of treaties that established the EEC and the EU offered little in terms of tax coordination. It was broadly accepted that a single market requires tax neutrality on international business operations, and the European Commission had consistently tried to advance the subject in the 1960s, but not much had been achieved (Radaelli and Kraemer 2005). The

Commission established a fiscal and financial committee whose 1962 report called for tax harmonization across the EEC. Unsuccessful attempts at harmonization of tax codes followed in 1975 and 1985.

The 1997 Code of Conduct on Business Taxation changed all that. The code does not have the status of a legal instrument, but it provides an informal approach to regulation, which proved surprisingly effective (Radaelli 2003). In adopting this code, member states work to eliminate several harmful tax competition practices and avoid new ones. Whereas the OECD campaign is limited to financial and other services, the EU Code looks at business activities in general, with greater emphasis on mobile activities. It thereby avoids charges of a bias against mobile capital lodged by Luxembourg and Switzerland in their dissenting letters to the OECD's 1998 report.

The code of conduct also overturned another traditional objection of tax havens. To avoid the charge of imperialism, the code does not elaborate a principle of "just taxation" nor imposes it on recalcitrant states. Instead, taking a line adopted by the OECD, the code accepts the principle of tax competition, allowing states freedom of choice in this matter. However, the EU insists that the tax regime's rules be applied equally on all businesses in the jurisdiction, domestic and foreign. The code targets the practice whereby nonresidents are provided "a more favorable tax treatment that which is generally available in the Member State concerned." The code sought to root out formal or informal rules that created:

- an effective level of taxation that is significantly lower than the general level of taxation in the country concerned
- tax benefits reserved for nonresidents
- tax incentives for activities that are isolated from the domestic economy and therefore have no impact on the national tax base
- the granting of tax advantages even in the absence of any real economic activity
- profit determination for companies in an MNE group departing from internationally accepted rules, in particularly those approved by the OECD
- lack of transparency

The code confronts jurisdictions that have created a niche for themselves in the global economy by distinguishing resident and nonresident companies for tax purposes. Citing the code, for example, in 2006 the Commission forced Luxembourg to abandon its 1929 holding companies. Similarly, the adoption of new tax regimes by Jersey, Guernsey, and the Isle of Man from 2008 on (notably the zero percent tax rate on business profits) may be taken to task for not respecting the code.

Harmonization of Business Taxation in the EU

The EU is also pushing for the harmonization of company taxation across the continent. Multinational companies with subsidiaries in more than one European country pay taxes in countries where they operate, but they tend to shift profits to the lowest-tax country through complex systems of transfer pricing.

The EU is proposing a European-wide tax base that would reduce the incentives to shift profits by applying a "formulary apportionment." In this process group profits will be taxed just once in the EU, and tax revenues will be distributed among countries according to an agreed criterion (e.g., amount of capital invested or sales turnover) as is already done among U.S. states and among Canadian provinces. There is a long way to go to consensus, but Germany and France support the proposal. The United Kingdom and Ireland, predictably, oppose it, for they fear that harmonization of the tax base will be followed by harmonization of tax rates. The proposal is also opposed by the Baltic states and Slovakia, which fear that a harmonized tax base will be narrower and will allow more exemptions than their existing regimes. The Commission gave itself until 2008 to come up with a directive for company taxation, but the Irish 2008 no vote in the referendum on the Lisbon treaty, partially won on the claim that the EU supposedly threatens the Irish tax system, has delayed the directive.

European Withholding Tax

Any state can serve effectively as a tax haven by sheltering savings from taxation. The EU put forward a clear set of proposals to deal with this sort of abuse as well. In 1989, a first draft proposed a pan-European withholding tax of 15% for all savings income, including investments by nonresidents of the European Union. It was abandoned under pressure from Luxembourg, which was reluctant to give up its bank secrecy laws. A second draft was presented in 1998 and then relaunched in June 2000 as part of the great international mobilization against tax havens. A European directive was introduced in July 2001 and finally implemented in July 2005.

Since July 2005 all member states are required to exchange information with the relevant national authorities. Austria, Belgium, and Luxembourg retained their bank secrecy rules but are required to impose a withholding tax on earnings from deposits starting at a rate of 15% from 2005 to 2007, rising to 20% from 2008 to 2010, and to 35% thereafter. Their compliance depended on the application of equivalent measures to the principal non-EU competitors (Andorra, Liechtenstein, Monaco, San Marino,

Switzerland) plus all the dependencies and associated territories of member states (the Channel Islands, Isle of Man, and the Caribbean dependencies). Despite general pessimism about the idea, agreement was achieved.

The European Court of Justice

The European Court of Justice (ECJ) proved to be the main force of change for European taxation from the mid-1980s on. An important court ruling in 1985 left direct taxation to the responsibility of each member state, but it called on states to devise their tax laws to respect treaty obligations. In the twenty years thereafter, the ECJ has delivered more than fifty judgments along these lines.

The ECJ has adopted a far more aggressive attitude since 2005. Until then it tended to side with individuals and corporations and not with member states seeking to protect their revenues. But in a landmark judgment of April 2005, the Halifax case (C-255/02), the Court ruled that European law forbids transactions whose sole purpose is to create a tax advantage. This interpretation was reaffirmed in a case involving Cadbury Schweppes in May 2006, when the court condemned what it called "wholly artificial" subsidiaries in tax havens. In another important judgment delivered on March 13, 2007 (the so-called thin-cap affair), the Court ruled that states could restrict freedom of establishment of wholly artificial structures devoid of economic reality and having tax avoidance as their principal objective. The Court reaffirmed its position again in July of that year.

The battle lines have been drawn, but the struggle has a long way to go. The European Union has taken several positive steps forward. It is more than likely that with the new Obama administration, the United States will join forces with the EU to stem tax and regulatory abuse.

Conclusion

The late 1990s witnessed a marked shift in policy toward tax havens, from bilateralism to multilateralism, from low-key pressure politics to the name and shame tactics adopted by international organizations. In the late 1990s, it looked as though the most significant initiative was the OECD's campaign on harmful tax competition. A host of other initiatives were pursued through all of the leading international financial institutions. Yet international initiatives against tax havens fizzled out five or six years later, not least because of the Bush administration's policies. Meanwhile, the European Union emerged as the most significant player in the international battle against tax havens. There is growing evidence that European directives are beginning to have a serious impact on the European and European-dependency tax havens.

The sheer amount of money that goes through tax havens, reported in chapter 2, inevitably generates deeply entrenched vested interests on both sides of the debate. We doubt whether international organizations have the capacity, the will, or the legitimacy to pursue policies that might seriously affect tax havens, not least because there are so many tax havens and they have the sovereign right to write their laws. However, in the EU and the United States under President Obama—both undergoing one of the deepest recessions ever experienced by capitalist economies and both seeking ways of augmenting their depleted revenues without affecting consumer demand—the pendulum has swung very clearly against tax havens. We have returned to the more traditional bilateral approaches toward tax havens. This time, however, the two largest economies in the world are likely to take a much more aggressive attitude. The golden years of tax havens are over.

Chapter 10

Tax Havens in the Twenty-First Century

If there is a recurring theme in the story of the tax havens, it is their continuous development in the face of opportunity and opposition. Indeed, one of the most remarkable features of the last decade has been their ongoing growth. Rawlings's survey of companies doing business in tax havens showed that the net effect of the various campaigns was to increase the cost of tax havens but little else (Rawlings 2005; see also Sharman and Mistry 2008). Yet opposition to tax havens is mounting. The major states are, through collective organizations, opposing almost every aspect of their activity.

One reason for the mounting opposition is a growing awareness of the scale and figures involved. Policymakers are perfectly aware of the demands on their budgets, and tax avoidance and evasion is a hot topic. Civil society groups also play a crucial role in raising the profile of the fight against tax havens. These themes provide us with opportunity to muse, if only briefly, on what might happen next.

Tax Havens and Civil Society

We cannot ignore the role civil society groups have played in raising awareness of tax abuses. At the turn of the twenty-first century, one of the world's largest development NGOs—Oxfam—based in the UK, issued a report titled "Tax Havens: Releasing the Hidden Billions for Poverty Eradication" (Oxfam 2000). The argument was simple and direct. Oxfam said that offshore tax havens are an increasingly important obstacle to poverty reduction because they are depriving governments in developing countries of the revenues they need to invest in basic services and the infrastructure upon which broad-based economic growth depends. The report estimated that the cost of tax evasion and avoidance to developing countries was at least $50 billion a year. Little noticed at the time of its publication, the report has had enormous impact since, because some of those involved in its writing went on to help create the Tax Justice Network in 2002.

The first reaction to tax havens came elsewhere. As we saw in the previous chapter, Republicans obtained the upper hand in U.S. politics with the 2000 election of George W. Bush to the White House. U.S. support for the OECD and other initiatives against tax havens had always appeared dependent on a Democratic president. The Heritage Foundation, backed by substantial financial resources and with a commitment to free market economics, low taxation, and tax competition—all of which it believed were supported by the existence of tax havens—grabbed the opportunity that a change in president presented. Their response was the Center for Freedom and Prosperity (CFP), whose sole goal was to challenge the OECD initiative against tax havens (for details see Sharman 2006).

Unsurprising, the CFP won many friends among the members of the Bush administration, as well as support from the tax havens. CFP characterized the OECD and its member states as economic monopolists or "rent-seeking" governments, wishing to preserve their own special status in the world by oppressing smaller competitors. They argued that a Republican White House should not side with monopolists and high-tax states (Sharman 2006).

Some of the tax havens formed the International Tax and Investment Organization (ITIO), to which the Commonwealth Secretariat lent its support, reflecting the presence in its membership of many British Overseas Territories. They demanded to be treated on what they called a "level playing field." At its core, this request meant two things. First, they asked the OECD to apply the same rules to its members. Their target (or rather somewhat unhappy ally) was Switzerland and more broadly the intermediate tax havens, as well as smaller U.S. states such as Delaware. Second, they argued that they should have a role in the regulatory process and from which they were currently excluded by the OECD.

In July 2001, the tax havens and the CFP got their way: the White House withdrew its support for the OECD initiative when U.S. Treasury Secretary Paul O'Neill told a congressional committee that he would seek bilateral treaties to share information with tax havens rather than support curbs on preferential tax regimes. By doing so, he made it clear that he had required the OECD to stop implementation of defensive measures against tax havens until those measures came into effect for all OECD members.

The effect was immediate. The OECD initiative was holed beneath the waterline, and the confidence of tax havens soared. Various events—the aftermath of Enron's collapse, the U.S. tax mis-selling scandals, and the impact of post–9/11 legislation—appeared to constrain tax haven activity, as did the requirement that they put FATF-inspired rules on their statute books. But in reality the bankers, lawyers, and accountants who operate the OFC sector in the tax havens believed that they had won a new freedom from external regulation. Some of the most striking evidence of this claim comes from statements made available in June 2008 following charges and plea bargaining disclosures made by a former UBS employee (*United States of America vs. Bradley Birkenfeld 2008*). Bradley Birkenfeld's testimony makes clear that, in his opinion, from 2001 to 2006 UBS knowingly and deliberately encouraged U.S. taxpayers to hold assets offshore in contravention of the U.S. tax code, using the sort of sham trusts and nominee corporations we have described in this book. It is hard to believe that the bank would have done so without at least two good reasons.

The first is that there was considerable money to be made. Birkenfeld estimates that UBS managed some $20 billion of assets through this operation, securing revenues for the bank of at least $200 million a year. The second reason must have been a belief that the activity would either not be discovered or would not lead to retribution against UBS. In this second belief the bank was wrong. The tax havens might have won a battle in 2001, but the war against tax havens has gone on.

Civil society has played an important role in highlighting these abuses. In 2002, the Tax Justice Network (TJN) was formed following a meeting between NGOs from several European countries in Florence in November. The TJN, which is led from the United Kingdom but has affiliate branches in many countries, has brought together academics, concerned professionals from the financial services sector, development NGOs, and others to campaign against tax havens on the basis that they harm the capacity of developing countries to create effective taxation systems capable of supporting a stable, democratic government that is not dependent upon aid. Their campaign has had considerable impact and has been widely noted in the tax havens and by the CFP. More important, by 2008, the campaign was being supported by major NGOs in the UK and throughout Europe, giving it a broad support base that the tax haven lobby cannot reach and a press appeal that has brought the debate into the mainstream media.

The mobilization of civil society organizations is affecting the fight against illegal financial practices, according to Moisés Naím (2005, 201–8). Although constrained by financial resources, activist networks help to gather information, disseminate ideas, and maintain media interest in the subject.

Activists target not only the major states, advising revenue officials and the like, but also the corporations and indeed, with less success, the professional services at the heart of the tax haven phenomenon. It appears that the concept of corporate social responsibility, in particular, has some traction. Fifty-seven percent of respondents in a poll of 223 CFOs of British companies conducted in late 2005 considered ethics an important factor in tax planning. Equally, the respondents to a KPMG (2005) survey of 250 large multinational firms showed awareness of the changing public perception of tax avoidance schemes. A clear sign of the times is that the four major accounting firms—KPMG, Ernst & Young, Deloitte, and Pricewaterhouse-Coopers—published papers in 2005 underlining the growing reputation risk faced by companies with questionable tax practices (Sullivan 2007b). Loughlin Hickey, head of KPMG's tax department, caused a sensation in September 2005 by declaring that the distinction between tax avoidance and evasion is not sufficiently robust. However, we should not overstate the changes. In 2005 issue of *Tax Business Magazine*, that same Loughlin Hickey declared himself "proud" that his company is present in all the major tax havens and felt that "tax experts are poorly understood" (Tax Business Magazine 2005). Similarly, Peter Athanas, CEO of the Swiss branch of Ernst & Young, said during a panel discussion at Davos in late January 2006 that "the problem of tax havens is no longer an issue of great importance."[1] Yet the mere fact that the issue was being discussed in Davos is important in and of itself.

The Publish What You Pay (PWPY) Campaign

One effective contribution pioneered jointly by the Tax Justice Network and the Publish What You Pay (PWYP) coalition has been the promotion of a new accounting concept. PWYP calls for country-by-country reporting. Proposed by one of the authors of this book, Richard Murphy, it has been used to campaign for greater transparency in the extractive industries. It is widely believed that tax havens are extensively used in the industry for the payment of bribes, the advance of oil-backed loans that contravene international agreements, and transfer pricing abuse.

Country-by-country reporting makes three demands. First, a company should declare every country in which it has an operation and the names of all its subsidiaries in that place, so that the company can be held accountable for its actions. This move would immediately draw attention to those companies using tax havens as part of their business structure. Second, a shortened profit and loss account and balance sheet should be published for every country in which the multinational corporation trades,

---

1. Meeting attended by one of the authors of this book.

without exception. With additional disclosures required on the number of employees, payments made to employees, and mineral resources extracted, these data would allow calculation of a form of unitary apportionment for a group, which would show if its profit and tax allocation between states accorded with the economic substance of the transactions it was undertaking. This move would likely have a significant impact on the way in which corporate entities behaved. Third, regarding the control of transfer pricing, country-by-country reporting would require that both sales and purchases be split between transactions with third parties and those undertaken on an intra-group basis.

Publish What You Pay has another attraction: disclosure within many countries that host the extractive industries is remarkably poor, and contractual restrictions often guarantee secrecy. These restrictions can be overridden only if an international convention makes it necessary. Publish What You Pay and the Tax Justice Network have lobbied the International Accounting Standards Board for the adoption of country-by-country reporting, arguing that it would ensure massively improved transparency in the extractive industries, revelation of the nature of intra-group trade, and a greater understanding of the geographic risk to which the company is exposed. To date, the PWYP campaign had its greatest success in November 2007 when the European Parliament requested that the International Accounting Standards Board develop a standard on this basis for use by the extractive industries. Discussions are now in progress. Civil society organizations have been changing the game.

Policies against Tax Havens: Evolving Tactics

Multilateral Efforts I: The OECD's Seoul Declaration

Other organizations also have been changing their game. The OECD has, after losing the bulk of its tax haven initiative, moved to campaign for greater transparency and accountability. It has done so largely by the way of Tax Information Exchange Agreements between its member states and tax havens.

It has also taken note of the role of tax professionals in OFCs. In 2006 it issued its Seoul declaration, resulting in investigation of the role of tax intermediaries (as the OECD calls them) in creating abusive tax structures. In recent OECD meetings the change in tone is noticeable. The OECD now recognizes the importance and increased sophistication of tax avoidance practices, and particularly the roles played by financial intermediaries and law, tax, and accounting professionals. All are threatened with legal sanction. The role of transfer mispricing is also acknowledged.

The consequences were the establishment of a directory of aggressive tax planning schemes and a report submitted to an OECD meeting in Johannesburg in 2008. That report largely exonerated accountants and lawyers when it came to creating complex structures, on the curious grounds that tax malpractice resulted from the demand for sophisticated products from taxpayers rather than from supply by professionals. All examples of aggressive tax schemes presented in the report were clearly supplied and proposed by these very professionals. Many observers think that the OECD has taken this rather contradictory view because state-based taxation systems require the cooperation of these professionals for the effective management of taxation revenues. Bankers got off less lightly: their role in creating complex tax-driven structures was more clearly condemned and remains under review.

Others have not been so kind to accountants and lawyers. In particular in the United States, as we saw, Senator Carl Levin as chair of the Senate Permanent Subcommittee on Investigations has led several investigations into tax haven activity. The most recent was published in August 2006 and concentrated almost entirely on the activity of U.S. citizens in the Isle of Man. The senator was brusque about the role of professional firms in organizing the structures investigated, saying:

> U.S. persons, with the assistance of lawyers, brokers, bankers, offshore service providers, and others, are using offshore trusts and shell corporations in offshore tax havens to circumvent U.S. tax, securities, and anti-money laundering requirements. (2006, 9)

We can find the same attitude elsewhere, especially in the wake of the disclosure of significant tax evasion in Liechtenstein in February 2008. The OECD secretary general said in response to this revelation:

> Disclosures concerning alleged widespread tax evasion by German citizens through Liechtenstein highlight a much broader challenge in today's globalized economy: how to respond to countries and territories that seek to profit from tax dodging by residents of other jurisdictions. (OECD 2008b)

Others went much further, but in practice Germany's reactions were typical of efforts by major tax jurisdictions over the last few years, as they have sought to collect revenue lost to tax havens. The United States has tackled credit card fraud based in Cayman, the British Virgin Islands, and other Caribbean centers. Ireland made a particularly successful attack upon the Crown Dependencies, and in 2007 the UK followed suit, tackling the same territories and the bank accounts held by the UK-resident persons in branches of the five large UK high-street banks in those territories. Over 60,000 people admitted to having undisclosed accounts.

Multilateral Efforts II: The Road to Doha

While the OECD is renewing its efforts, development agencies are beginning to see the link between development and tax havens. Since 2005, the influential NGO Transparency International changed its focus in the investigation of corruption. It now recognizes the role of tax havens in corruption and the incongruous fact that many of the states that have scored very highly in its *Corruption Perceptions Index* are tax havens used to hide funds stolen from developing countries. Another NGO, Christian Aid (2008), argued that tax havens cost the lives of more than 250,000 children a year in the developing world, because of capital flight and lost tax revenue. The Norwegian government has created a task force to look at these issues and chaired a UN conference in Doha in November 2008 to examine innovative forms of funding for development. In preparation, the Norwegians solicited the views of activist organizations and commissioned a report by the TJN (2007). The collection of taxes lost because of the abuse of tax havens featured prominently.

The Doha Declaration raised all the issues discussed in this book, including tax evasion, money laundering, and corruption, but it does not name or even mention tax havens. The declaration simply affirms the signatories' support for the various international efforts to fight abuse (UN 2008). The declaration appears fairly anodyne—but it would have been unimaginable at the turn of the century. Although some of the direct initiatives to tackle tax havens may have made little progress, much has changed as more becomes known about tax haven activity, and resentment rises at the loss of revenue and control of assets that result from it.

The European Commission's International Financial Diplomacy

The European Commission's response to charges of interventionism and imperialism was ingenious: rather than getting embroiled in a messy argument about levels of taxation, the European Union targeted the favorable treatment of nonresidents. Countries could still select their own level of taxation, but they had to apply these rules to everyone, including their own population. Ireland has responded by enacting 12.5% uniform taxation on all Irish corporations, and so did Cyprus. Jersey and the Isle of Man first tried a more canny policy: they reduced corporate taxation to zero but introduced a "voluntary contribution" from local businesses to the value of 10%. This effective tax is unlikely to succeed.

The EU is perfectly aware of the dangers of simply shifting funds from European tax havens to other regions in the world, and so European financial diplomacy has targeted non-European tax havens. In early 2006, the Cayman Islands and Montserrat agreed to information exchange in principle, and the British Virgin Islands and Turks and Caicos opted for a withholding tax.

The European Commission admits that some of Europe's offshore capital has simply fled to Asia as a result of the introduction of its directives. This realization has prompted the EU to widen the geographical scope of its initiative, and it is seeking to open negotiations with Hong Kong, Singapore, Macau, and Japan, as well as with Canada, Bahrain, Dubai, and the Bahamas. Since March 2007, there have been clear indications that the Commission has targeted several loopholes and is working to identify how best to close them. The Liechtenstein affair in early 2008 reinforced France and Germany's resolve to increase the scope of the European Savings directive.

The EU will have to persuade the tax havens to follow suit on the savings directive as it has already done with the original directive. The struggle against tax havens has a long and difficult road ahead. However, we should recognize that the European Union has already taken several positive steps and seems to want further progress.

Another Possible Future: The Buenos Aires Response

A significant if largely unnoticed development has taken place in Argentina, and comes from the Buenos Aires authorities (for detail see Meinzer 2005). During the 2001 Argentinean financial crisis, several offshore shell companies were suspected of serving as fronts for domestic speculators in a particularly virulent Latin American version of the round-tripping game. Thereafter the City of Buenos Aires took the bold step of banning all investment from shell companies held in tax havens. The new regulations were issued in 2003 and came into force in 2005. The General Inspectorate of Justice (IGJ) stated that "every company situated in low, no tax jurisdiction must either prove they have genuine economic activity there (similar to that which they wish to undertake in Buenos Aires), or they have to transform into a national Argentinean company." In addition, every anonymous company such as the Uruguay SAFIS must provide detailed information about their shareholders, ultimate owners, and amounts of shares to obtain business accreditation from the IGJ.

At the time of this writing, the development of these new regulations are slow and their effects unclear.[2] The Buenos Aires approach, however,

---

2. Meinzer, personal communication, July 2009.

may become a model. It is founded on the methods of combating flag of convenience (FOC) abuse. In the case of flags of convenience, the major industrialized countries demand an inspection for safety and labor regulation purposes of FOC vessels that wish to dock in their ports. Thus, developed countries raised standards for the world's shipping. If the same method is adapted to tax havens, companies would be able to set up shop in tax havens or offshore, but in order to trade or invest onshore they would need to open their books. The scope for abuse will be greatly reduced.

The Future

Where is change likely to lead us? Anyone making predictions in this area has to accept that the one constant factor in the development of tax havens has been its unpredictability. In 2008, the UK Parliament's Treasury Select Committee announced that it would investigate tax haven activity but with a primary focus on transparency. This has become a collective theme: even some tax havens acknowledge it, making much of their having agreed to implement the EU Savings Tax Directive and other information-exchange agreements. Yet at the same time, as we were concluding the writing of this book, Jersey announced plans to spend £100,000 to promote its banking privacy (Herbert 2008). Nonetheless, we think three things are likely.

First, as the subprime crisis continues to unfold, we will see enormous pressure on corporations to increase their transparency and accountability. Our prediction is that not much will result. Securitization, derivatives, and OFCs are the Bermuda Triangle of international capital flows. To demand that financial intermediaries, whose profits are at least partly founded on their capacity to maintain opacity, become ever more transparent is unrealistic.

Second, in the fallout from the Liechtenstein affair, we will see increasing pressure to exchange information. This pressure will be compounded as the transitional arrangements for the introduction of the EU Savings Tax Directive come to an end by 2013. Then, all states who are party to the directive either will have to withhold tax at 35% or will have to exchange information in full on all interest earned within their territories. Tax withholding at that rate will be unattractive to all but a few tax evaders who do not wish to disclose the source of their offshore capital, and so the pressure for full disclosure will increase. The European Union may well extend the directive to other sources of income, and we believe this will happen. If it does, and the directive is extended to private companies and trusts, the activities of many havens would cease to be attractive. All those located in Europe would probably cease to function, as would others that operate under the protection of the UK and the Netherlands. The geography of tax havens would be transformed.

Third, funds will flow to those few sovereign states beyond the reach of European regulation and, potentially, that of a United States under the presidency of Barack Obama. He has already put his name to the Stop Tax Haven Abuse Act in the U.S. Senate, along with Senators Carl Levin and Norm Coleman.

Of course this is a bold vision of a future that will take time to develop, but it is already clear that the vast majority of tax havens no longer control their own future. To quote one commentator:

> Does the future of the Swiss banking system rest on the outcome of the US presidential race? Yes, definitely. (Mathiason 2008)

Conclusion

The central argument of this book is that tax havens not only are conduits for tax avoidance and evasion but belong more broadly to the world of finance—to the business of managing the monetary resources of an organization, country, or person. Individually, tax havens may appear small and insignificant; combined, they play a central role in the world economy, serving as one of the key pillars of what has been described as "neoliberal globalization."

We define tax havens as jurisdictions that deliberately create legislation to ease transactions undertaken by people who are not resident in their domains, with a view to avoiding taxation and/or regulations, which they facilitate by providing a legally backed veil of secrecy to make it hard to determine beneficiaries. Throughout the book we have emphasized *intentionality*: that is, the deliberate creation of law and policy—by those states we believe are acting as tax havens—to provide nonresidents with an alternative low-tax and largely unregulated secrecy space. Tax havens do so with the active support of a large, sprawling, and highly lucrative, "respectable," professional industry of accountants, lawyers, bankers, and tax experts.

Of course the majority of states offer a plethora of fiscal incentives to selected industries and sectors—incentive packages that are described in academic and policy jargon as Preferential Tax Regimes (PTRs). Typically, PTRs do not make a distinction between domestic and nonresident constituents. Tax havens, in contrast, deliberately aim at the nonresident market. Ironically, some tax havens, such as Jersey and Liechtenstein, are particularly harsh in sanctioning their own population against the use of other tax havens to avoid paying local taxes.

We suggest that tax havens are continually evolving, developing new types of legislation, new entities, and even new sectors, partly in response to the tightening of the rules by OECD countries and partly in response to new opportunities opened up by the Internet and the World Wide Web.

Like Freud's famous borrowed kettle argument (I returned the kettle last year . . . anyway it was broken . . . anyway I never borrowed a kettle), tax havens have consistently argued over the years that:

1. They are not tax havens;
2. It is not their fault that other parties use them as tax havens;
3. They are doing their best to cooperate with other countries to root out abuse;
4. They are highly regulated economies.

We have produced evidence to show that many jurisdictions are indeed tax havens, and even if the phenomenon originated in a complex and sometimes haphazard manner, over time all tax havens became the product of intentional policy decisions. In addition, we have shown that they are very reluctant to cooperate, always dragging their feet, and that they change only in response to sustained pressure. When they do change, they often develop new laws and policies to replace the very laws they have agreed to change with the aim of achieving the same effect as the regulation they have replaced.

In light of the multilateral campaigns that began in the late 1990s, a new kettle-type argument has developed:

1. Tax havens are highly regulated, respected countries that are able to maintain efficient government and low taxation;
2. They are subject to a new imperialism from OECD countries;
3. All countries are tax havens.

Some of these recent arguments have hit home (Sharman 2006). But rhetoric, however cleverly presented, cannot change some fundamental facts. Although the existing data are still rough, the unavoidable conclusion must be that tax havens are not marginal phenomena but a core component of the modern, globalized economy. Clever rhetoric cannot help recover the billions of lost tax revenue for countries that have to borrow heavily to sustain their economies in times of extreme economic crisis. In addition, clever politicking cannot help to regulate a financial system that has driven itself to the edge of the precipice and beyond; and feigned innocence cannot prevent multinational businesses, criminal organizations, and corrupt tyrants from siphoning off billions in desperately needed capital to Swiss, London, and Cayman Island accounts.

Policy toward tax havens had to change, and, as we showed in the case of the EU, it has changed in ingenious ways. The debate concerning tax havens has centered, as we saw, on three core issues: tax avoidance and evasion; regulation, particularly financial regulation and prudential supervision; and criminality, including money laundering, trafficking, and embezzlement. Throughout the book we have stressed that none of these issues, and in particular any policy responses, can be understood outside the context of the very building blocs of the contemporary international order. Tax havens raise important questions about the sovereign rights of smaller countries; they also raise questions about the nature of sovereignty more broadly, especially where the rights of one state impinge, or are perceived to impinge, on the sovereign rights of other states; and they raise important ideological and practical questions about market efficiency and state regulation. Ultimately, they raise questions about power and wealth in an increasingly integrated world economy.

If there is a fundamental change in policy toward tax havens, and we believe that such a change is happening, then that change must herald a deeper change in the very nature of the international order. A change from a so-called neoliberal type of globalization to what we can only describe at this point, the beginning of the process, as a post-neoliberal globalization.

The Liechtenstein Effect—and the Reason for Change

Two thousand eight and 2009 were extraordinary years for the world's tax havens. For a long time the United States and the European Union were unwilling to cooperate in a battle against tax havens, but the election of Barack Obama to the U.S. presidency more or less guarantees that the topic will remain on the agenda. When Jeffrey Owens, long-time head of taxation at the OECD and the man behind its attempts to tackle tax havens, was quoted in the *Financial Times* in December 2008 saying that "The political climate on the issue of tax havens has changed dramatically over the past three months" (Houlder 2008b), clearly any conclusion we might draw can be no more than tentative.

And yet conclusions can be drawn. Tax havens have been subjected to a decade of consistent criticism. We know a lot more about them as a result, even if there is still much to learn. Two developments in 2008 serve as the basis for our conclusion that change is happening.

The first is the Liechtenstein debacle, where an informant, previously an employee of the LGT bank (owned by the principality's royal family), stole a computer disk that contained information about more than 4,000 bank customers, all of whom had assumed they could rely on banking secrecy to avoid disclosure. He sold it for reportedly more than €4 million to the German tax authorities, who have since made the information available to other jurisdictions around the world. This incident generated a crisis for all tax havens for which they hold some degree of collective responsibility.

The Liechtenstein debacle clarified the feature of tax havens that many see as defining—that is, secrecy. It is not by chance that the proposed Stop Tax Haven Abuse Act in the United States calls these locations "secrecy jurisdictions" as much as tax havens. Campaigning organizations such as the Tax Justice Network, which has emerged as the leading anti-haven group over the last few years, are doing the same thing. The logic in both cases is that low tax is not the sole lure: rather, secrecy is the key attraction, and in many cases tax advantage would not be available if secrecy did not protect it from discovery. Liechtenstein excelled as a tax haven because of the secrecy it provided. Absolute bank secrecy, a refusal to sign information exchange agreements, a refusal to cooperate with the OECD on tax haven issues or even to express any future intent to do so—all these measures were based on the belief that for a small community such as Liechtenstein, banking secrecy is its sole selling point and the foundation for its financial industry. Liechtenstein had never imagined that someone would ever break its code of silence.

All this was already common knowledge among those who studied these esoteric locations. But this time it was different. Clear and unambiguous evidence showed that secrecy jurisdictions create what might in economic terms be called an "artificial factor of production." The structures they permit are intended for use solely or mainly by nonresidents in order to undermine the regulation of the state in which the beneficial owner resides—and this is possible only because tax havens offer legally enforced secrecy so that other states, whose regulations are undermined, cannot identify what is happening or who is doing it.

Liechtenstein may have taken secrecy to an extreme, but the difference between Liechtenstein and other tax havens is a matter of degree, not of principle. It is true that during 2008 some havens, and the Isle of Man in particular, signed OECD-inspired Tax Information Exchange Agreements with major trading partners, such as the United States and the Scandinavian countries. However, one of the longest established agreements, between the United States and Jersey, signed in 2002, had by 2008 been used just four times (Houlder 2008a). The implications are clear: many havens may have protested that they are transparent, that they have signed all the necessary information agreements, and that they are well regulated, but the world remains unconvinced. The available evidence does not prove their good intentions.

This is the view taken by the European Commission. Experience with the European Union Savings Tax Directive (STD) gives good reason to doubt the havens' claims. As the Commission reported in November 2008 when issuing proposals for a revised STD, "The European Commission on 13 November 2008 adopted an amending proposal to the Savings Taxation Directive, with a view to closing existing loopholes and better preventing tax evasion." The EU thus recognizes that a directive, unambiguously issued for the sole reason of tackling tax evasion, has not been markedly successful in doing so, and in no small part because of the combined actions of tax havens within and outside the European Union. Cayman and Luxembourg alike offered investors the opportunity to avoid their obligations under the STD by arranging for entities considered Undertakings for Collective Investment in Transferable Securities (UCITS), which were subject to the STD, to reregister as non-UCITS entities and so outside its scope—an obscure arrangement that is only now coming to light. It is rumored that Swiss private banks have been bulk-buying Panama corporations through which their customers could remain outside the scope of the directive, which applied solely to individuals. Individuals who pose as corporations can avoid the STD. As we reported earlier, two of the largest Swiss banks, UBS and Credit Suisse, have set up large training facilities in Singapore for private banking operations—presumably anticipating the shift of such activities from Europe to Asia. The trust regimes in the UK Crown Dependencies and Overseas Territories are rumored to be doing much the same thing. None of the tax havens showed any willingness to subscribe to automatic information exchanges under the directive. It is hard to explain their failure to do so other than their desire to protect the financial services industry and its tax-evading customers. A commitment to information exchange and transparency, which underpinned the directive, has been notable for its absence.

The focus on offshore structures that have effects outside the domain of their creation has, however, delivered a powerful new weapon to the havens' critics. When the focus was on tax haven jurisdictions, the havens had sentiment and sovereignty on their side—a combination they used to powerful effect to tackle the 1998 OECD initiative (Sharman 2006). They argued that it was their right to set their own tax rates without interference, and the world was powerless to dispute their claims at a time when low taxation was the mantra for governments that subscribed to the Washington Consensus.

Secrecy is a different matter altogether. Secrecy is now perceived for what it is, a weapon used to undermine the sovereignty of other states. The sovereignty argument that sheltered tax havens for so long has become an Achilles heel. Following the EU's lead, those now attacking the havens do not challenge their right to set whatever tax rate they choose, but they insist that other states must also have the right to set their own rates. The opacity of tax havens prevents those other states from exercising their sovereign right to determine tax rates, for tax havens undermine the rule of law with regard to taxation. This reversal of the argument on sovereignty may prove a tipping point in the international politics of tax havens. So far neither the havens nor their advocates have provided any robust response.

Lessons from the Financial Crisis

The second important development is the global credit crisis, one result of which has been much additional attention for tax havens. We can be emphatic here: *tax havens did not cause this crisis.* But there is little comfort for them in that truth, for there is no doubt that they facilitated it.

Throughout this book we have reported on the absence of solid research into the functioning of tax havens as genuine financial centers. Barack Obama may have underestimated when he remarked: "You've got a building in the Cayman Islands that supposedly houses 12,000 corporations. That's either the biggest building or the biggest tax scam on record." The U.S. General Accounting Office reports that "the sole occupant of Ugland House [an address at the center of Georgetown, Grand Cayman] is Maples and Calder, a law firm and company-services provider that serves as registered office for 18,857 entities it created as of March 2008" (GAO 2008, 2). Yet there are reasons to believe that some havens (especially those closely linked to major financial centers, such as Cayman with New York, Jersey with London, and Switzerland with both) have moved beyond mere booking locations and become significant nodes of investment banking. Some specialist law and accounting firms, such as the Mourants of Jersey, have set up branches in other tax havens, although they are still a small minority. While still subservient to the financial services industry, they have developed the capacity to create, or rather replicate, financial innovations. This is a characteristic they exploited in three areas that helped create the crisis—securitization, orphan companies, and hedge funds.

Securitization is an umbrella term that refers to a great variety of financial instruments. The types of securitization implicated in the current crisis involved first assembling debt and then channeling it into special purpose vehicles, many of which, it is believed, were registered offshore. The vehicles then assisted in the financing of the debt through the issue of bonds. All of this activity remained, by and large, off the balance sheet of the entity responsible for collecting liabilities from customers and so serviced the cash flow of the whole structure—although in some cases it remained on balance sheet as well. This arrangement, when it involved an onshore debt-accumulating company and an offshore SPV, was also crucial to what is described euphemistically as "true sale" of debt: a legal technique of separating the insolvency risk of the originator of the loans from the insolvency risk of the bonds issued by the SPV. "True sale" was imperative for the business of credit ratings agencies (CRAs), which in turn ranked the SPV-issued bonds, making them tradable and "liquid" in the marketplace.

The company originating the debt existed onshore, but the offshore environment facilitated the rapid expansion of this market because of its low costs, light regulation, and relaxed approach to some governance and legal issues—but mostly because splitting the arrangements across international boundaries offered a considerable regulatory advantage. What portion of the securitization market operated such onshore/offshore arrangements? We simply do not know, although anecdotal evidence suggests that the majority were registered offshore. For reasons discussed in chapter 7, we believe that the majority of British banks certainly used such techniques. The GAO investigation into the Cayman Islands (GAO 2008) suggests that a considerable portion of the U.S. securitization market used such techniques. Corroborating evidence emanates from European bankers as well. The advantages of these arrangements can be summed up quite simply: speed, cost, and the fact that no regulator could look at the deal as a whole.

Nowhere was this more useful to those issuing debt than in the case of the "orphan" companies in which Jersey specialized—although it is not clear whether Jersey-type orphan companies were used as pervasively in the U.S. market. An organization wishing to offload debt from its balance sheet, or to raise bulk funds to issue new mortgages (the mechanism being the same in either case), creates a charitable trust, often but not always in a tax haven, whose professional trustees are nominally independent of and yet in practice work in accordance with the wishes of the originating corporation. The trustees then supposedly arrange the creation of an SPV to issue bonds that finance the debt of the originating organization, often through a web of related entities in more than one jurisdiction.

We doubt that many of the participants knew precisely what each stage in the arrangement was meant to achieve. It is obvious that many arrangements lacked any economic substance whatsoever. They were almost wholly hidden from view: the customers whose debts were assigned to them were unaware of the fact; the charities that supposedly benefited were blissfully unaware of their existence. This opacity has now brought them and the jurisdictions that allowed their creation into the limelight—the last place they wished to be. Precisely because tax havens facilitated rising levels of debt, and did so in ways that most find hard to fathom, they have been subjected to harsh criticism. There is a demand for change. And not just with regard to tax: serious questions about governance have arisen from the reliance on such structures. And how could directors believe that such artificial fabrications were really operating within the spirit of good governance?

The trend is confirmed as one inquires into another aspect of finance widely believed to have created the financial crisis. The hedge fund industry seems to operate primarily through offshore jurisdictions. As we have mentioned, in August 2008 a spokesperson for the UK Financial Services Authority was quoted as saying "Nobody ever registers hedge funds in the UK. If somebody did, we'd be scratching our heads over how to deal with it. We'd have to devise something" (Clark 2008). The issue has become all too obvious to both politicians and the public: what is structured offshore has a significant impact onshore. The perception of that impact is, rightly or wrongly, negative. Hedge funds undoubtedly shorted shares in U.S., UK, French, and other banks and helped bring at least one, HBOS, to a position of needing state aid and forcing it into a merger. The sector has assumed no accountability and is tainted by the combination of very high earnings subject to very little tax.

The Impact of the Financial Crisis on Tax Havens

The crisis of 2007-9 may prove, as we have noted in the introduction, another important watershed in the evolution of regulatory response to tax havens. At the time of writing, the G-20 meeting in London issued an important communiqué about financial reforms across many sectors of the financial system, including, importantly for us, tax havens. The G-20 communiqué states that "It is essential to protect public finances and international standards against the risk posed by non-cooperative jurisdictions" and vows to "stand ready to take agreed action against those jurisdictions which do not meet international standard for exchange of information" (G-20, 2009). To achieve these aims, the G-20 agreed on a "toolbox of effective counter measures for countries to consider."

The G-20 communiqué alludes to many of the abuses detailed in this book and, in that sense, it has already achieved what appeared impossible only a year ago. Most important, the G-20 has recognized the concerns of a few dedicated scholars and campaigners who have for many years pointed out the persistent abuses by tax havens in the world economy. Yet we believe the G-20 proposals remain unsatisfactory. To begin with, the criterion proposed by the G-20 for establishing lists of tax havens is grossly inadequate: it simply requires the signing of twelve OECD standard information exchange agreements. As we argued in chapter 9, this fails to acknowledge the role of OECD countries such as the Netherlands, or the state of Delaware, in providing tax haven facilities. Predictably, under pressure from China, Hong Kong and Macao were not included in the list of suspected tax havens, while the British tax havens of Jersey, Guernsey, and the Isle of Man were in the so-called white list, the criteria for which may have been set to ensure this outcome was possible, no other alternative explanation for having established such a low standard for respectability having been offered. Ireland is also seen, oddly enough, as a virtuous country. Needless to say, the City of London, Delaware, and Nevada do not face risk of the sanctions included within the G20 "toolbox." The obvious political compromises that these observations hint at will, without doubt, create continuing tensions as this process progresses, compromises which are in turn bound to delay or dilute any planned outcome.

More important, the G-20 use of the system of Tax Information Exchange Agreements (TIEAs) as indicators of OECD acceptability is deeply problematic. As we have argued in this book, TIEAs have proved to be almost wholly ineffective while the system of creating TIEAs is extremely cumbersome, time-consuming, and expensive. To operate an existing TIEA, a tax authority must first present the jurisdiction requesting information with evidence of fraud and tax evasion linked unambiguously to a person resident in their domain—precisely the kind of evidence that is difficult to obtain because of tax haven secrecy. Tax campaigners claim that only a system of automatic exchange of information, such as the one introduced by the EU, will have the necessary deterrence effect and at the same time provide the "smoking gun" evidence that the TIEA system needs. Until this happens, and there is no date set for its occurrence, the era of banking secrecy will not be over, contrary to what the G-20 claims in its communiqué.

The Battle against Secrecy

What, then, is the next step in the battle against tax havens? The answer, we believe, at this point is to tackle secrecy. Without the deliberate veil of secrecy that tax havens create, those using tax havens for the purpose of tax and regulatory avoidance would be readily identifiable. Take away secrecy, and they would desist from doing so of their own volition, for fear of the effect on their reputation or for fear of prosecution, or they could actually be prevented from doing so by the states in which they really undertake their economic activities. Tackling secrecy, however, is likely to be insufficient by itself. There remain legacy issues arising from the existing international architecture that will have to be addressed. Our suggestions are clustered around these two themes.

Secrecy is created within tax havens under the pretense that as sovereign jurisdictions it is their sovereign right to write their laws as they wish. The impact of these provisions, however, is felt outside tax havens. Those who wish to address secrecy have choices: they can try to break the secrecy that these jurisdictions create from within those places, or they can seek to break it in the places where it has impact, or they can try to work around the issue. Despite tremendous pressure from civil society groups, tax havens have been very reluctant to give up their secrecy provisions. We do not believe that they are likely to change their position in the short term, particularly when reform in the United Kingdom, Delaware, Nevada, and other locations appears to be a necessary prerequisite to any action inside the secrecy jurisdictions.

Consequently, attempts to break secrecy from outside are now receiving greater attention. One line of attack is a proposed extension of the EU Savings Tax Directive. This directive was a substantial step forward when first introduced, but it was limited in its impact because all privately owned trusts and companies were excluded from its scope. The EU's November 2008 proposed amendment is sweeping in its impact. It seeks to link together the information that banks must hold on the beneficial ownership of the entities with which they contract and the obligation either to exchange information with the country of residence of the beneficial owner of an account or to withhold tax of up to 35% from payments made. This requirement will apply to all paying agents who operate within the EU and any additional states that apply this directive. This proposal, in effect, means that the actual beneficial owners of entities located in tax havens must be known and identified, and be subject to tax because of their association with their normal country of residence. Offshore entities such as International Business Companies or offshore trusts will consequently be ignored when determining whether information exchange should take place or not. Information will be exchanged with the countries where the beneficial owners reside, bypassing the jurisdictions where the entities are registered.

This is an extraordinary breakthrough: it sweeps aside all the tax planning that is undertaken offshore and says that the income paid to the entities in question must be taxed in the countries in which their beneficial owners reside. There are, of course, obstacles: the Directive must be supported by all EU states, and it is not yet clear if that support exists, with particular opposition coming from Luxembourg. But the mere presence of this proposal gives a clear indication of the direction in which the EU wishes to proceed.

Similar indications are available from the United States. The Stop Tax Haven Abuse Act, drafted legislation before the U.S. Senate, has President Barack Obama's name on it from the time when he served in that body. The fundamental presumption of the act is that the person who engages with a tax haven entity has control of it, enjoys the benefit of its income, and unless he or she can prove the contrary has the duty to declare that income in the United States. Legislation with similar intent was tabled in Germany in January 2009. Germany is also seeking to deny tax relief on payments made to tax haven entities, even if done so within commercial groups of companies. In both cases, this is blunt legislation that presumes the taxpayer guilty until proved innocent. No doubt, this will be the basis on which it is criticized.

Another approach to tackling secrecy has been proposed for multinational corporations. With minor exceptions, the vast majority of corporations have to prepare accounts in accordance with the requirements of the International Accounting Standards Board (IASB) or its U.S. equivalent, the Federal Accounting Standards Board (FASB). Under the rules of both bodies, multinational corporations have to submit consolidated accounts to their members. These eliminate all intra-group transactions from view, including therefore all that involve transfer pricing. In addition, under the now common rules issued by the two bodies, almost no geographical reporting of an entity's transactions is required. As a result it is almost impossible to establish where a multinational group of companies trades, where it makes its profit, where it locates its assets, and where it pays its tax.

Civil society groups, led by the Publish What You Pay coalition and the Tax Justice Network, have argued that these corporations should be required to account on a country-by-country basis; an accounting development originally proposed by one of the authors of this book. This means that they would report sales by location, including intra-group sales, their costs split in similar fashion, where they employ their staff and what they pay them, what profit they make in each country in which they operate, what tax they pay on that profit, and what assets they have located in each country. They argue that this reform would substantially reduce shareholder risk; that it would enhance the allocation of assets and reduce the cost of capital within groups of companies, thus bringing economic benefits; and that it would make these corporations accountable for the actions they undertake in all countries in which they trade. By arguing that this disclosure should be made for all jurisdictions without consideration of size or the volume of trade undertaken there, the disclosure would also expose the use of secrecy jurisdictions for both third-party trading and intra-group transactions. The latter has particular significance for transfer pricing issues, where it is thought that much of the tax abuse of developing countries is perpetrated.

This proposal, in common with those from the EU, the United States, and Germany, works around the secrecy provisions offered by tax havens. The consent of those locations would not be required for the policy to work, or for a corporate accounting for their actions to be put on public record. The direction of policy is indicative of the state of frustration that has been reached: negotiating for the reduction of secrecy in the jurisdictions is not working. It is widely acknowledged that the Tax Information Exchange Agreements that should supposedly ensure information exchange between havens and majors states is not giving rise to any meaningful exchange, and so measures to attack secrecy are needed that do not require the havens' consent.

Considerable problems within the jurisdictions need to be addressed as well. There is an obvious and continuing problem with regard to the regulation of banking in these places. As has been shown by banking failures in Iceland, Ireland, and the Isle of Man, the capacity of small governments to support the depositors of a bank that fails is very limited. It exposes those who have acted in good faith to unnecessary risk, potentially burdens the population of these places with debts that they cannot reasonably afford, and ultimately transfers risk to the rest of the banking system.

In the same vein, it has also been suggested that regulatory reform might require that parent company directors of these banks be responsible for the activities of their tax haven subsidiaries. In addition, the major financial centers have to decide if they wish to bring funds, notionally resident in tax havens, inside a domain for regulatory purposes on the basis that funds management is located within their territory. Their right to do so is obvious: as the liquidation of hedge funds managed by Bear Stearns in the Cayman Islands revealed, there was no local substance to the Cayman Islands management of these entities; all decisions were taken in New York. If that is true for liquidation purposes, it is equally true for regulatory purposes: it is up to the regulators to make this point, and to claim their right to regulate these entities, which would become substantially more transparent. All of these reforms follow the familiar theme, noted above, of imposing control from outside the tax havens.

Some jurisdictions will refuse to cooperate. Many have reacted to previous attempts to regulate them by promoting yet more secrecy, providing ever more sophisticated and obscure financial entities. This trend may well continue in some locations, such as Panama, Dubai, and Singapore, which remain largely outside the political control of other states. They have made clear their commitment to secrecy as the basis of their financial services industries.

For these states, sanctions are needed to ensure their compliance with internationally agreed standards of conduct. The cost of financial failure has now been identified, and its imposition on the ordinary taxpayer of the world will in due course be quantified. As a result it is likely that the political will to reduce risks will be substantial. Those small states that refuse to participate are likely to be subjected to considerable pressure. Many will succumb without much of a struggle. For example, all those jurisdictions under the influence of the United Kingdom will almost certainly be brought within the regulatory environment as a result of EU action. Others, such as Bermuda and Switzerland, are clearly in the U.S. sight lines. As they are targeted, the pressure on the remaining secrecy jurisdictions will increase. Then, and only then, will sanctions be imposed because further capital flight to another location will be eliminated as the number of available territories is reduced.

How far away is this sea change? It is hard to tell. Few would have predicted the progress in the battle against secrecy abuse in 2008, or the change in the political climate that it created. The Obama administration is already taking the lead in putting additional pressure on tax havens. In May 2009 President Obama proposed several measures addressing the use of tax havens by the wealthiest Americans and the multinationals. In Europe, France and Germany continue to exert pressure on tax havens with another meeting to coordinate their action scheduled in June 2009. Prime Minister Gordon Brown, meanwhile, sent a remarkably robust letter to the British Overseas territories—Bermuda, the Cayman Islands, the British Virgin Islands, as well as the Crown Dependencies—during April 2009, demanding that they to go far beyond the minimum standards set by the OECD to eliminate tax evasion while, at the same time, threatening to increase the pressure on them if they did not act quickly in response to the G20. He has also demanded that they act to tackle tax avoidance—although as yet there is no indication as to what change in behavior he expects as a consequence.

There are other pressures in existence. For example, as the governments' experience of owning banks progresses they will realize that the use of the capital they provide to support secrecy jurisdictions is not in their best interests. Then we can expect change. It may come sooner than anyone might have predicted. There is nothing like self-interest to spur action.

Glossary

ACU Asian Currency Unit. Singapore's version of IBF (see below). Established 1968.

Aggressive tax avoidance the use of complex schemes of uncertain legality to exploit taxation loopholes for the benefit of taxpayers who can afford the fees charged by professional advisers to create such arrangements.

Anstalt a specialty of Liechtenstein, it is a complex hybrid between the foundation (see below) and the trust (see below).

Article 47 refers to the corresponding article of the Swiss Banking Act of 1934, which places bank secrecy under the protection of criminal law (see banking secrecy).

Banking secrecy laws strengthen the normal contractual obligation of confidentiality between a bank and its customer by providing criminal penalties to prohibit banks from revealing the existence of an account or disclosing account information without the owner's consent.

Capital flight deliberate and illicit disguised expatriation of money by those resident or taxable within the country of origin.

Derivatives so-called secondary financial instruments typically based on an underlying commodity, financial instrument or an index, or even an event, like a default or a bankruptcy. From their origins in guaranteeing the price of commodities such as sugar of wheat, derivatives have become key instruments in the trading of risks in the financial system today.

Double tax treaty an agreement between two sovereign states or territories to ensure, as far as possible, that income arising in one and received in the other is taxed only once.

Eurodollars U.S. dollars deposited and lent outside the U.S. territory. The market where these transactions take place is called the Euromarket. There is a Euromarket for any currency exchanged outside of its territory of origin.

EU Code of Conduct on Business Taxation was set out in the conclusions of the Council of Economics and Finance Ministers (ECOFIN) of December 1, 1997. The Code is not a legally binding instrument but it clearly does have political force. By adopting this Code, the Member States have undertaken to roll back existing tax measures that constitute harmful tax competition and refrain from introducing any such measures in the future. The code covers tax measures (legislative, regulatory, and administrative), which have, or may have, a significant impact on the location of business in the European Union.

EU Savings Tax Directive (STD) was adopted to ensure the proper operation of the internal market and tackle the problem of tax evasion. It was approved in 2003 and came into effect on July 1, 2005. The main method is exchange of information between tax authorities. However, an alternative withholding tax arrangement has been allowed for some countries, which is intended to be provisional.

Foundation a form of trust (see below) that is recognized as having separate legal existence akin to a limited company. It has no owners or shareholders. It is set up to manage assets whose income must serve a specific goal, as stated by the foundation.

Hedge fund describes a great variety of investors employing a diverse set of generally aggressive and risky investment strategies. They are generally either unregistered or registered in offshore financial centers in order to minimize both regulatory supervision and tax.

Incorporeal property lacks physical substance but can be traded on a market through the exchange of property titles. Finance deals with contracts for the exchange of property titles on currencies, equities (shares), debt instruments (bonds), claims on existing and future earnings, etc.

International Banking Facility (IBF) legal space within a territory enabling banking institutions to offer deposit and loan services to foreign residents and institutions free of national regulations.

International Business Corporation (IBC) limited liability companies that are set up either as subsidiaries of onshore companies or as independent companies in tax havens and OFCs. They are used for a variety of purposes; the principal among them is to shift the profitable portion of a business to a low tax country.

Inversion the act of a parent company whose headquarters are located within one jurisdiction switching registration with an offshore subsidiary they own to secure location within that offshore jurisdiction in order to secure a tax advantage. Mainly occurs in the United States.

Offshore legal space that decouples the real and the legal location of a transaction with an aim to avoid some or all kind of regulation (tax regulation, financial regulation, etc.). There are offshore financial centers, offshore vessels registration centers (flags of convenience), and so on.

Offshore financial center (OFC) financial center located in any country and offering financial services to non-resident clients with an aim to avoid some or all kind of regulation. According to Y. S. Park, there are four types of OFCs:

primary centers serve a worldwide clientele and are banking and financial market center ; booking centers are banking centers at best and do not have capital markets; funding centers play the role of inward financial intermediaries; outward centers engage in outward financial intermediation.

Offshore financial center community the firms of accountants together with the lawyers, bankers, tax experts, and financial traders, who build the instruments that make the offshore world—whether in tax haven or offshore financial centers—possible.

Over the Counter (OTC) trading in stocks, debt securities and other financial instruments such as derivatives, through a dealer network and not on any one of the formal exchanges.

Preferential tax regime (PTRs) wide array of policies and regulations put in place by States and designed to attract foreign capital.

Race to the bottom the downwards trend of tax rates and regulatory requirements on capital arising from competition between sovereign states to attract and retain investment.

Round-tripping locally owned money being invested in its country of origin via an offshore location to benefit from a preferential tax regime.

Special Purpose Vehicle (SPV or SPEs) subsidiaries or affiliates of large companies normally established to serve as a risk management tools. Due to weaknesses and ambiguity in accounting they are also used to take advantage of less restrictive regulations, issue complex financial instruments, and hide debt. They can be located onshore or offshore.

Structured Investment Vehicle (SIV) SPVs (see above) that use structured investment to make a profit from the difference between short-term borrowing and longer-term returns.

Tax avoidance the term given to the practice of seeking to minimize a tax bill without deliberate deception (which would be tax evasion or fraud).

Tax gap the difference between what taxpayers should pay and what they actually pay on a timely basis

Tax haven are considered generally as countries that offer one of the three facilities or a combination of all three: zero or near zero taxation for nonresidents; robust secrecy provisions and anonymity; easy, speedily, and flexible rules of incorporation.

Tax Information Exchange Agreement (TIEA) bilateral agreements signed to establish exchange of information for tax purposes.

Tax planning devices used by companies aiming at reducing taxation on earnings and relying on the knowledge of tax practitioners of the various loopholes and cracks in regulation within a territory or around the world (then called international tax planning).

Transfer pricing the price companies charge for intra-group cross-border sales of goods and services.

Trust relationship in which a person or entity (the trustee) holds legal title to certain property (the trust property) but is bound to exercise that legal control for the benefit of one or more individuals or organizations (the beneficiary).

In other words, it as a contractual agreement between two private individuals to create a barrier between the legal owner of an asset and its beneficiary.

Withholding tax tax deducted from a payment made to a person outside the country. Generally applied to investment income, such as interest, dividends, royalties, and license fees.

References

Altman, Oscar L. 1969. Eurodollars. In *Reading in the Euro-Dollar*, ed. Eric B. Chalmers. London: W.P. Griffith.

Avery Jones, John F. 1996. Tax law: Rules or principles? *Fiscal Studies* 17(3):63–89.

Baker, Raymond W. 2005. *Capitalism's Achilles heel: Dirty money and how to renew the free-market system.* London: John Wiley and Sons.

Baldacchino, Godfrey. 2006. Managing the hinterland beyond: Two ideal-type strategies of economic development for small island territories. *Asia Pacific Viewpoint* 47(1):45–60.

Baldwin, R., and P. Krugman. 2004. Agglomeration, integration and tax harmonization. *European Economic Review* 48(1):1–23.

Balzli, Beat, and Frank Hornig. 2008. Europe, US battle Swiss bank secrecy. *Der Spiegel Online International*, May 20.

Beauchamp, A. 1983. *Guide mondial des paradis fiscaux.* Paris: Grasset.

Becht, Marco, Colin Mayer, and Hannes F. Wagner. 2006. Where do firms incorporate? CEPR Discussion Paper no. 5875, October.

Becker, Brandon, and Colleen Doherty-Minicozzi. 2000. Hedge funds: A reprise of 1999's 'Where do we go from here' program. Panel Discussion, ABA Section of Business Law, Columbus, Ohio.

Beja, Edsel L. Jr. 2005. Capital flight: Meanings and measures. In *Capital flight and capital controls in developing countries*, ed. Gerald Epstein. Cheltenham, UK: Edward Elgar.

——. 2006. Was capital fleeing Southeast Asia? Estimates from Indonesia, Malaysia and the Philippines and Thailand. *Asia Pacific Business Review* 12(3):261–83.

Belotsky, Vincent P. 1987. The prevention of tax havens via income tax treaties. *California Western International Law Journal* 17:43–101.

Beltran, Daniel O., Laurie Pounder, and Charles Thomas. 2008. Foreign exposure to asset-backed securities of U.S. origin. Board of Governors of the Federal Reserve System, International Finance Discussion Papers, 939. August 6. http://www.federalreserve.gov/pubs/ifdp/2008/939/ifdp939.pdf.

Bertrand, Benoit, and Vanessa Houlder. 2008. Trounced on tax. *Financial Times*, March 6.

Berle, A. A. 1950. Historical inheritance of American corporation. In *Social meaning of legal concepts*. Vol. 3: *The power and duties of corporate management*. New York: New York University School of Law.

Bestley, T., and A. C. Case. 1995. Incumbent behavior: Vote-seeking, tax-setting, and yardstick competition. *American Economic Review* 85:25–45.

Bhattacharya, Anindya. 1980. Offshore banking in the Caribbean. *Journal of International Business Studies*. 11(3):37–46.

BIS. 1995. The BIS statistics on international banking and financial market activity. Monetary and Economic Department, Basle, Switzerland.

——. 2000. Guide to the international banking statistics. Monetary and Economic Department. Basle, Switzerland.

——. 2003a. Shell banks and booking offices. Basel Committee on Banking Supervision, Basle, January.

——. 2003b. Parallel-owned banking structures. Basel Committee on Banking Supervision. Basle, January.

——. 2005. 75th annual report. Basle, June.

Blum, Jack A., Michael Levi, R. Thomas Naylor, and Phil Williams. 1998. Financial havens, banking secrecy and money laundering. A study prepared on behalf of the United Nations under the auspices of the Global Programme against Money Laundering. Office for Drug Control and Crime Prevention, Vienna, December.

Blum, R. H. 1984. *Offshore haven banks, trusts, and companies: The Business of crime in the Euromarket*. New York: Praeger.

Boyrie, Maria E., Simon J. Pak, and John S. Zdanowicz. 2001. The impact of Switzerland's money laundering law on capital flows through abnormal pricing in international trade. CIBER Working Paper.

——. 2005. Estimating the magnitude of capital flight due to abnormal pricing in international trade: The Russia–USA case. *Accounting Forum* 29(3):249–70.

Bräutigam, Deborah, Odd-Helge Fjeldstad, and Mick Moore, eds. 2008. *Taxation and state-building in developing countries: Capacity and consent*. Cambridge: Cambridge University Press.

Brittain-Caitlin, William. 2005. *Offshore: The dark side of the global economy*. New York: Farrar, Strauss and Giroux.

Browning, Lynneley. 2008. A one-time tax break saved 843 U.S. corporations $265 billion. *New York Times*, June 24.

Brueckner, J. K., and L. A. Saavedra. 2001. Do local governments engage in strategic property tax competition? *National Tax Journal* 54:203–29.

Burn, Gary. 1999. The state, the city and the Euromarket. *Review of International Political Economy* 4(2):225–60.

——. 2005. *Re-emergence of global finance*. London: Palgrave.

Burton, John. 2008. Singapore: From guns to bankers in colonial bungalow. *Financial Times*, June 20.

Calcutta Jute Mills, Limited v. Nicholson (Surveyor of Taxes), Cesena Sulphur Company, Limited v. Nicholson (Surveyor of Taxes), (1876) I TC 83, 88 (HL).

Campbell, Greg. 2002. *Blood diamonds: Tracing the deadly path of the world's most precious stones*. Boulder, CO: Westview Press.

Capgemini, and Merrill Lynch. 2007. World wealth report 2007. http://www.ml.com/media/79882.pdf.

Case, A. C. 1993. Interstate tax competition after TRA86. *Journal of Policy Analysis and Management* 12:136–48.

Cassard, M. 1994. The role of offshore centers in international financial intermediation. IMF Working Paper no. 107, Washington, DC.

Cavalier, G. A. 2005. Tax havens and publics international law: The case of the Netherlands Antilles. *Bepress Legal Series*. Working Paper 567. http://law.bepress.com/expresso/eps/567.

Cayman Island Government. 2004. Budget 2004/5, Tabled in the Legislative Assembly 16 March 2004. Strategic Policy Statement, Caymans Islands. http://www.radiocayman.gov.ky/pls/portal30/docs/FOLDER/SITE83/LOCALISSUES/BDGTSPSOSX.PDF.

CBO. 2005. Why does U.S. investment abroad earn higher returns than foreign investment in the United States? Economic and budget issue briefs. November 30. http://www.cbo.gov/ftpdocs/69xx/doc6905/11-30-Cross-BorderInvestment.pdf.

Chaikin, David. 2005. Policy and fiscal effects of Swiss bank secrecy. *Revenue Law Journal* 15(1):90–110.

Chambost, Eduard. 1977. *Guides des paradis fiscaux*. Paris: Fabre.

Chavagneux, Christian. 2001. Secret bancaire: une légende helvétique. *Alternatives Economiques* no. 188, January.

———. 2004. *Economie politique internationale*. Paris: La Découverte.

———. 2009. *Les dernières heures du libéralisme*. Paris: Editions Perrin.

Chavagneux, Christian, and Ronen Palan. 2006. *Paradis Fiscaux*. Paris: La Découverte (Edition Repères).

Chee Soon Juan. 2008. Singapore's future as a financial centre. Singapore's Democrats. http://yoursdp.org/index.php/perspective/special-feature/1513-singapores-future-as-a-financial-centre-part-i.

Christian Aid. 2008. Death and taxes. London. http://www.christianaid.org.uk/getinvolved/christianaidweek/cawreport/index.aspx.

Clark, Andrew. 2008. How to set up a hedge fund. *Guardian*, August 6.

Clarke, William M. 2004. *How the City of London works*. London: Sweet & Maxwell.

Clausing, K., and A. Calusing. 2007. Closer economic integration and corporate tax systems. Paper presented at the conference Tax Havens and tax competition, Universita Bocconi.

Clegg, David. 2006. The morality of taxation. Ernst & Young. http://www.schmidtreport.co.uk/Subscribers/offshore/offshore4.html.

Cobb, Corkill. 1998. Global finance and the growth of offshore financial centers: The Manx experience. *Geoforum* 29:7–21.

Commons, John. [1924] 1959. *The Legal foundations of capitalism*. Madison: University of Wisconsin Press.

Corporation of London. 2005. *The competitive position of London*. http://www.zyen.com/Knowledge/Research/LCGFC.pdf.

Council on Foreign Relations. 2002. Terrorist financing. Task Force Report, Washington, DC.

Couzin, Robert. 2002. *Corporate residence and international taxation*. Amsterdam: IBFD.

Crombie, Roger. 2008. Bermuda in-depth series part I: lighting and fire. *Risk and Insurance*, January 1.

CRS Report. 1998. The 1997–98 Asian financial crisis. http://www.fas.org/man/crs/crs-asia2.htm.

Desai, Mihir, A. C. Fritz Foley, and James R. Hines Jr. 2002. Dividend policy inside the firm. NBER Working Paper no. 8698.

———. 2004a. Foreign direct investment in a world of multiple taxes. *Journal of Public Economics* 88:2727–44.

———. 2004b. Economic effects of tax havens. *NBER Working Paper* no. 10806.

——. 2005. The degradation of reported corporate profits. *Journal of Economic Perspectives* 19(4):171–92.

——. 2006. The demand for tax haven operations. *Journal of Public Economics* 90:513–31.

Dev, Kar, and Devon Cartwright-Smith. 2008. *Illicit financial flows from developing countries: 2002–2006*. Washington, DC: Global Financial Integrity. www.gfip.org.

Devereux, M., R. Griffith, and A. Klemm. 2002. Corporate income tax reforms and international tax competition. *Economic Policy* 35:449–96.

Dharmapala, Dhammika A., and James R. Hines. 2006. Which countries become tax havens? *NBER Working Paper* no. 12802.

Diamond, Walter, and Dorothy Diamond. 1998. *Tax havens of the world*. New York: Matthew Bender Books.

Dill, T. M., and L. M. Minty. 1932. Bermuda laws and franchise. *J. Comp. Legis. & Int'l L.* 3d ser. 216.

Dinmore, Gary, and Hugh Williamson. 2008. Italy gripped as names of Liechtenstein accounts holders leak out. *Financial Times*, March 20.

Dixon, Liz. 2001. Financial flows via offshore financial centers. *Financial Stability Review* 10:104–15.

Doggart, Caroline. 2002. *Tax havens and their uses*. 10th ed. London: Economist Intelligence Unit.

Doyle, Michelle, and Anthony Johnson. 1999. Does offshore business mean onshore economic gains. Central Bank of Barbados Working Papers 1999, pp. 95–111.

Duménil, Gerard, and David Lévy. 2004. *Capital resurgent*. Cambridge, MA: Harvard University Press.

Dupuis-Danon, M. C. 2004. *Finance criminelle*, 2nd edition. Paris: PUF.

ECOFIN. 1999. Code of conduct business taxation council of the European Union. Brussels. http://ec.europa.eu/taxation_customs/resources/documents/primarolo_en.pdf.

Eden, Lorraine, and Robert Kudrle. 2005. Tax havens: Renegade states in the international tax regime? *Law & Policy* 27:100–127.

Edwards, Andrew. 1998. Review of financial regulation in the Crown Dependencies: A report." The Edwards report, London, Home Office.

Epstein, Edwin. 1969. *The corporation in American Politics*. Englewood Cliffs, NJ: Prentice Hall.

Ernst & Young. 2008. Global transfer pricing report for 2007. http://www.ey.com/.

European Commission. 2006. Taxation papers: A history of the "tax package." The Principles and issues underlying the community approach. Working Paper no. 10.

Evans, N. 2002. Bermuda: The new standard setter?" *Euromoney*, January.

Federal Reserve Bank of New York (FRBNY). 2007. International Banking Facilities. FedPoints. http://www.newyorkfed.org/aboutthefed/fedpoint/fed20.html.

Fehrenbach, R. R. 1966. *The gnomes of Zurich*. London: Leslie Frewin.

Feld, Lars P., and Emmanuelle Reulier. 2005. Strategic tax competition in Switzerland: Evidence from a panel of the Swiss cantons. Cesifo Working Paper no. 1516 Category 1: Public Finance, August.

Financial Action Task Force on Money Laundering (FATF). 2000. Report on noncooperative countries and territories. February 14, OECD, Paris.

Financial Stability Forum (FSF). 2000. Report of the Working Group on Offshore Centers. www.fsformum.org/Reports/RepOFC.pdf.

——. 2005. FSF Announces a New Process to Promote Further Improvements in Offshore Financial Centers (OFCs). Press Release. Ref 11/2005. March 11. http://www.fsforum.org/press/pr_050311b.pdf?noframes=1.

Fleming, Donald M. 1974. The Bahamas tax paradise. *Tax Executive* 27:217–24.

Frank, Robert. 2007. *Richistan: A journey through the 21st century wealth boom and the lives of the new rich.* London: Piatikus.

G-20. 2009. Declaration on strengthening the financial system—London, 2 April. http://www.g20.org/pub_communiques.aspx.

Garretsen, Harry, and Jolanda Peeters. 2006. Capital mobility, agglomeration and corporate tax rates: Is the race to the bottom for real? De Nederleandsche Bank (DNB) Working Paper no. 113.

Gates, Carolyn L. 1998, *The merchant republic of Lebanon: Rise of an open economy.* Oxford: I.B. Tauris.

Genschel, Philip. 2002. Globalization, tax competition, and the welfare state. *Politics and Society* 30(2):245–75.

———. 2005. Globalization and the transformation of the tax state. *European Review* 13:53–71.

Gerakis, A. S., and A. G. Roncesvalles. 1983. Bahrain's offshore banking center. *Economic Development and Cultural Change*, 31(2):271–93.

Ginsburg, Anthony S. 1991. *Tax havens.* New York: New York Institute of Finance.

Global Witness. 2006. Heavy mittal? A state within a state: The inequitable mineral development agreement between the government of Liberia and Mittal Steel holdings NV. A Report by Global Witness, October. http://www.globalwitness.org/media_library_detail.php/156/en/heavy_mittal.

Glos, George E. 1984. Analysis of a tax haven: The Liechtenstein Anstalt. *International Lawyer* 18(4):929–36.

Godefroy, T., and P. Lascoumes. 2004. Le *capitalisme* clandestin. L'illusoire régulation des places offshore. Paris: La Découverte.

Goodfriend, Marvin. 1998. Eurodollar. In Instruments of money market, ed. Timothy Q. Cook and Robert K. Laroche. 7th ed. Richmond, VA: Federal Reserve Bank of Richmond.

Gordon Report. 1981. Tax Havens and their use by U.S. taxpayers. Report prepared for the Internal Revenue Service Washington, DC.

Gorton, G., and N. S. Souleles. 2005. Special purpose vehicles and securization. Federal Reserve Bank of Philadelphia Working Paper no. 05–21.

Gourvish, T. R. 1987. British business and the transition to a corporate economy: Entrepreneurship and management structures. *Business History* 29(4):18–45.

Government Accounting Office (GAO). 2000. Suspicious banking activities: Possible money laundering by U.S. corporations formed for Russian entities. Report to the Ranking Minority Member, Permanent Subcommittee on Investigations, Committee on Governmental Affairs, U.S. Senate Washington, DC.

———. 2004. Tax administration comparison of the reported tax liabilities of foreign and U.S.-controlled corporations, 1996–2000. Report to Congressional Requesters, February. http://www.gao.gov/new.itemsUnited States General Accounting Office/d04358.pdf.

———. 2008. Cayman Islands: Business and tax advantages attract U.S. persons and enforcement challenges exist. Report to the Chairman and Ranking Member, Committee on Finance, U.S. Senate, July.

Gray, Simon. 2005. Vista trusts allow BVI to sough off past and attract global business. *The Lawyer.com*, 17 January.

Gruber, H., and J. Mutti. 1991. Taxes, tariff and transfer pricing in multinational corporate decision making. *Review of Economics and Statistics* 73(2):285–93.

Grundy, Milton. 1987. *Grundy's tax havens: A world survey.* London: Sweet and Maxwell.

Guex, Sebasiten. 1998. *L'argent de l'état: Parcours des finances publiques au xxe siécle.* Lausanne : Réalités sociales.

———. 1999. Les origines du secret bancaire suisse et son rôle dans la politique de la confédération au sortir de la Seconde Guerre mondiale. *Genèses* 34.

Gutcher, Lianne. 2006. Banks braced for demands to hand over offshore information. *The Scotsman,* May 4.

Haiduk, Kiryl. 2007. The political economy of post-Soviet offshorization. In *After deregulation: Global finance in the new century,* ed. Libby Assassi, Duncan Wigan, and Anastasia Nesvetailova. London: Palgrave.

Hampton, Mark. 1996. *The offshore interface: Tax havens in the global economy.* Basingstoke: Macmillan.

———. 2007. Offshore finance centers and rapid complex constant change. Kent Business School Working Paper no. 132.

Hampton, M. P., and John Christensen. 1999. Treasure island revisited. Jersey's offshore finance centre crisis: Implications for other small island economies. *Environment and Planning* 31:1619–37.

———. 2002. Offshore pariahs? Small island economies, tax havens and the reconfiguration of global finance. *World Development* 30(9):1657–73.

Hanzawa, Masamitsu. 1991. *The Tokyo offshore market. In Japan's Financial Markets.* Tokyo: Foundation for Advanced Information and Research.

Hedge Fund Research Inc. 2006. HFR industry report—Year end 2006. http://www.hedgefundresearch.com.

Hejazi, Walid. 2007. Offshore financial centres and the Canadian economy. http://www.rotman.utoronto.ca/facBios/file/canadianeconomy.pdf.

Helleiner, Eric. 1994. *States and the reemergence of global finance.* Ithaca: Cornell University Press.

Her Majesty's Revenue & Customs (HMRC). 2007. Taxation of the foreign profits of companies: a discussion document. http://customs.hmrc.gov.uk/channelsPortal WebApp/downloadFile?contentID=HMCE_PROD1_027592.

———. 2008. Company residence: Guidance originally published in the International Tax Handbook. http://www.hmrc.gov.uk/manuals/intmanual/INTM120150.htm.

Herbert, Christine. 2008. £100,000 PR campaign. *Jersey Evening Post,* June 27.

Heyndels, B., and J. Vuchelen. 1997. Tax mimicking among Belgian municipalities. *National Tax Journal* 51:89–101.

Higonnet, René P. 1985. Eurobanks, eurodollars and international debt. In *Eurodollars and international banking,* ed. Paolo Savona and George Sutija. Basingstoke: Macmillan.

Hines, J. R. 1999. Lessons from behavioural responses to international taxation. In *Location and competition,* ed. S. Brakman and H. Garretsen. London: Routledge.

Hines, James R., and Eric M. Rice. 1994. Fiscal paradise: Foreign tax havens and American business. *Quarterly Journal of Economics* 109:149–82.

Hinks, Gavin. 2008. UK corporations moving overseas: Will they stay or will they go? *Accountancy Age,* May 14.

Hodess, Robin. 2004. Introduction: Transparency International. Where did the money go? Global Corruption Report 2004. London: Pluto.

Hodjera, Zlatan. 1978. The Asian currency market: Singapore as a regional financial centre. International Monetary Fund Staff Papers, 252: 221–53.

Hong, Qing, and Michael Smart. 2007. In Praise of Tax Havens: International Tax Planning and Foreign Direct Investment. http://www.fatf-gafi.org/document/9/0,2340,en_32250379_32236920_34032073_1_1_1_1,00.html.

Hoskins, Patrik. 2007. HBOS bails out own fund as effect of credit crisis spreads. *Times*, August 22.

Houlder, Vanessa. 2008a. Accord puts suspected tax evaders in spotlight. *Financial Times*, October 29.

——. 2008b. Harbours of resentment, *Financial Times*, December 1.

Huber, Nick. 2008. Offshore tax havens: Crackdown. *Accountancy Age*, November 27.

Hübsch, Marc. 2004. Economic development policy in the context of EU enlargement: The case of Luxembourg. Paper presented at the workshop on small states, University of Iceland, September.

Hudson, Alan C. 1998. Reshaping the regulatory landscape: Border skirmishes around the Bahamas and Cayman offshore financial centers. *Review of International Political Economy* 5(3):534–64.

Hug, Peter. 2000. Les vraies origines du secret bancaire, démontage d'un mythe. *Le Temps*, April 27.

IFSL. 2007a. 2007 Hedge Funds. International Financial Services, City Business Series. http://www.ifsl.org.uk/upload/CBS_Hedge_Funds_2007.pdf.

——. 2007b. International Financial Markets in the UK. www.IFSL.org.uk/research.

IMF. 2000. Offshore Financial Centers. IMF Background Paper. Prepared by the Monetary and Exchange Affairs Department, June.

INCSR. 2008. U.S. International Narcotics Control Strategy Report, vol. 2, U.S. Department of State, Bureau for International Narcotics and Law Enforcement Affairs. March 2008.

Irish, Charles R. 1982. Tax havens. Vanderbildt Journal of Transnational Law, pp. 49–510.

Ise, William H. Boston College. *Indus. & Com. L. Rev.* 194 1969–1970, Secret Swiss bank accounts as a mechanism for violating United States securities laws: An analysis of proposed solutions legislation, *J. Comp. Legis. & Int'l L.* 3d ser. 216.

Jao, Y. C. 2003. Shanghai and Hong Kong as international financial centres: Historical Perspective and contemporary analysis. Hong Kong Institute of Economics and Business Strategy, no. 1071. http://www.hiebs.hku.hk/working_paper_updates/pdf/wp1071.pdf.

Jersey Financial Services Commission (JFSC). (no date). Report of the Working Group on Offshore Centres. http://www.jerseyfsc.org/the_commission/international_co-operation/evaluations/independent_reportofworkinggroup.asp#7.

Jersey Police Report. 2006. http://www.taxresearch.org.uk/Documents/Statesof JerseyPoliceAnnualReport2006.pdf.

Jeune, Philip. 1999. Jersey hits back over tax haven allegations. *Financial Times*, September 25.

Johns R. A. 1983. *Tax havens and offshore finance: A study of transnational economic development*. New York: St. Martin's Press.

Johns, R. A., and C. M. Le Marchant. 1993. *Finance centres: British isle offshore development since 1979*. London: Pinter.

Kane, Daniel R. 1983. *The eurodollar market and the years of crisis*. London and Canberra: Helm.

Kakazu, H. 1994. *Sustainable development of small island economies*. Oxford: Westview Press.

Kim, Woochan, and Shang-Jon Wei. 2001. Offshore Investment funds: Monster in Emerging Markets? HKIMR Working Paper no. 05/2001. http://papers.ssrn.com/sol3/papers.cfm?abstract_id=1009446#PaperDownload.

KPMG. 2005. Transfer Pricing Surveys 2005–2006.

———. 2007. *The KPMG Corporate Tax Rate Survey 1993 to 2006.* http://www.kpmg
.com/NR/rdonlyres/D8CBA9FF-C953-45FA-940A-FAAC86729554/0/KPMG
CorporateTaxRateSurvey.pdf.

Kudrle, Robert T. 2003. Hegemony strikes out: The U.S. global role in antitrust, tax evasion, and illegal immigration. *International Studies Perspectives* 4(1):52–71.

Kudrle, Robert T., and Lorraine Eden. 2003. The campaign against the tax havens: Will it last? Will it work? *Stanford Journal of Law, Business and Finance* 9:37–68.

Kuenzler, Roman. 2007. Les paradis fiscaux. M.A. thesis, University of Geneva.

Kynaston, D. 2001. *The city of London. A club no more, 1945–2000.* London: Chatto & Windus.

Les paradis fiscaux. 1999. *L'economie politique.* vol. 4.

LeRoy, Greg. 2006. The great American jobs and tax scam. *Tax Justice Focus* 2(4).

Levin, Carl. 2003. U.S. tax shelter industry: The Role of accountants, lawyers and financial professionals. Statement by Senator Carl Levin before U.S. Senate Permanent Subcommittee on Investigations, November 18. http://levin.senate.gov/newsroom/release.cfm?id=216379.

———. 2006. Tax havens abuses: The enablers, the tools and secrecy. Senate Permanent Subcommittee on Investigations. U.S. Senate. Committee on Homeland Security and Government Affairs, August 1. http://levin.senate.gov/newsroom/supporting/2006/PSI.taxhavenabuses.080106.pdf.

———. 2007. Levin, Coleman, Obama introduce Stop Tax Haven Abuse Act. Press Office of Senator Carl Levin. http://levin.senate.gov/newsroom/release.cfm?id=269479.

Likhovski, Assaf. 2007. The law and public opinion explaining IRC v. Duke of Westminster. In *Studies in the history of tax law,* ed. John Tiley, vol. 2. Oxford: Hart.

Lindholm, Richard W. 1944. *The corporate franchise as a basis of taxation.* Austin: University of Texas Press.

Looijestijn-Clearie, Anne. 2000. Centros LTD: A complete u-turn in the right of establishment for companies? *International and Comparative Law Quarterly* 49(3):621–42.

Maillard, De J. 1998. *Un monde sans loi. La criminalité financière en image.* Paris: Stock.

———. 2001. *Le Marché fait sa loi. De l'usage du crime par la mondialisation.* Paris: Mille et une nuits.

Maingot, Anthony P. 1995. Offshore secrecy centers and the necessary role of states: Bucking the trend. *Journal of Interamerican Studies and World Affairs* 37(4): 1–24.

———. 1998. Laundering drug profits: Miami and Caribbean tax havens. *Journal of Interamerican Studies and World Affairs* 30(2): 167–87.

Marias, Saul G. 1957. Liechtenstein—A corporate home away from home. *Business Lawyer* 1956–57.

Marshall, Don D. 1996. Understanding late-twentieth-century capitalism. *Government and Opposition* 31:193–214.

Masciandaro, Donato, ed. 2004. *Global financial crime: Terrorism, money and offshore centers.* London: Ashgate.

Mathiason, Nick. 2008. Tax scandal leaves Swiss giant reeling. *Observer,* June 29.

Maurer, Bill. 1998. Cyberspatial sovereignties: Offshore finance, digital cash, and the limits of liberalism. *Indiana Journal of Global Legal Studies* 52:493–519.

McClam, Warren D. 1974. Monetary growth and the euro-currency market. In *National monetary policies and the international financial system,* ed. Robert Z. Aliber. Chicago: Chicago University Press.

Meinzer, Marcus. 2005. Buenos Aires bans investment from offshore companies. *Tax Justice Focus* 1(2):10.

Merrill Lynch, Gapgemini, Ernst & Young. 2002. *World Wealth Report 2002.* New York.

Moffett, Michael H., and Arthur Stonehill. 1989. International banking facilities revisited. *Journal of International Financial Management and Accounting* 1(1):88–103.

Morgenthau, Henry. 2006. Note du Trésor sur la fraude et l'évasion fiscales. *L'economie politique*, no. 19, July.

Murphy, Richard. 2006. The price of offshore. TJN Briefing Paper. http://www.taxjustice.net/cms/front_content.php?idcatart=134.

———. 2007. UK subsidises the Isle of Man to be a tax haven. Tax Justice Network. http://www.taxresearch.org.uk/Documents/TRIoM3-07.pdf.

———. 2008a. *The missing billions: The UK tax gap*. Touch Stone Pamphlets. www.tuc.org.uk/touchstonepamphlets.

———. 2008b. The Direct Tax Cost of Tax Havens to the UK. Tax Research. http://www.taxresearch.org.uk/Documents/TaxHavenCostTRLLP.pdf.

Naím, Moisés. 2005. *Illicit: How smugglers, traffickers, and copycats are hijacking the global economy*. New York: Doubleday.

National Audit Office (NAO). 2007. Managing Risk in the Overseas Territories. Report by the Comptroller and Auditor General. London: The Stationery Office.

Naylor, R. T. 1987. *Hot money and the politics of debt*. London: Unwin Hyman.

———. 2002. *Wages of crime: Black markets, illegal finance and the underworld economy*. Ithaca: Cornell University Press.

Nesvetailova, Anastasia. 2007. *Fragile finance: Debt, speculation and crisis in the age of global credit*. Basingstoke: Palgrave.

Neveling, Nicholas. 2007a. Mass opposition to HMRC's disclosure changes as a head. *Accountancy Age*, January 18.

———. 2007b. Darling on the offensive against UK "tax havens" claims. *Accountancy Age*, July 19.

Norregaard, John, and Tehmina S. Khan. 2007. *Tax policy: Recent trends and coming challenges*. International Monetary Fund: IMF Working Paper, WP/07/274.

Novack, J., and L. Saunders. 1998. The hustling of rated shelters. *Forbes*, December 14.

OECD. 1987. International tax avoidance and evasion: Four related studies. Issues in International Taxation. no. 1. OECD Committee on Fiscal Affairs. Paris: OECD.

———. 1998. *Harmful tax competition: An emerging global issue*. Paris: OECD. http://www.oecd.org/dataoecd/33/0/1904176.pdf.

———. 1999. *OECD benchmark definition of foreign direct investment*. 3rd ed. http://www.oecd.org/dataoecd/10/16/2090148.pdf.

———. 2000. *Improving access to bank information for tax purposes*. Paris: OECD. http://www.oecd.org/dataoecd/24/63/39327984.pdf.

———. 2001. Transfer pricing guidelines for multinational enterprises and tax administrations. Paris: OECD. http://www.oecd.org/document/34/0,3343,en_2649_33753_1915490_1_1_1_1,00.html.

———. 2002. Intra-industry and intra-firm trade and the internationalisation of production. OECD Economic Outlook 71. June. http://stats.oecd.org/Index.aspx?DataSetCode=EO71_MAIN.

———. 2004. *The OECD's Project on harmful tax practices: The 2004 progress report*. Paris: OECD.

———. 2006. Third meeting of the OECD forum on tax administration, 14–15 September, 2006, Final Seoul Declaration. Paris: OECD.

———. 2007. *Revenue statistics, 1965–2006*. Paris: OECD.

———. 2008a. 4th Meeting of the forum on tax administration. Cape Town, 10 January 2008. Address by Trevor Manuel, MP, Minister of Finance of the Republic of South Africa.

———. 2008b. Tax disclosures in Germany part of broader challenge, says OECD Secretary-General. http://www.oecd.org/document/34/0,3343,en_2649_201185_40114018_1_1_1_1,00.html.

Olson, P. 2002. Testimony of Pamela Olson before the House Committee on ways and means on corporate inversion transactions. Office of Public Affairs, U.S. Treasury.

Oppenheimer, Peter M. 1985. Comment on Aliber, Robert Z. Eurodollars: An economic analysis. In *Eurodollars and international banking*, ed. Paolo Savona and George Sutija. Basingstoke: Macmillan.

Oxfam. 2000. Tax havens: Releasing the hidden billions for poverty eradication. Policy Paper. http://www.taxjustice.net/cms/upload/pdf/oxfam_paper_-_final_version__06_00.pdf.

Pack, S. J, and J. S. Zdanowicz. 2002. US Trade with the world. An estimate of 2001 lost U.S federal income tax revenues due to over-invoiced imports and under-invoiced exports. Study for Senator Byron Dorgan.

Palan, Ronen. 1998. Luring buffaloes and the game of industrial subsidies: A critique of national competitive policies in the era of the competition state. *Global Society* 12(3):323–41.

——. 2002. Tax havens and the commercialisation of state sovereignty. *International Organization* 56(1):153–78.

——. 2003. *The offshore world: Sovereign markets, virtual places, and nomad millionaires.* Ithaca: Cornell University Press.

Palan, Ronen, and Jason Abbott. 1996. *State strategies in the global political economy.* London: Pinter.

Palan, Ronen, and Richard Murphy. 2007. Tax subsidies and profits: Business and corporate capitalisation. In *After deregulation: Global finance in the new century*, ed. Libby Assassi, Duncan Wigan, and Anastasia Nesvetailova. London: Palgrave.

Papke, Leslie E. 2000. One-way treaty with the world: The U.S. withholding tax and the Netherland Antilles. *International Tax and Public Finance* 7:295–313.

Park, Y. S. 1982. The economics of offshore financial centers. *Columbia Journal of World Business.* 17(4):31–35.

Paris, Roland. 2003. The globalization of taxation? Electronic commerce and the transformation of the state. *International Studies Quarterly* 47(2):153–82.

Payne, P. L. 1967. The emergence of the large-scale company in Great Britain, 1870–1914. *Economic History Review* 20(3):519–42.

Pearson, Robin. 2006. Introduction to *The history of the company: The development of the business corporation 1700–1914*, ed. Robin Pearson, James Taylor, and Mark Freemen. London: Pickering and Chato.

Peillon, V., and A. Montebourg. 2000. La Principauté du Liechtenstein: paradis des affaires et de la délinquance financière. *Rapport d'information de l'Assemblée nationale*, no. 2311, 18/2000.

——. 2001. La Cité de Londres, Gibraltar et les Dépendances de la Couronne: des centres offshore, sanctuaires de l'argent sale. *Rapport d'information de l'Assemblée nationale*, no. 2311. 52/2001.

Picciotto, Sol. 1992. *International business taxation.* London: Weidenfeld and Nicolson.

——. 1999. Offshore: The state as legal fiction. In *Offshore finance centres and tax havens: The rise of global capital*, ed. Mark Hampton and Jason Abbott. Basingstoke: Macmillan.

Piketty, Thomas. 2001. *Les hauts revenus en France au XXe siècle: inégalités et redistributions, 1901–1998.* Paris: Grasset.

Piotrowska, Joanna, and Werner Vanborren. 2008. The corporate income tax rate-revenue paradox: Evidence in the EU. European Commission taxation papers. http://ideas.repec.org/p/tax/taxpap/0012.html.

Powers, William C., Raymond S. Troubb, and Herbert S. Winokur. 2002. Report of investigation by the Special Investigative Committee of the Board of Directors of Enron Corp. Austin, TX, February 1.

President Kennedy appeal to the Congress for a tax cut. 1961. http://www.national center.org/JFKTaxes1961.html.

President's Commission on Organized Crime. 1984. Organized Crime of Asian Origins. Record of Hearing III—October 23–25, New York, NY. Washington DC: Government Printing Office.

Quiet flows the dosh: A piece on capital flight out of Russia. 2000. *Economist*, December 7.

Radaelli, Claudio M. 2003. The code of conduct against harmful tax competition: Open method of coordination in disguise? *Public Administration* 81(3):513–31.

Radaelli, Claudio M., and Ulrike S. Kraemer. 2005. *The rise and fall of governance legitimacy: The case of international direct taxation.* http://huss.exeter.ac.uk/politics/research/readingroom/.

Radelet, Steven, and Jeffrey Sachs. 1998. The onset of the East Asian financial crisis. Harvard Institute for International Development, March 30. http://www.cid .harvard.edu/archive/hiid/papers/eaonset2.pdf.

Ramati, U. E. 1991. *Liechtenstein's uncertain foundation: Anatomy of a tax haven.* Dublin: Hazlemore LTD. tax publications.

Rawlings, Greg. 2004. Laws, liquidity and eurobonds: The making of the Vanuatu tax haven. *Journal of Pacific History* 393:325–41.

———. 2005. Mobile people, mobile capital and tax neutrality: Sustaining a market for offshore finance centres. *Accounting Forum* 29:289–310.

Rawlings, Greg, and Brigitte Unger. 2005. Competing for Criminal Money. Utrecht School of Economics discussion paper series 05–26.

Ridley, Timothy. 2007. What makes the Cayman Islands a successful international financial services centre? Background paper presented at the Caribbean Investment Forum, Montego Bay, Jamaica, June. *BIS Review* 72/2007 1.

Riesco, Manuel, Gustavo Lagos, and Marcos Lima, 2005. The "pay your taxes" debate: Perspectives on corporate taxation and social responsibility in the Chilean mining industry. UN Research Institute for Social Development. http://www .taxjustice-usa.org/index2.php?option=com_content&do_pdf=1&id=151.

Rixen, Thomas. 2008. *The political economy of international tax governance.* Basingstoke: Palgrave.

Robbie, K. J. H. 1975/6. Socialist banks and the origins of the euro-currency markets. *Moscow Narodny Bank Quarterly Review* (Winter):21–36.

Robé, J-P. 1997. Multinational enterprises: The constitution of a pluralist legal order. In *Global law without a state*, ed. Gunther Teubner. Aldershot, UK: Dartmouth.

Roberts, Susan. 1994. Fictitious capital, fictitious spaces: The geography of offshore financial flows. In *Money, power and space*, ed. Stuart Corbridge, Ron Martin, and Nigel Thrift. Oxford: Blackwell.

Rose, Andrew K., and Mark M. Spiegel. 2007. Offshore financial centres: Parasites or symbiotics? *Economic Journal* 117(523):1310–55.

Schenk, Catherine R. 1998. The origins of the eurodollar market in London, 1955–63. *Explorations in Economic History* 21:1–19.

Schmidt Report. 1999. General principles relating to the use of offshore tax havens. http://www.schmidtreport.co.uk/Subscribers/offshore/offshore4.html.

Select Committee on Trade and Industry. 1998. Examination of Witnesses Questions 112–122, Professor P. Sikka, Tuesday 1 December 1998. http://www.parliament .the-stationery-office.co.uk/pa/cm199899/cmselect/cmtrdind/59/81201a19.htm.

Sharman, Jason C. 2005. South Pacific tax havens: From leaders in the race to the bottom to laggards in the race to the top? *Accounting Forum* 29:311–23.

———. 2006. *Havens in a storm: The struggle for global tax regulation.* Ithaca, NY: Cornell University Press.

———. 2007. The future of offshore. Paper Presented at the International Studies Association Annual Conference, San Francisco, March.

Sharman, Jason, and Percy S. Mistry. 2008. *Considering the consequences: The development implications of initiatives on taxation, anti-money laundering and combating the financing of terrorism.* London: Commonwealth Secretariat.

Sharman, Jason, and Greg Rawlings. 2006. National tax blacklist: A comparative analysis. *Journal of International Taxation* 17(9):38–47.

Shaxson, N. 2007. *Poisoned wells: The dirty politics of African oil.* Basingstoke: Palgrave Macmillan.

Sikka, Prem. 2003. The role of offshore financial centres in globalization. *Accounting Forum* 27:365–99.

Slemrod, Joel. 1994. Free trade taxation and protectionist taxation. NBER Working Paper no. 4902.

———. 2004. The economics of corporate tax selfishness», *NBER Working Paper* no. 10858, October.

Slemrod, Joel, and John D. Wilson. 2006. Tax Competition with Parasitic Tax Havens. Ross School of Business Working Paper Series, no. 1033, Michigan State University, March.

Sorensen, P. B. 2006. Can capital income taxes survive? And should they? *CESifo Economic Studies* 53(2):172–228.

Srinivasan, Kannan. 2005. Capital flight recycling in India. *Tax Justice Focus* 1(4):1–2.

State of Jersey. 2005. Survey of financial institutions 2005, Statistics Unit. St. Peter Port, State of Jersey.

Step Survey 2004. 2004. *STEP Journal.* www.step.org.

Stewart, Jim. 2005. Fiscal incentives, corporate structure and financial aspects of treasury management. *Accounting Forum* 29:271–88.

Stockman, Farah. 2008. Shell firms shielded U.S. contractor from taxes. *Boston Globe,* May 4.

Strange, Susan. 1988. *States and markets: An introduction to international political economy.* New York: Basil.

Sullivan, Martin A. 2004a. Data show dramatic shift of profits to tax havens. *Tax Notes,* September 13:1190–1200.

———. 2004b. Economic analysis: Profit shift out of U.S. grows, costing treasury $10 billion or more. *Tax Analysts,* September 28.

———. 2007a. Lessons from the last war on tax havens, *Tax Notes* 116: 327–37.

———. 2007b. Tax analysts offshore project. *Tax Notes Today,* October 10. http://www.taxanalysts.com/www/features.nsf/Articles/C3C3ACF3CB7036637852573770076DFAD?OpenDocument.

Summers, Lawrence. 2008. A strategy to promote healthy globalization. *Financial Times,* May 4.

Sunderland, Ruth, and Nick Mathiason. 2007. Into the lion's den. *Observer,* June.

Suss, E., O. Williams, and C. Mendis. 2002. Caribbean offshore financial centers: Past, present, and possibilities for the future. IMF Working Paper, wp/02/88, Revised 6/26/02.

Swank, Duane. 2006. Tax policy in an era of internationalization: Explaining the spread of neoliberalism. *International Organization* 60:847–82.

Sylla, Richard. 2002. United States banks and Europe: Strategy and attitudes. In *European banks and the American challenge: Competition and cooperation in international banking under Bretton Woods,* ed. Stefano Battilossi and Youssef Cassis. Oxford: Oxford University Press.

Taylor, David. 2006. A political technology of information technology: Assessing the developmental impact of the Eastern Caribbean Securities Exchange. PhD diss., University of Sussex.

Tiebout, Charles M. 1956. A pure theory of local expenditure. *Journal of Political Economy* 64:416–24.

Tikhomirov, V. 1997. Capital flight from post-Soviet Russia. *Europe-Asia Studies* 49(4):591–615.

TJN. 2005. Tax us if you can. http://www.taxjustice.net/cms/upload/pdf/tuiyc_-_ eng_-web_file.pdf.

Tolley's Tax Havens. 1993. Croydon: Tolley.

Toniolo, Gianni. 2005. *Central bank cooperation at the Bank for International Settlements, 1930–1973.* Cambridge: Cambridge University Press.

Tranoy, Bent Sofus. 2002. Offshore finance and money laundering: The politics of combating parasitic strategies. SNF project no. 1370, Institute for Research in Economics and Business Administration, Bergen, April.

Tschoegl, Adrian E. 1989. The benefits and costs of hosting financial centres. In *International banking and financial centres*, ed. Yoon S Park and M. Essayyad. Amsterdam: Kluwer.

UNCTAD. 2005. *World Investment Report 2005.* Geneva: UNCTAD.

United States Department of Treasury. 2001. Treasury Secretary O'Neill statement on OECD tax havens. Office of Public Affairs for Immediate Release May 10, 2001 PO-366, Washington, DC.

U.S. Senate. 1983. *Crime and secrecy.* Washington, DC: U.S. Government Printing Office.

———. 2002. The role of the board of directors in Enron's collapse. Report Prepared by the Permanent Subcommittee on Investigations of the Committee on Governmental Affairs, United States Senate, 107th Congress, 2nd Session, 107–70. Washington, DC: U.S. Senate.

———. 2003. U.S. Tax shelter industry: The role of accountants, lawyers and financial professionals, U.S. Senate Committee on Homeland Security and Governmental Affairs, Permanent Subcommittee on Investigations. http://hsgac.senate.gov/ public/index.cfm?Fuseaction=Hearings.Detail&HearingID=f5bce0f9-8780-456e -bb1b-c2e6b6ad525.

United States of America v. Bradley Birkenfeld. 2008. United States District Court, Southern District of Florida, Case no. *08-CR-60099-ZLOCH.* http://www.gfip.org/storage /gfip/documents/birkenfeld%20statement%20of%20facts.pdf.

UN. 1999. International convention for the suppression of the financing of terrorism. http://untreaty.un.org/english/Terrorism/Conv12.pdf.

———. 2008. Follow-up international conference on financing for development to review the implementation of the monetary consensus, Doha, Qatar, November 29—December 2.

Van Dijk, Michiel, Francis Weyzig, and Richard Murphy. 2006. *The Netherlands: A tax haven.* Amsterdam: Centre for Research on Multinational Corporations (SOMO).

Van Fossen, Anthony B. 2002. Norfolk Island and its tax haven. *Australian Journal of Politics & History* 48(2):210–25.

———. 2003. Money laundering, global financial instability, and tax havens in the Pacific Islands. *Contemporary Pacific* 15(2):237–75.

Vleck, William. 2008. *Offshore finance and small states: Sovereignty, size and money.* London: Palgrave Macmillan.

Warf, Barney. 2002. Tailored for Panama: Offshore banking at the crossroads of the Americas. *Geografiska Annaler* 84(1):33–47.

Warner, Philip, J. 2004. *Luxembourg in international tax planning.* Amsterdam: IBFD publication.

Webb, Michael. 2004. Defining the boundaries of legitimate state practice: Norms, transnational actors and the OECD's project on harmful tax competition. *Review of International Political Economy* 11(4):787–827.

Wechsler, William F. 2001. Follow the money. *Foreign Affairs* 80:40–57.

Weichenrieder, Alfons. 1996. Fighting international tax avoidance: The case of Germany. *Fiscal Studies* 171:37–58.

World Bank. 2006. Utilization of repatriated Abacha loot. www.gov.je/statistics.

Yeandle, Mark, Michael Mainelli, and Adrian Berendt. 2005. *The competitive position of London as a global financial centre.* London: Corporation of London.

Zoromé, Ahmed. 2007. Concept of offshore financial centers: In search of an operational definition. IMF Working paper no. 07/08.

Zuill, L. 2005. Bermuda lags behind Cayman as hedge fund domicile. *Royal Gazette*, September 21.

Index